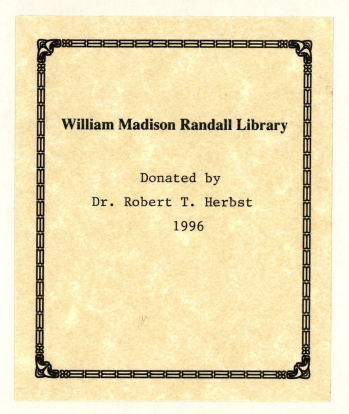

# DATABASE DESIGN FUNDAMENTALS

## A STRUCTURED INTRODUCTION TO DATABASES AND A STRUCTURED APPLICATION DESIGN METHODOLOGY

NAPHTALI RISHE

*Florida International University*

PRENTICE HALL, Englewood Cliffs, New Jersey 07632

Library of Congress Cataloging-in-Publication Data

Rishe, Naphtali.
    Database design fundamentals.

Bibliography.
Includes index.
1. Data base management.   2. Electronic data processing
—Structured techniques.   I. Title.
QA76.9.D3R55 1988          005.7   87-11443
ISBN 0-13-196791-6

Editorial/production supervision: Carolyn D. Fellows
Cover design: George Cornell
Cover art: M. C. Escher, *Knots*, 1966
                © M. C. Escher Heirs
                c/o Cordon Art
                Baarn–Holland
Manufacturing buyer: Gordon Osbourne

## To Bella and Rudolf Rishe

 © 1988 by Prentice Hall
A Division of Simon & Schuster
Englewood Cliffs, New Jersey 07632

Printed in the United States of America

10  9  8  7  6  5  4  3  2  1

ISBN 0-13-196791-6   025

Prentice-Hall International (UK) Limited, *London*
Prentice-Hall of Australia Pty. Limited, *Sydney*
Prentice-Hall Canada Inc., *Toronto*
Prentice-Hall Hispanoamericana, S.A., *Mexico*
Prentice-Hall of India Private Limited, *New Delhi*
Prentice-Hall of Japan, Inc., *Tokyo*
Simon & Schuster of Asia Pte. Ltd., *Singapore*
Editora Prentice-Hall do Brasil, Ltda., *Rio de Janeiro*

# CONTENTS

# PREFACE

## Uses of this book

- an undergraduate course on databases;
- a college course for future systems analysts and programmers;
- an "updating" course for software engineers, systems analysts, and programmers;
- suitable for a self-educating professional;
- a supplement for a graduate course on databases;
- a quick-reference manual and glossary of database terminology.

## Knowledge to be gained

- the logical aspects ("the externals") of databases and database management systems;
- how to design and develop a high-quality database for any given enterprise;
- how to to select an appropriate database management system;

- how to program in the database environment;

- how to solve information access problems by use of database languages without programming;

- how to comprehend easily and critically the user manuals of commercial database management systems.

Most other textbooks devote their primary attention to the "internals" of database management systems and to theoretical aspects of databases. Neither of these issues is among the practical goals of the majority of the students, because they are future *users* of database management systems. They are users at the logical level of databases: *application* software engineers, systems analysts, and logical database designers, rather than developers of database management *systems* or theoreticians. Thus, the most important issues of the database study are:

- software design methodology for databases and programs, and

- application-world-oriented comprehension of database concepts.

### Database design methodology

A novel methodology for logical design of databases is presented in this textbook. In the first step, a conceptual description of an enterprise is designed using a semantic binary model. Then, this description is converted into the relational, network, or hierarchical database design, in a form suitable for commercial database management systems. A high-quality database is produced as a result.

Chapter 4 explains why this methodology is significantly easier than and superior to (produces databases of higher quality) the methodologies based on the relational database theory, such as the normalization methodology. The normalization methodology used to be popular in the academic world, but was not practical enough or advantageous enough to be widely accepted by the industry.

### Database models

The Relational, Network, and Hierarchical database models and languages are presented in this text as restricted forms of the semantic model in which the initial conceptual description of the user's enterprise is done. This reduces the reader's effort by minimizing the number of concepts to be learned. Although the different models have different terminology, the concepts are similar. After introducing the concepts, the text translates them into the terminology of each model. Most other textbooks introduce the terminology of each database model without relation to the other models. That causes quadruplication of the number of concepts to be understood by the student.

## Database languages

Two classes of database languages are studied in detail. They are represented by two abstracted model-independent languages:

- a fourth-generation structured extension of a structured third-generation programming language (*Pascal* taken as an example), and

- a non-procedural language based on Logic.

These abstracted languages are used in all the database models to comprehend the specific languages of those models and of their database management systems. Several languages which are not strictly within the above classes of languages, but yet are very widely used in some database models, are also presented in this text. These languages are: SQL, Relational Algebra, and the CODASYL network navigation language. The presentation of SQL is very extensive. This text can be used as a reference manual and a user guide for those languages.

## Prerequisites

Structured programming is required, preferably in Pascal or a similar language. Those who do not know Pascal or a similar language may wish to skip the sections on data manipulation extensions of programming languages. Those sections are not prerequisite to the other sections, and the other sections do not use Pascal.

No knowledge is needed of file organization or data structures.

## Structure of the book

The book is composed primarily of explanations of concepts and examples. The examples are offset and boxed, so that the experienced reader or browser can easily skip them.

The concepts being defined are set in bold face. They are also referenced by the index.

The examples constitute a continuous case study of one application, for which databases are designed in different models, application programs are written in different languages, *etc*.

Most sections are followed by problems. Many of the problems are solved in the last chapter of the book. Page-number pointers direct the reader from the problems to their solutions.

If after reading a chapter the reader fails to solve a problem marked 'Advanced' or 'Optional', it does not mean a lack of understanding of the chapter. (It rather means the lack of mathematical knowledge or experience, which is not prerequisite to the reading of this book.)

The sections marked with '*' contain optional, usually advanced, material, and may be skipped. Optional advanced material within the regular sections is given in the footnotes.

## Acknowledgment

I am grateful to the Computer Science Department of the University of California, Santa Barbara, for providing facilities and an environment conducive to writing this book, and to the following students, whose comments on the manuscript were very helpful: Shih-Chao Chang, Changlin Chen, Wentsung Chen, Janine Felzer, David Galvin, Lionel Geretz, Alok Jain, John King, Nina Lewis, Ben Lipkowitz, Ernest Liu, Hemant Madan, Brigit Prochazka, Eric Rapin, Jack Schwartz, Donald Traub, and Narayanan Vijaykumar.

I thank the staff of Prentice Hall, especially Valerie Ashton, Carolyn Fellows, and Cynthia Scheel, for their excellent professional work.

I would like to express my deep gratitude to Professors Allen Reiter and Alan Konheim, whose guidance and support were of great value in my professional development.

# 1
# DATABASES AND SEMANTIC MODELING

*"Database — From DATA and BASE (adj = low, mean, vile, etc). A place where data can be lost in a structured manner.*

*"DBMS (Database Management System) — The software needed to set up highly complex inter-relational data structures, so that files can be lost in any convenient sequence (e.g. Index before data; First-in-last-out)."*

From a folklore dictionary.

This chapter introduces the basic concepts of databases and logical representation of real-world information in databases.

## 1.1. Databases

**General-purpose software system** — a software system that can serve a variety of needs of numerous dissimilar enterprises.

> *Example 1-1.*
> A compiler for Pascal.

**Application** — a software system serving the special needs of an enterprise or a group of similar enterprises.

> *Example 1-2.*
> The registration of students in a university.

**Application's real world** — all the information owned by, and subject to computerization in an enterprise, *or* all such information which is relevant to a self-contained application within the enterprise.

> *Example 1-3.*
>
> The examples of this text constitute a case study. Its application world is the educational activities of a university. The information contains
>
> - a list of the university's departments (including all the full and short names of each department)
> - personal data of all the students and their major and minor departments
> - personal data of all the instructors and their work information (including all the departments in which the instructor works and all the courses which the instructor teaches)
> - the list of courses given in the university catalog
> - the history of courses offered by instructors
> - the history of student enrollment in courses and the final grades received

**Database** — an updatable storage of information of an application's world *and* managing software, that conceals from the user the physical aspects of information storage and information representation. The information stored in a database is accessible at a *logical* level without involving the physical concepts of implementation.

> *Example 1-4.*
>
> Neither a user nor his program will try to seek the names of computer science instructors in track 13 of cylinder 5 of a disk or in "logical" record 225 of file XU17.NAMES.VERSION.12.84. Instead, the user will communicate with the database using some *logical* structure of the application's information.

Normally, a database should cover *all* the information of one application; there should not be two databases for one application.

**Database Management System, DBMS** — a general-purpose software system which can manage databases for a very large class of the possible application worlds.

> *Example 1-5.*
>
> A DBMS is able to manage our university database and also completely different databases: an Internal Revenue Service database, an FBI *WANTED* database, a UN database on world geographical data, an Amtrak schedule, *etc.*

**Instantaneous Database** — all the information represented in a database at a given instant of time. This includes the historic information which is still kept at that time.

The actual information stored in the database changes from day to day. Most changes are additions of information to the database.

> *Example 1-6.*
>
> A new student, a new instructor, new events of course offerings.

Fewer changes are deletions of information.

> *Example 1-7.*
>
> Historic information past the archival period;
> a course offering which was canceled before it was given.

Some changes are replacements: updates; correction of wrongly recorded information.

---

*Example 1-8.*

Update of the address of a student;

correction of the student's birth year (previously wrongly recorded).

---

Hence the life of a database can be seen as a sequence of instantaneous databases. The first one in the sequence is often the empty instantaneous database — it is the state before any information has been entered.

**Database Model** — a convention of specifying the concepts of the real worlds in a form understandable by a DBMS. (Technically, it is an abstract data structure such that every possible instantaneous database of nearly every application's world can be logically represented by an instance of that data structure.)

The following database models will be studied in this text:

- **Binary** (also called *Semantic Binary* or *Conceptual Binary*), in which the information is represented by logical associations (relations) between pairs of objects and by classification of objects into categories;

- **Relational**, in which the information is represented by a collection of printable tables;

- **Network**, in which the information is represented by a directed graph of records;

- **Hierarchical**, in which the information is represented as a tree of records.

The Binary Model is the most natural of the above models. It is the most convenient for specifying the logical structure of information and for defining the concepts of an application's world. In this text, the other models will be derived from the Binary Model. The Relational, Network, and Hierarchical models are dominant in today's commercial market of database management systems.

## 1.2. Categories

**Object** — any item in the real world. It can be either a concrete object or an abstract object as follows.

> *Example 1-9.*
>
> *Consider the application world of a university.*
>
> I am an object, if I am of interest to the university. My name is an object. The Information Systems Department and its name "Information Systems Department" are two distinct objects.

**Value**, or **Concrete Object** — a printable object, such as a number, a character string, or a date. A value can be roughly considered as representing itself in the computer, or in any formal system.

> *Example 1-10.*
>
> My name and the name "Computer Science Department" are concrete objects. The grade 70 which has been given to a student in a course is also a concrete object.

**Abstract Object** — a non-value object in the real world. An abstract object can be, for example, a tangible item (such as a person, a table, a country), or an event (such as an offering of a course by an instructor), or an idea (such as a course). Abstract objects cannot be represented directly in the computer.

This term is also used for a user-transparent representation of such an object in the Semantic Binary Model.

> *Example 1-11.*
>
> The Management Science Department, the student of the department whose name is Alex Johnson, and the course named "Chemistry" are three abstract objects.

**Category** — any concept of the application's real world which is a unary property of objects. At every moment in time such a concept is descriptive of a set of objects which possess the property at that time.

Unlike the mathematical notion of a set, the category itself does not depend on its objects: the objects come and go while the meaning of the category is preserved in time. Conversely, a set *does* depend on its members: the meaning of a set changes with the ebb and flow of its members.

Categories are usually named by *singular* nouns.

---

*Example 1-12.*

*STUDENT* is a category of abstract objects. The set of all the students relevant to the application today is different from such a set tomorrow, since new students will arrive or will become relevant. However, the concept *STUDENT* will remain unaltered.

---

An object may belong to several categories at the same time.

---

*Example 1-13.*

One object may be known as a person, and at the same time as an instructor and as a student.

---

---

*Example 1-14.*

Some of the categories in the world of our university are: *INSTRUCTOR, PERSON, COURSE, STUDENT, DEPARTMENT.*

---

**Disjoint categories** — Two categories are *disjoint* if no object may simultaneously be a member of both categories. This means that at every point in time the sets of objects corresponding to two disjoint categories have empty intersection.

---

*Example 1-15.*

The categories *STUDENT* and *COURSE* are disjoint; so are *COURSE* and *DEPARTMENT* (even though there may be two *different* objects, a course and a department, both named "Physics").

   The categories *INSTRUCTOR* and *STUDENT* are not disjoint; neither are *INSTRUCTOR* and *PERSON*.

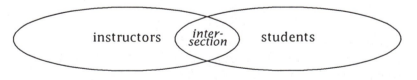

---

**Subcategory** — A category is a *subcategory* of another category if at every point in time every object of the former category should also belong to the latter. This means that at every point in time the set of objects corresponding to a category contains the set of objects corresponding to any subcategory of the category.

*Example 1-16.*

The category *STUDENT* is a subcategory of the category *PERSON*. The category *INSTRUCTOR* is another subcategory of the category *PERSON*.

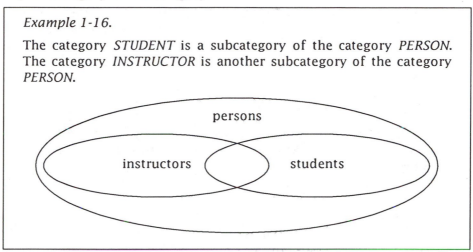

**Abstract category** — a category whose objects are always abstract.

**Concrete category, category of values** — a category whose objects are always concrete.

*Example 1-17.*

*STUDENT* and *COURSE* are abstract categories. *STRING*, *NUMBER*, and *DIGIT* are concrete categories.

Many concrete categories, such as *NUMBER*, *STRING*, and *BOOLEAN*, have constant-in-time sets of objects. Thus, those concrete categories are actually indistinguishable from the corresponding sets of all numbers, all strings, and the Boolean values ({TRUE, FALSE}).

**Finite category** — A category is *finite* if at no point in time an infinite set of objects may correspond to it in the application's world.

*Example 1-18.*

The categories *STUDENT*, *COURSE*, and *DIGIT* are finite. The category *NUMBER* may be infinite.

Every abstract category is finite.

---

*Example 1-19.*

If there were infinitely many atoms in the universe, then we would not be able to create a database registering all the atoms in the universe. This would result in an infinite abstract category *ATOM*.

---

## 1.3. Binary Relations

**Binary Relation** — any concept of the application's real world which is a binary property of objects, that is, the meaning of a relationship or connection between two objects.

---

*Example 1-20.*

*WORKS-IN* is a relation relating instructors to departments. *MAJOR-DEPARTMENT* relates students to departments. *NAME* is a relation relating persons to strings. *BIRTH-YEAR* is a relation relating persons to numbers.

---

At every moment in time, the relation is descriptive of a set of pairs of objects which are related at that time. The meaning of the relation remains unaltered in time, while the sets of pairs of objects corresponding to the relation may differ from time to time, when some pairs of objects cease or begin to be connected by the relation.

*Notation:* "$x R y$" means that object $x$ is related by the relation $R$ to object $y$.

---

*Example 1-21.*

To indicate that an instructor $i$ works in a department $d$, we write:
$$i \; WORKS\text{-}IN \; d$$

---

**Types of binary relations:**

- A binary relation $R$ is **many-to-one** (**m:1, functional**) if at no point in time $xRy$ and $xRz$ where $y \neq z$.

---

*Example 1-22.*

*BIRTH-YEAR* is an **m:1** relation because every person has only one year of birth:

$person_1$     *BIRTH-YEAR*     1970
$person_2$     *BIRTH-YEAR*     1970
$person_3$     *BIRTH-YEAR*     1969
$person_4$     *BIRTH-YEAR*     1965

*Example 1-23.*

*MAJOR-DEPARTMENT* is also an **m:1** relation, since every student has at most one major department:

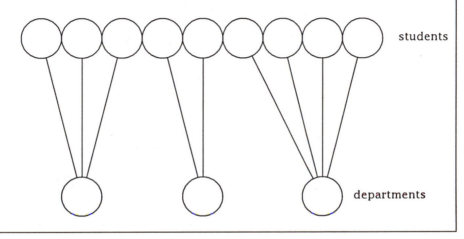

- A binary relation $R$ is **one-to-many** (**1:m**) if at no point in time $xRy$ and $zRy$ where $x \neq z$.

*Example 1-24.*

The relation *MAJOR-DEPARTMENT* is not **1:m**, since a department may have many major students.

If, instead of the relation *MAJOR-DEPARTMENT*, we have the relation *MAJOR-STUDENT* between departments and students, then this relation would be **1:m**, since every student can have at most one major department.

- Relations which are of neither of the above types are called **proper many-to-many** (**m:m**).

*Example 1-25.*

*WORKS-IN* is a proper **m:m** relation because every instructor can work in many departments and every department may employ many instructors:

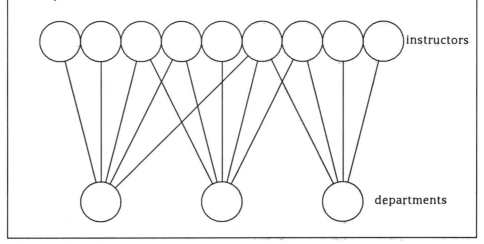

instructors

departments

- A binary relation which is both *m:1* and *1:m* (always) is called **one-to-one (1:1)**.

*Example 1-26.*

If courses are identified by their names, then the relation *COURSE-NAME* is **1:1**, meaning that every course has at most one name, and no character string is the name of two different courses:

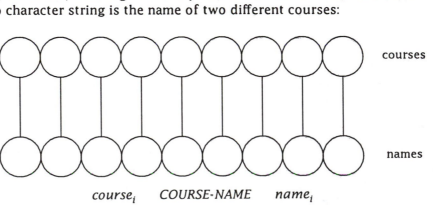

courses

names

*course$_i$*          *COURSE-NAME*          *name$_i$*

*Example 1-27.*

Suppose that in the current situation in our real world, the following is true:

(a) every registered person has at most one name, and no two persons have the same name.

This does not mean that *NAME* is a **1:1** relation between persons and strings. *NAME* would be a 1:1 relation if the condition (a) were true *at all times*: past, present, and future.

The following diagram shows the classification of all relations:

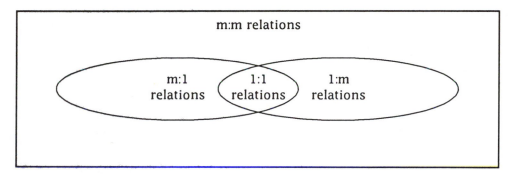

- A binary relation is **proper m:1** if it is *m*:1 and not 1:1.
- A binary relation is **proper 1:m** if it is 1:*m* and not 1:1.

*Example 1-28.*

All of the types of relations mentioned in the previous example are proper.

Since the *COURSE-NAME* is 1:1, it is also **1:m, m:1** and **m:m**. Since this relation is *proper* 1:1, it cannot be *proper* **1:m, m:1** or **m:m**.

**Domain** and **range** of a binary relation:

A category $C$ is the domain of $R$ if it satisfies the following two conditions:

a.   whenever $xRy$ then $x$ belongs to $C$ (at every point in time for every pair of objects); and

b.    no proper subcategory of *C* satisfies (a).

A category *C* is the range of *R* if:

a.    whenever *xRy* then *y* belongs to *C* (at every point in time for every pair of objects); and

b.    no proper subcategory of *C* satisfies (a).

---

*Example 1-29.*

The domain of *COURSE-NAME* is the category *COURSE* and its range is the category *STRING*. The domain of *WORKS-IN* is *INSTRUCTOR* and the range is *DEPARTMENT*.

---

**Total** binary relation — A relation *R* whose domain is *C* is *total* if *at all times* for every object *x* in *C* there exists an object *y* such that *xRy*. (At different times different objects *y* may be related to a given object *x*.)

*Note*:  No relation needs to be *total* on its domain.

---

*Example 1-30.*

Though the domain of the relation *BIRTH-DATE* is the category *PERSON*, the date of birth of some relevant persons is irrelevant or unknown.  Thus, the relation *BIRTH-YEAR* is not total.

---

*Problem 1-1.*

For each of the following relations determine the type (proper m:m/1:m/m:1/1:1).

- Relation **works-in** from *INSTRUCTOR* to *DEPARTMENT*   (*?:?*)

- Relation *name* from *DEPARTMENT* to the category of values  *String*   (*?:?*) (A department may have several names, but every name is unique.)

- Relation *last-name* from *PERSON* to the category of values  *String*   (*?:?*)

- Relation *first-name* from *PERSON* to the category of values  *String*   (*?:?*)

- Relation *birth-year* from *PERSON* to the category of values  *1870..1990*  (*?:?*)

- Relation *address* from *PERSON* to the category of values  *String*   (*?:?*)

- Relation **major** from *STUDENT* to *DEPARTMENT*   (*?:?*)

- Relation **minor** from *STUDENT* to *DEPARTMENT*   (*?:?*)

- Relation *year* from *QUARTER* to the category of values  *1980..1995*   (*?:?*)

- Relation *season* from *QUARTER* to the category of values *String*   (*?:?*)
- Relation *name* from *COURSE* to the category of values *String*   (*?:?*)

Solution on page 279.

*Problem 1-2.*

(*Optional, combinatorics*)

Given:

R is an m:m relation.
A is a category.
The domain of R is A.
The range of R is also A.
Presently, two objects belong to the category A:   objects *a1* and *a2*.

List the different sets of pairs of objects that may presently correspond to R.

Solution on page 279.

*Problem 1-3.*

(*Optional, combinatorics*)

Given:

R is a total m:1 relation.
A is a category.
The domain of R is A.
The range of R is also A.
The set of objects that presently corresponds to A is {a1, a2, a3, a4}.

How many different sets of pairs of objects may presently correspond to R?

Solution on page 280.

*Problem 1-4.*

(*Optional, combinatorics*)

Given:

R is an m:1 relation (not total).
A is a category.
The domain of R is A.
The range of R is also A.
The set of objects that presently corresponds to A is {a1, a2, a3, a4}.

How many different sets of pairs of objects may presently correspond to R?

Solution on page 280.

## 1.4. **Non-binary Relationships**

**Non-binary relationships** — real-world relationships that bind more than two objects in different roles.

> *Example 1-31.*
>
> There is a relationship between an instructor, a course, and a quarter in which the instructor offers the course.

Such complex relationships are regarded in the Binary Model as groups of several simple relationships.

> *Example 1-32.*
>
> The non-binary relationship of the previous example is represented in the Binary Model by a fourth object, an offering, and three binary relations between the offering and the instructor, the quarter, and the course:
>
>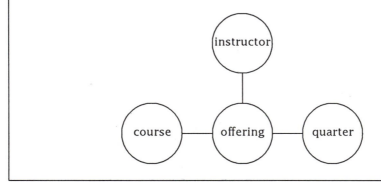

In general, the Binary Model represents any non-binary relation as:

    a.    An abstract category of events. Each event symbolizes the existence of a relationship between a group of objects.

    b.    Functional binary relations, whose domain is the category (a). Each of those functional binary relations corresponds to a role played by some objects in the non-binary relation.

Thus, the fact that objects $x_1, \ldots, x_n$ participate in an n-ary relation $R$ in roles $R_1, \ldots, R_n$, is represented by:

a.    an object $e$ in the category $R'$, and

b.    binary relationships $eR_1x_1, \ldots, eR_nx_n$.

---

*Example 1-33.*

The information of offering a course by an instructor during a quarter could be considered a ternary relation between instructors, courses, and quarters. In the Binary Model, we solve this problem by representing this information as a category *COURSE-OFFERING* and three functional relations from *COURSE-OFFERING*: *THE-INSTRUCTOR*, *THE-COURSE*, and *THE-QUARTER*.

Instructor $i$ has offered course $c$ in quarter $q$ if and only if there exists a course-offering $o$, such that:

$o$ *THE-INSTRUCTOR i*, and

$o$ *THE-COURSE c*, and

$o$ *THE-QUARTER q*.

---

## 1.5.  Instantaneous Databases

**Formal representation of an instantaneous binary database** — as a set of **facts**, unary and binary:

**Unary fact** — a statement that a certain abstract object belongs to a certain category.

---

*Example 1-34.*

(The person whose name is "Jane Howards") is a *student*.

---

**Binary fact** — a statement that there is a certain relationship between two given objects.

---

*Example 1-35.*

The *birth-year* of (the person whose name is "Jane Howards") is 1968.

---

*Example 1-36.*

(The instructor whose name is "John Smith")
*works in*
(the department whose name is "Information Systems")

---

*Example 1-37.*

The *final grade* of

(the enrollment of (the student whose name is "Jack Brown") in (the offering of (the course named "Basic Chemistry") by (the instructor named "Veronica Hammer") during (the Fall 1900 quarter)))

is 100.

Although this fact relates to old times, it is still relevant, and thus is a part of today's instantaneous database.

---

*Note:* In order to be in the current instantaneous database, the fact must have been explicitly or implicitly entered at some time and never canceled since.

## 1.6. Semantic Binary Schemas

**Semantic Binary Model** is a data structure generating all the binary instantaneous databases.

A **semantic binary schema** is a description of the names and the properties of all the categories and the binary relations existing in an application's world.

All the instantaneous databases under the schema should have only those categories and relations listed in the schema. The sets of pairs of objects corresponding, in the instantaneous database, to the categories, and the sets of pairs of objects corresponding to the relations, should satisfy the properties indicated in the schema.

The schema should list the following properties of the categories and relations: the subcategories, the domains and ranges of the relations, and the types of the relations (*proper m:m, proper m:1, proper 1:m, 1:1*).

## 1.7.  Graphic Representation of Schemas

1.    In a schema, categories are shown by rectangles.

---

*Example 1-38.*

   •   Category *STUDENT*

**STUDENT**

---

2.    Relations from abstract categories to concrete categories are shown inside the boxes of the domain-categories as follows:

*relation* **:** *range type*

The *range* is specified as a programming language data-type. (We will use the style of *Pascal* here.)

---

*Example 1-39.*

   •   Category *DEPARTMENT*
   •   Relation *name* from *DEPARTMENT* to the category of values *String* (*1:m*)  (A department may have several names, but every name is unique.)

**DEPARTMENT**

*name: String  1:m*

---

Usually, relations between abstract and concrete categories are *m:1*. This is the *default type of relations whose ranges are concrete categories*, and it need not be explicitly specified in the schema for such relations.

*Example 1-40.*

- Category *PERSON*
- Relation *last-name* from *PERSON* to the category of values *String*  (*m:1* )
- Relation *first-name* from *PERSON* to the category of values *String*  (*m:1* )
- Relation *birth-year* from *PERSON* to the category of values *1870..1990*  (*m:1* )
- Relation *address* from *PERSON* to the category of values *String*  (*m:1* )

**PERSON**

*last-name: String*
*first-name: String*
*birth-year: 1870..1990*
*address: String*

3.  Relations between abstract categories are shown by arrows between the categories' rectangles.  (The direction of the arrow is from the domain to the range.)   The name and type of the relation are indicated on the arrow.  The *default for the type of relations between abstract categories* is *m:m*.

*Example 1-41.*

- Category *DEPARTMENT*
- Category *INSTRUCTOR*
- Relation **works-in** from *INSTRUCTOR* to *DEPARTMENT* (*m:m*)

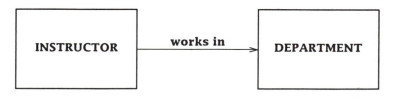

4.  Subcategories' rectangles are connected to their supercategories' rectangles by arrows with dashes.

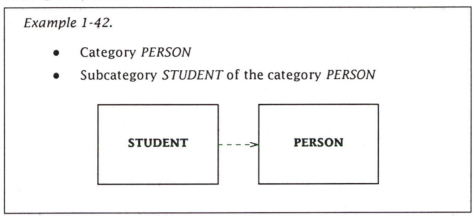

*Example 1-42.*

- Category *PERSON*
- Subcategory *STUDENT* of the category *PERSON*

5.  The disjointness of categories is indicated implicitly:

   a.   Two categories which have a subcategory in common are *not* disjoint. (The common subcategory does not have to be their *immediate* subcategory, that is, it may be a subcategory of a subcategory, and so on.)

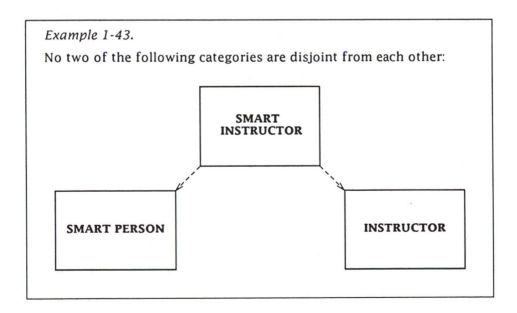

*Example 1-43.*

No two of the following categories are disjoint from each other:

b. Two categories which are subcategories of one category (not necessarily immediate subcategories) are considered *not* disjoint, unless otherwise declared in an appendix to the schema.

*Example 1-44.*

No two of the following categories are disjoint from each other:

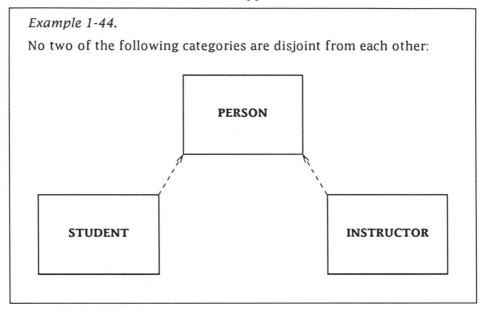

c. The other categories are disjoint from each other, unless otherwise declared in an appendix to the schema.

*Example 1-45.*

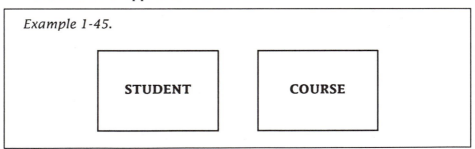

*Example 1-46.*

A binary schema for a university application is given at the end of this book. This will be the principal reference schema used in the examples throughout the book.

## 1.8.  Storage Structure: Abstracted Implementation

The physical implementation of a database is a responsibility of the DBMS. The implementation of the database should be completely transparent to the database users, including the database designers and systems analysts.

Nevertheless, it may be helpful to the reader to have a general idea on how the database may be implemented. This section shows a possible idea of database implementation. This is a simplistic implementation. Efficiency is not a concern here. It would be, of course, a concern in any actual implementation.

We can represent the abstract objects as integers. The DBMS will enumerate all the abstract objects. The numbers assigned to the objects will be invisible to the user, as will be all the implementational details.

We can represent the instantaneous database as a large table. Every row contains a fact: a unary fact (*object — category*), or a binary fact (*object — relation — object*). This table can be implemented as a file.

---

*Example 1-47.*

The following is a fragment of a file representing an instantaneous database. The fragment consists of one unary fact and three binary facts.

---

| object# | relation or category | object# or value |
|---------|----------------------|------------------|
| o21     | COURSE-ENROLLMENT    |                  |
| o21     | THE-STUDENT          | o18              |
| o21     | THE-OFFERING         | o17              |
| o21     | FINAL-GRADE          | 100              |

---

*Example 1-48.*

The following figure shows an implementation of an instantaneous database for the university application. It specifies the instantaneous database which will be used in examples throughout this book.

---

| category | object# | relation | object# or value |
|---|---|---|---|
| DEPARTMENT | o1 | NAME | Computer Science |
| | o1 | NAME | CS |
| | o2 | NAME | Mathematics |
| | o2 | NAME | Math |
| | o3 | NAME | Physics |
| | o4 | NAME | Arts |
| | o5 | NAME | Economics |
| COURSE | o6 | NAME | Databases |
| | o7 | NAME | Gastronomy |
| | o8 | NAME | Football |
| QUARTER | o9 | YEAR | 1987 |
| | o9 | SEASON | Fall |
| | o10 | YEAR | 1987 |
| | o10 | SEASON | Winter |
| | o11 | YEAR | 1987 |
| | o11 | SEASON | Spring |
| INSTRUCTOR | o12 | LAST-NAME | Brown |
| | o12 | FIRST-NAME | George |
| | o12 | BIRTH-YEAR | 1956 |
| | o12 | ADDRESS | 112 Lucky Dr. |
| | o12 | WORKS-IN | o1 |
| | o12 | WORKS-IN | o2 |
| | o13 | LAST-NAME | Whatson |
| | o13 | FIRST-NAME | Mary |
| | o13 | BIRTH-YEAR | 1953 |
| | o13 | ADDRESS | 231 Fortune Dr. |
| | o13 | WORKS-IN | o3 |
| | o14 | LAST-NAME | Blue |
| | o14 | FIRST-NAME | John |
| | o14 | BIRTH-YEAR | 1950 |
| | o14 | ADDRESS | 536 Orange Dr. |
| | o14 | WORKS-IN | o2 |

**Figure 1-1.** An instantaneous binary database for the university application.

| category | object# | relation | object# or value |
|---|---|---|---|
| COURSE-OFFERING | o15 | THE-INSTRUCTOR | o12 |
|  | o15 | THE-COURSE | o6 |
|  | o15 | THE-QUARTER | o9 |
|  | o16 | THE-INSTRUCTOR | o12 |
|  | o16 | THE-COURSE | o7 |
|  | o16 | THE-QUARTER | o9 |
|  | o17 | THE-INSTRUCTOR | o12 |
|  | o17 | THE-COURSE | o8 |
|  | o17 | THE-QUARTER | o9 |
| STUDENT | o18 | LAST-NAME | Victory |
|  | o18 | FIRST-NAME | Elizabeth |
|  | o18 | BIRTH-YEAR | 1966 |
|  | o18 | ADDRESS | 100 Sun St. |
|  | o18 | MAJOR | o1 |
|  | o18 | MINOR | o5 |
|  | o19 | LAST-NAME | Howards |
|  | o19 | FIRST-NAME | Jane |
|  | o19 | BIRTH-YEAR | 1965 |
|  | o19 | ADDRESS | 200 Dorms |
|  | o19 | MAJOR | o4 |
|  | o19 | MINOR | o5 |
|  | o20 | LAST-NAME | Wood |
|  | o20 | FIRST-NAME | Michael |
|  | o20 | BIRTH-YEAR | 1964 |
|  | o20 | ADDRESS | 110 Dorms |
|  | o20 | MAJOR | o4 |
|  | o20 | MINOR | o5 |
| COURSE-ENROLLMENT | o21 | THE-STUDENT | o18 |
|  | o21 | THE-OFFERING | o17 |
|  | o21 | FINAL-GRADE | 100 |
|  | o22 | THE-STUDENT | o19 |
|  | o22 | THE-OFFERING | o17 |
|  | o22 | FINAL-GRADE | 70 |
|  | o23 | THE-STUDENT | o19 |
|  | o23 | THE-OFFERING | o15 |
|  | o23 | FINAL-GRADE | 80 |

*Problem 1-5.*

Design a binary schema for a wholesaler, covering the following information for each product:

- the name and the address of the manufacturing firm;
- for each sale and for each purchase of the product: the date, the quantity of the product, the name and address of the firm selling or buying, and the dollar value of the transaction.

Solution on page 280.

*Problem 1-6.*

Design a binary schema for a movie studio, covering the following information:

- the title and the directors of each film;
- the names and addresses of the personnel and the occupations of each person: actor, technician, director, other.
- partitioning of the films into scenes; for each scene, its location, its actors, the props used in it, and the persons assisting in shooting the scene.

Solution on page 281.

*Problem 1-7.*

A *clan* is a group of living and past relatives sharing one last name. The last name can be received from the father at birth or from the husband at marriage. Design a database to store the relations within a clan (by birth and by marriage.)

Solution on page 281.

*Problem 1-8.*

Design a binary schema to record sale transactions of items. A *sale* is a transaction of a merchandise of an *item-type* for a *price* between the *seller* and the *buyer*. The database also contains a bill of material of item-types, that is, the components of each item-type are known.

Solution on page 282.

*Problem 1-9.*

Design a binary schema to store information which describes a printed circuit board in terms of the component devices contained thereon and the circuits which connect between the electrical terminals (pins) of the devices. The components of the circuit board are chosen from among a set of component types. Each component has an identifier which distinguishes it from all other components, of like or different type, on the circuit board. Each component has a number of electrically separate terminals (pins) to which wires may be connected. Pins are numbered to distinguish among the pins of a given component. Wires may connect a pin to one or more pins of the same or of other components on the circuit board. A set of such wires which are electrically common (interconnected) is referred to as a circuit. All of the wires of a circuit will be the same color.

# 1.9. Integrity Constraints

**Integrity Law, Integrity Constraints, Integrity Rules** — rules attached to a database in order to detect obvious user errors when updating the database.

1. **Static integrity constraints** — rules to detect instantaneous databases which cannot correspond to any probable state of the application's world in the past, present, or future, regardless of the database's update history.

> *Example 1-49.*
>
> These are some static integrity constraints in our university:
>
> - no one has two last names;
> - every student has at most one major department;
> - first names of people are composed only of letters;
> - no student may participate in a course before he was born or receive a grade in a course before he is 15 years old.

A static integrity law can be regarded as a Boolean function from the set of all the instantaneous databases which are well-formed according to the schema or the database model. This function assigns the value *false* to those instantaneous databases which cannot correspond to any probable state of the application's world.

2. **Dynamic integrity constraints** — as above, but the domain of the function is the set of transitions between instantaneous databases, and *false* is assigned to highly improbable transitions between states of the application's world.

> *Example 1-50.*
>
> The following is a dynamic integrity constraint:
>
> - the catalog of courses is unerasable — a course, once entered, may not be removed.

> *Example 1-51.*
>
> If we wish to record the sex of persons in our data base and we are sure that nobody's sex is ever recorded wrongly (this is usually a

dangerous and unreasonable assumption), and we further assume that a woman cannot become a man, then the following would be another dynamic constraint:

once the sex of *x* is *female* in an instantaneous database, the sex of *x* is *female* in the next instantaneous database also.

*Note*:

(i) Very often some of the integrity constraints are captured by the schema.

(ii) Integrity constraints should be distinguished from *implementational restrictions*:

**Implementational restrictions** — the inability of the database to represent some possible situations of the application's world, or the inability to represent them in a logical, natural, non-redundant, error-avoiding, flexible way.

Implementational restrictions are caused by considerations such as hardware, software, database model, effort, time, and expenses.

---

*Example 1-52.*

If for the application world of the university we use a database model less powerful than the Semantic Binary Model, then our implementational considerations may require that every instructor is uniquely identified by his social security number. This is not the case in the real world of the university, because sometimes an instructor receives a social security number only several months *after* being hired and becoming of relevance to the university database.

The aforementioned is a static implementational restriction. To cope with it we have either to delay the recording of new instructors or to supply them with some temporary numbers.

If our implementation further requires that the social security number of a person should remain constant in time, then this would constitute a dynamic restriction. Supplying temporary numbers would not help then. Also, this dynamic restriction would not allow for correction of a wrongly recorded social security number (due to a data-entry clerk's mistake). In practice, such a correction may be possible, but with an extremely high cost in terms of the

> programming effort, and with a chance to inadvertently corrupt the database.

## 1.10.  Quality of Schemas

We have defined the term *schema* for the Semantic Binary Model. The following is a more general definition of the term, regardless of the database model.

**Schema** — a description, in terms of a database model, of the concepts and the information structure of an application's world. It may be the actual data structure of a database. A schema describes all the possible instantaneous databases for one given application's world.

> *Example 1-53.*
>
> A schema for our university application should outline the basic relevant concepts of the university, such as *student, instructor, etc.,* and the kinds of information to be gathered about them. The schema will not allow the database to contain information about salaries of the instructors or about girl/boyfriends of students as these are outside the scope of the application's world.

A schema is called **high quality** or **conceptually adequate** if it satisfies the following criteria:

1.  The schema describes the concepts of its application's world **naturally**:

    - The schema describes the objects, categories and relations as they are in the real world.

    - The users can translate ideas easily in both directions between the concepts of the schema and the natural concepts of the application world.

2.  The schema contains very little or **no redundancy**. *Redundancy* is the possibility of representing a fact of the application's world more than once in the same instantaneous database (so that if one of the representations is removed from the database, no information is lost, that is, all of the information represented by the instantaneous database remains unaltered).

    The redundancy should be avoided *not* in order to improve the storage efficiency — the storage is not that expensive nowadays. Moreover, the redundancy in the schema is not directly related to the redundancy in the physical storage: a logically non-redundant schema may be physically implemented by a redundant physical structure in order to improve the access-time efficiency.

The redundancy should be avoided primarily in order to prevent inconsistency of the database and its update anomalies. When two facts in the database represent the same information, and that information is updated, the user may forget to update both facts. In this case, after the update the two facts would contradict. This contradiction may cause unpredictable behavior of many application programs. The ramifications would be much beyond the local incorrectness of a fact in the database.

When the redundancy is needed for the convenience of the users, it should be introduced into the userviews (to be defined in the next section), but not into the schema.

---

*Example 1-54.*

The following is a fragment of a redundant *WRONG* schema:

> **COURSE**
> **ENROLLMENT**
>
> *final-grade: 0..100*
> *student's-address: String*

Suppose a student $s$, whose address is $a$, has two enrollments, $e_1$ and $e_2$. Then, the following facts (among others) are logically recorded in the database:

a.   $s$ *ADDRESS* $a$

b.   $e_1$ *THE-STUDENT* $s$

c.   $e_2$ *THE-STUDENT* $s$

d.   $e_1$ *STUDENT'S-ADDRESS* $a$

e.   $e_2$ *STUDENT'S-ADDRESS* $a$

The facts (d) and (e) can be inferred from the facts (a)—(c). Thus, (d) and (e) can be omitted from the database without altering the information represented by the database. These facts are redundant; the schema should not have allowed their entrance in the first place.

> If the following relation were omitted from the above wrong schema,
>
> - Relation *address* from *PERSON* to the category of values *String*  (*m:1* )
>
> then the schema would still remain redundant and wrong, because fact (e) can be inferred from fact (d). (Additionally, it would be a problem to record the address of a student who has no enrollments yet).

In some database models we cannot eliminate the redundancy completely. When we have to have some redundancy, we should at least bind it by integrity constraints. When such constraints are implemented, the user is forced to update all the related facts simultaneously.

> *Example 1-55.*
>
> If we cannot avoid having the redundant schema of the previous example, we can at least try to enforce the following integrity constraint:
>
> Whenever
>
> >  *s ADDRESS a*    and    *e THE-STUDENT s*
>
> then
>
> >  *e STUDENT'S-ADDRESS a*

3.   The schema does **not impose implementational restrictions**, that is, every situation probable in the real world of the application is fully representable under the schema.

> *Example 1-56.*
>
> A schema containing the following relation would prevent very senior citizens from entering our university:
>
> - Relation *birth-year* from *PERSON* to the category of values *1900..2000*  (*m:1* )
>
> This schema imposes an avoidable implementational restriction, and thus it is *WRONG*.

4.  The schema covers by itself as many **integrity constraints** as possible, that is, the class of instantaneous databases formally possible according to the schema is not much larger than the class of all possible situations of the real world.

    Constraints that are *not* expressed in the schema cause these problems:

    - They are hard to formulate and to specify.

    - They are seldom enforced by the DBMS. Thus, they require a substantial application programming effort for their enforcement, are often implemented incorrectly, and usually prevent direct interaction between the user updating the database and the DBMS (the user may not use the standard language for simple updates, which is supplied by most DBMS).

    - The users and application programmers often forget or misunderstand such constraints.

---

*Example 1-57.*

The following is a fragment of a *POOR* schema, with respect to the coverage of the integrity constraints by the schema:

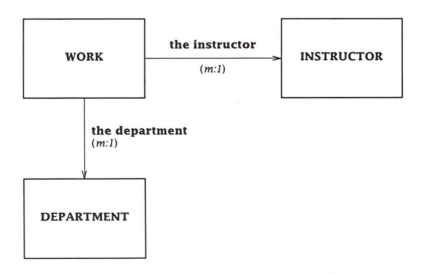

It requires an integrity constraint not expressed in the schema:

For no instructor there are two events of his work in the same department.

---

A better schema fragment is:

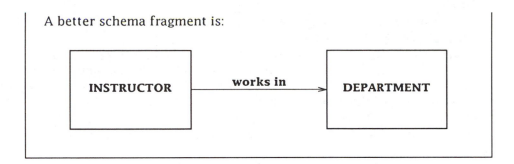

5.  The schema is **flexible**: if probable changes in the *concepts* of the application world occur, the schema would not have to undergo drastic changes.

6.  The schema is **conceptually-minimal**: it does not involve concepts which are irrelevant in the application's real world, and limits the accumulation of information which is irrelevant in that world.

---

*Example 1-58.*

The following would be irrelevant and *WRONG* in the schema of our university:

- Subcategory *BEAUTIFUL* of the category *STUDENT*

---

*Example 1-59.*

The following would be irrelevant and *WRONG* in the schema of our university, unless it is unavoidable due to technical problems:

- Relation *enrollment-number* from *ENROLLMENT* to the category of values *Integer* (*m:1* )

---

The most important issue of the database design is the design of a high-quality schema within the restrictions of the available DBMS and database model. A low-quality schema increases the chances of corruption of the data, makes it very hard to use and maintain the database, and makes it very hard, if not impossible, to adjust the database to the changing concepts of the application's real world.

It is easy to design a high quality schema in the Semantic Binary Model. The task is much harder in most other models. Moreover, it is usually impossible to describe an application world by a schema in the Relational,

Network, or Hierarchical model with the same high quality as with which that application can be described in the Semantic Binary Model.

The following chapters will introduce methodologies to design conceptually adequate schemas in the Relational, Network, and Hierarchical models. Those schemas will be close to the highest quality possible within the restrictions of the respective models. In those methodologies, a semantic binary schema is designed first, and then the schema is translated into the model supported by the DBMS which will service the application.

*Problem 1-10.*

Design a binary schema for a simple medical application covering the following information:

1.  A catalogue of names of known diseases.

2.  A catalogue of descriptions of known symptoms

    -   their names and

    -   the units in which the magnitude of their intensity/acuteness is measured.

3.  For every disease there is a list of possible symptoms, in which

    for every possible symptom $s$

    for some magnitudes $m$ of the symptom's acuteness

    there is an estimation of the probability that

    whenever a patient has the disease, he also has the symptom $s$ with acuteness $m$ at least.

4.  A catalogue of names of known drugs.

5.  For every disease there are lists of factors which may aggravate, cause or cure the disease. These factors are drugs, drug combinations, other diseases.

6.  Names, addresses, and dates of birth of patients; names and addresses of physicians. Some physicians are also known as patients. Some persons relevant to the database are neither patients nor physicians. (These other persons can be, for example, parents of patients, paramedical personnel.) For these persons we have only names and addresses.

7.  Physicians' areas of specialization (diseases).

8.  Every patient's medical history, including:

    •   all his/her present and past illnesses,

        -   their duration,

        -   their diagnosing physicians,

        -   drugs prescribed for them;

- all his/her reported symptoms with

    - the duration of the symptom's occurrences,

    - an indication of the magnitude of intensity/acuteness of the symptom's occurrence,

    - a record of the persons (names and addresses) who reported or measured the symptom's occurrence (a symptom can be reported by the patient himself, his relatives, or medical personnel),

    - and physicians who confirmed the symptom's occurrence.

Solution on page 283.

## 1.11. Userviews

**Subschema** — a part of the schema, provided this part in itself can constitute a schema for some application world.

---

*Example 1-60.*

The following figure shows a schema for a very small application world. The only relevant information in that world is the names of the courses.

```
+---------------------+
|                     |
|      COURSE         |
|                     |
|    name: String     |
|                     |
+---------------------+
```

This schema is a subschema of the University Binary Schema of Figure Ref-1.

---

A subschema of a binary schema can be obtained by removing some of the categories and some of the relations (provided, whenever a category is removed, every relation whose domain or range is the category is also removed.)

The primary use of the subschemas is to provide subpopulations of the database users with a partial view of the database information. The user of a subschema may regard it as the whole schema and need not be aware of the existence of the information beyond the subschema. The DBMS will conceal from such a user all the information beyond the subschema. This brings the following benefits:

- The user does not have to understand the information concepts which are irrelevant to his activities.

- The user is prevented from accidently corrupting the information which he had no business to access in the first place, but accessed in error instead of the relevant information.

- The malicious user is prevented from accessing information beyond that which he is entitled to access.

- When the database is extended by adding new concepts to the schema, and those new concepts do not affect some existing programs using subschemas, those programs need not be modified.

*Example 1-61.*

The following subschema covers the names of the courses and the seasons in which the courses are offered.

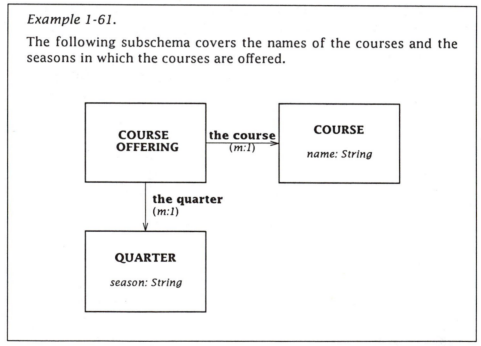

Normally, the schema is partitioned into non-disjoint subschemas according to the needs of the different divisions within the enterprise and the different sub-applications.

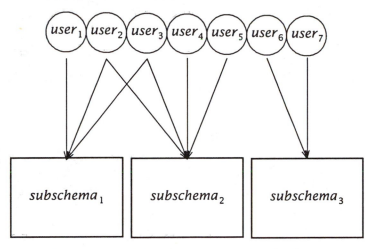

**Figure 1-2.**  The users access the database through subschemas.

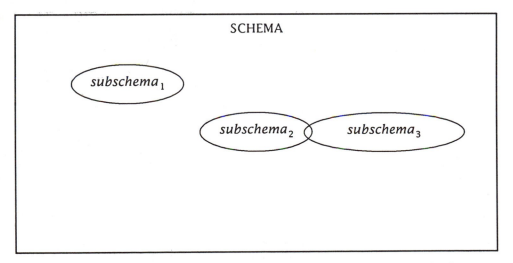

**Figure 1-3.**  The schema is partitioned into subschemas, which need not be disjoint.

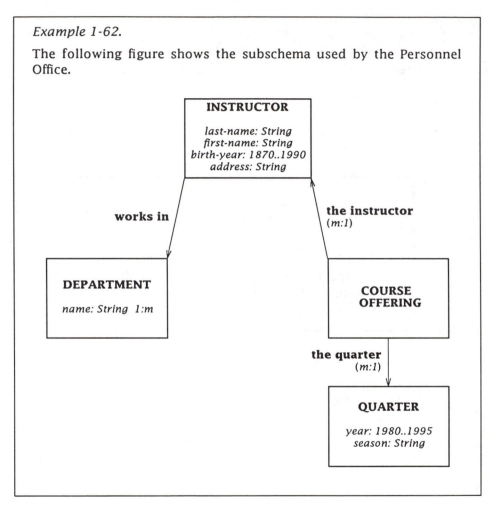

*Example 1-62.*

The following figure shows the subschema used by the Personnel Office.

A generalization of the *subschema* concept, the *userview*, is defined in the remainder of this section.

**Inference rules** — rules by which new information can be deduced from the information that the users have entered into the database.

*Example 1-63.*

The following are some parts of the information recorded in the university database:

- for every instructor, the classes he/she teaches;
- for every student, the classes he/she takes.

An inference rule:

- If *s* takes a class taught by *p* then *p* **teaches** *s*.

**Userview** — an alternative view on the application world.

A userview is a means of alternative comprehension of a part or all of the application world's information. A userview consists of an alternative schema and inference rules by which every instantaneous data base characterized by the original schema implies the (logical) instantaneous database characterized by the alternative schema.

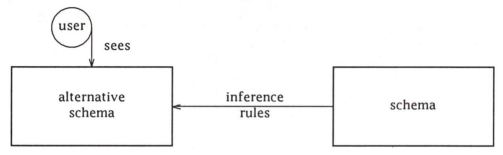

**Figure 1-4.** A userview.

*Example 1-64.*

The following is the alternative schema of the userview that covers the names of the courses and the seasons in which the courses are offered. It is more convenient to the user than the subschema of Example 1-61.

**COURSE SEASON**

*name: String*
*season: String  m:m*

One userview can be used by a subpopulation of the application world's users. Such a userview would conceal from those users all the information which is irrelevant for them. The remaining information is presented to these users in a form which is most convenient to these particular users.

---

*Example 1-65.*

The computer science faculty secretary might use a userview containing only the addresses of the faculty. The userview has the following alternative schema:

> **COMPUTER-SCIENCE-INSTRUCTOR**
>
> *last-name: String*
> *first-name: String*
> *address: String*

The inference rule for the category *COMPUTER-SCIENCE-INSTRUCTOR* is:

> A computer science instructor is an *INSTRUCTOR* who *WORKS-IN* the *DEPARTMENT* whose *NAME* is 'Computer Science'.

---

*Example 1-66.*

A subpopulation of the users is interested only in knowing who taught whom. Their userview has the following alternative schema:

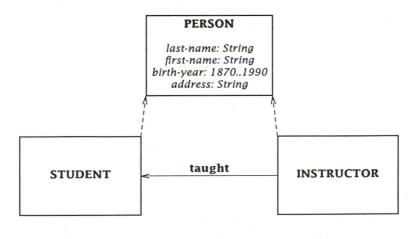

> The inference rule for the relation *TAUGHT* has been given in Example 1-63. The other concepts of the alternative schema are copied from the schema.

Some userviews do not omit any information and can be used by all the users. In this case, a userview presents the same information as the schema does, but in a form most suitable for some particular purposes.

All the information which can be deduced from an instantaneous database *idb* by a userview *u* is called *the instantaneous database corresponding to idb under u*.

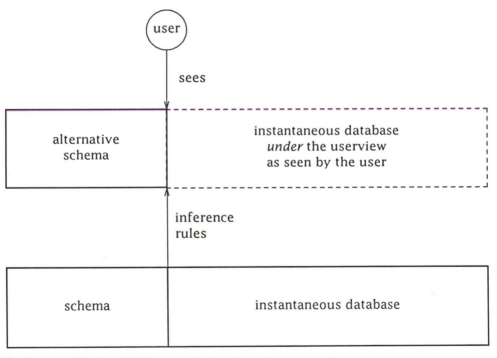

**Figure 1-5.** Instantaneous database *under* a userview.

Unlike the schema, the alternative schema of a userview may contain redundant information if it adds to the convenience of the users. This redundancy cannot cause inconsistency, as it would in the case of the schema redundancy, since the updates are translated into the terms of the schema updates, before the updates are actually performed.

The usage of userviews also greatly enhances the flexibility of the database. Suppose we have a program that uses a userview, and the concepts of the application world change.

— If the change does not affect the logical decisions of this particular program, then we would like to avoid the need to modify the program.

— So, we will define a new userview to be used by the program.

— The alternative schema of the userview would be identical to the alternative schema of the old userview, so the program would not notice the difference.

— The inference rules would be, of course, different.

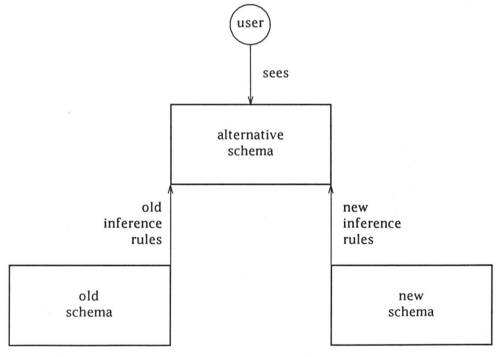

**Figure 1-6.** A change in the schema does not have to affect some users and programs.

*Example 1-67.*

Suppose we have some programs that use the information of the relation

- Relation **works-in** from *INSTRUCTOR* to *DEPARTMENT* (*m:m*)

Now, the university has become more sophisticated, and for certain future programs it will be important to know at what percentage of time do the instructors work for the departments. This new information is irrelevant to most old programs. The new schema will contain the following fragment:

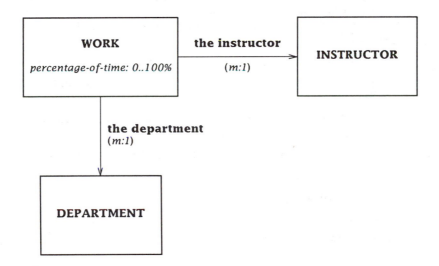

The alternative schema for the unaffected old programs will remain unchanged and will still contain the old relation *WORKS-IN*, but the inference rule of their new userview will be:

If there is a *WORK* whose department is *d* and whose instructor is *i*, then *i WORKS-IN d*.

*Note*:  A *subschema* is a userview whose alternative schema is a part or all of the original schema, and the inference rules are trivial: they copy the information of the alternative schema's concepts.

*Problem 1-11.*

Use the medical/binary schema (Figure 8-6 on page 287). Define a subschema covering a medical manual. The manual shall contain the following information:

- a.  A catalogue of names of known diseases and a catalogue of descriptions of known symptoms;

- b.  for every disease there is a list of its possible symptoms and a probability value is assigned to each such symptom.

*Problem 1-12.*

1.  Design a binary data base schema for a library. The database shall cover

   - For every copy of a book:  the title, the author, the subject, the publisher, the year of publication, the catalog number of the book, the copy number, and the name, address and phone of the vendor who supplied the book. Additionally, for the books that are currently on loan, the due-date and the customer.

   - For every customer:  the name, address, phone, and card number.

   - For every employee:  the name, address, phone, wage, and social security number.

   - For every late return of a book by a customer:  the date and amount of the fine imposed on the customer for the book.

2.  Design subschemas or userviews for the following uses in the library:

   - a.  Billing of customers

   - b.  Catalog searches

   - c.  Loaning books

   - d.  Statistical analysis of reading habits

Solution on page 288.

# 1.12. Services of DBMS

## 1.12.1. Languages

This section introduces the major types of languages supported by database management systems.

**Retrieval query** — a specification of information which a user wants to extract or to deduce from the data base without knowing the full extension of the instantaneous database.

---

*Example 1-68.*

The following is a retrieval query specified in English:

"What students failed the *Databases* course last year?"

Most DBMS do not understand English. Thus, a specification in a more formal language is needed. Such a formal language need not be a programming language. Most DBMS support some user-oriented formal language, in which the users can specify queries without writing programs.

---

**Query Language** — a non-programming language in which a user can formulate *retrieval queries* and possibly also update the database. 'Non-programming' means that the user does not have to specify an algorithm for the problem, but only to define the problem in a formal way.

Some query languages are simple enough to be used by the **end-user** — a database user who has no computer knowledge or experience.

Other, more complex, languages are used by computer professionals. Yet, the professional user can save a significant amount of time by using such a non-programming language rather than writing a program.

**Data Manipulation Language, DML** — a programming language that has a powerful capability of computations, flow of control, input/output, and also has syntactic constructs for database access (the update, retrieval, and dynamic exchange of information between the program and the database). The DML is used by the **application programmer**.

A data manipulation language may be

a.    A stand-alone, special-purpose language. In this case, the DBMS provides a compiler or an interpreter for the DML. The disadvantage of the stand-alone language is that it cannot be used for complex programs which perform some database access, but also simultaneously perform other tasks, for example numeric calculation or industrial assembly line monitoring.

b.    A **system call** interface. In this case, the user writes a program in a regular programming language. The user performs database access by subroutine calls to the DBMS. In a call, the user provides the system with a description of the user's request, with parameters of the request, and with output variables in which the system will produce the result of the database access.

*Example 1-69.*

The following is a fragment of a Pascal program with system calls.

```
        ...
last-name := 'Jefferson'
dbmscall (
        'Dear DBMS: Please find the instructor whose last name is
            given in the second argument of this call.  Place a
            reference to that instructor into the third argument of
            this call.  If everything is OK, set the fourth argument
            of this call to 0.  If there are several instructors by the
            given name, set the fourth argument to 1.  If there are
            no such instructors, set it to 2.  If another problem
            occurs, set the fourth argument to a number greater
            than 2.' (*  In a real program, of course, a code would
            be given instead of this "short story".  *),
        last-name, instructor-reference, return-code);
    if (return-code > 0)
        then write (' A DBMS error.')
        else begin
            dbmscall (
                'Dear DBMS: Please relate the instructor, referred
                    to by the second argument of this call, by the
                    relation BIRTH-YEAR to the number given in
                    the third argument.  If everything is OK, set
                    the fourth argument of this call to 0.  If a
                    problem occurs, set the fourth argument to a
                    number greater than 0.'    (*Of course, in a
                    real system call, one would abbreviate this
                    "short story" by a code*),
                instructor-reference, 1960, return-code);
            if (return-code > 0)
                then write (' A DBMS error.')
        end
```

The system-call interfaces are usually very unfriendly and hard to program in.

The system-calls are interpreted at run-time of the program. One ramification of this is that if a system call contains a syntactically incorrect request, or a request inconsistent with the schema, the user cannot be notified at compile time, but has to wait until the program aborts. Then, the partial effects of the aborted program would have to be undone.

Another ramification is the poor efficiency of the run-time interpretation versus the compilation.

c.  A database access extension of a general purpose programming language. The DML is said to be **embedded** in the **host** programming language. In a program, the host language statements are interleaved with DML statements.

---

*Example 1-70.*

The following is a two-statement fragment of an application program written in an embedded DML language whose host language is Pascal.

        **...**

    write ('This is a regular Pascal statement which prints this
        sentence.');

    **relate**: i *WORKS-IN* d (* This is a DML statement *)

---

The DBMS precompiles the program into a program in the host language without the DML statements. During the precompilation, the DBMS validates the syntax and the compatibility with the schema of the database. The DBMS may also perform optimization of the user's algorithm.

The resulting program is compiled by the host language compiler. When the program runs, it may communicate to the DBMS, but the system calls of this communication are transparent to the user.

**Report generator** — a language in which the user can specify a query together with requirements on the visual form of the output, such as nicely printed tables with titles, or bottom-of-page summaries.

**Data entry** language — a language in which the end-users can specify database updates on-line.

**Data Definition Language, DDL** — a language in which the logical structure of information in the application's world can be defined, together with its pragmatic interpretation for the management of a database, including: the schema, integrity constraints, and userviews.

Many DDL also allow for modification or redefinition of the database structure. This is needed when the concepts of the application world change and when the database designer finds a better description of the existing real world concepts (particularly during the initial database design process, which is often trial-and-error).

In many DBMS, the integrity constraints are specified in languages other than the DDL. In some DBMS the constraint are incorporated in DML programs.

Many DBMS do not provide any language at all to express the integrity constraints, other than those expressed in the schema. The other integrity constraints are left as the application programmer's responsibility. In this case, an application programmer should write a DML program which will

a.   collect the requests for updates from the users,

b.   check whether these requests would violate the integrity constraints,

c.   reject the requests that would violate the integrity, and

d.   submit to the DBMS the remaining good requests.

## 1.12.2.  Other services and utilities

Most database management systems provide some or all of the following services and utilities.

1.   **Integrity**:

a.   **Physical integrity** — prevention of a physical corruption of the database, such as placement of incorrect pointers or loss of an index when the power is shut off or the operating system fails.

b.   **Logical integrity** — enforcement of the integrity constraints.

2.   **Backup** and **recovery**:

a.   The DBMS keeps backup copies of the database, so that when the database is lost, or logically or physically corrupted, it can be restored to a previous state.

    b.    The DBMS keeps a log of the updates it performs in the database, so that when the database is restored to an old state, the correct updates kept in the log can be redone, in order to make the new database up to date.

    c.    When an application program is performing a complex update of the database, and the program gets aborted due to a run-time error, or violates the integrity of the database, or decides that it did not want that update after all, the DBMS can **undo** the update, that is, remove the partial effects of the update.

3.    **Subschemas, userviews, inference rules** — see Section 1.11.

4.    **Security**:

    a.    Prevention of persons who are not authorized database users from accessing the database. (This often involves verification of passwords or a similar procedure.)

    b.    Prevention of persons who are authorized users of a part of the database information from accessing other parts. This control is normally done through subschemas and userviews. A user may be allowed to read and update some information and be allowed to read-only some other information. More complicated services include the distribution and revocation of information access privileges.

    c.    Encryption of the particularly sensitive physical files, so that they could not be accessed by bypassing the DBMS.

5.    **Concurrency control**:

Several users and/or programs may access one database simultaneously.

Some of the major problems addressed by the concurrency control are:

    a.    an incorrect view of the database by one user during a database update being performed by another user; and

    b.    inconsistent simultaneous updates being performed by different users.

The logical side (the user's perspective) of these problems is addressed in Section 2.2.2.

6.    **Data dictionary**:

The information in the schema can be regarded as a small additional database. This database can be queried by the user.

*Example 1-71.*

A schema query:

> What relations have the category *STUDENT* as their domain?

This additional database can also accumulate useful information which is not a proper part of the schema. This may include text explaining the informal meaning of every schema concept.

*Example 1-72.*

A data dictionary explanation entry for the concept 'STUDENT':

*STUDENT* — "any person who is or was a registered student of the University at any time during the past fifteen years, excluding persons who only attended short Extension courses of less than 5 days duration. 'Registered' means 'paid the minimal registration fee at least once.' Insertion of a new student is initiated by the Office of the Registrar. Removal of a student from the database after the expiration of the 15-year period is performed automatically by the data manipulation program ARCHIVE, which is run every Sunday night. The removal of a student can also be explicitly performed by the Office of the Registrar as a correction of an error in inserting that non-student."

Some database management systems provide a "data dictionary" which can only assist the DML compiler in validating the program syntax. This is not a proper usage of the term, because such a "dictionary" facility is no more than a minimal support of the schema, which is essential in any reasonable database management system.

The update of the data dictionary is normally a responsibility of the **database administrator** — a person who is the technical manager of a database.

7. **Restructuring**:

When the schema changes, the instantaneous database may become inconsistent with the schema. *Restructuring* is a utility to transfer the old instantaneous database into a new instantaneous database under a new schema.

8.  **Distributed database**:

The database of a large enterprise may be physically partitioned into several subsets which are stored in different geographical sites, such as the branches of the enterprise. In order to avoid the costs and delays of telecommunication, each site physically contains the information which is most frequently used in that site.

---

*Example 1-73.*

Assume that our University has several campuses. In every campus we would physically store information most frequently used in that campus:

  a.   The departments of that campus.

  b.   The instructors who work in those departments.

  c.   The students whose majors or minors are among those departments.

  d.   The offerings of courses by those instructors.

  e.   The enrollments in those offerings.

---

Logically, the users at each site see the whole database (or the fractions thereof which they are authorized to see) regardless of the database's partition. When a user's query or update request necessitates the access to information which is beyond the user's site, the system performs this access in a way transparent to the user.

---

*Example 1-74.*

Assume that there is a student $a$ in campus $c_1$ who took some courses offered in another campus, $c_2$, by instructors of that campus $c_2$.

Now, an administrator of Campus $c_1$ submits a query:

'Calculate the grade-point-average of Student $s$.'

The administrator need not be aware of the physical distribution of the information. During the execution of the query, the DBMS will decide that it needs some information from Campus $c_2$, contact that campus's computer, and give the user the correct result as if all the data were available locally.

---

The physical subsets comprising the distributed database do not have to be disjoint.

---

*Example 1-75.*

    a.   The personal information about a student whose major is in one campus and whose minor is in another campus will be stored in both campuses. The enrollments of that student do not have to be duplicated, since enrollments are stored according to the offerings, which, in turn, are stored according to instructors, which are stored by departments.

    b.   The information about an instructor who works in Department $d_1$ of Campus $c_1$ and also in Department $c_2$ of Campus $c_2$ will be stored in both campuses.

    c.   The catalog of the names of all the courses can be duplicated in each campus, since it is frequently accessed in each campus.

---

The possible physical duplication of information introduces one of the major problems of the distributed database management: how to maintain consistency between the copies of information.

One of the other problems is the optimization of the routing of information between the sites during the execution of queries and update requests. Another problem is tolerance for failures: when one site or one communication line goes down, we do not want to shut the whole system down.

*Problem 1-13.*

A cable TV service needs to gather the following information:

    For every cable outlet: the outlet's location (the address and the room); the cable channels which can be viewed at the outlet; the name and the address of the customer.

    Additionally, for every customer: the monthly charge.

Design a binary schema for this application.

Solution on page 290.

*Problem 1-14.*

1.  Design a binary schema for a bus company. The database shall cover the following information:

    ●   The company owns a fleet of buses. For each bus, there is the year the bus was put in service, its license plate number, and the date of the next maintenance due. The buses are classified by their types. Each type has a name and number of seats. (All the buses of one type have the same capacity.)

    ●   The company operates a set of lines. For each line, there is a line-name, line-source, and destination.

    ●   The company schedules on a weekly basis, that is, the schedules of two weeks are identical. In each week, a set of trips is scheduled for each line. The trip goes from the line-source to line-destination. The different scheduled trips of one line differ in their days of the week, their times, their stops, and the types of buses they can use. Each scheduled trip will make several stops at known locations (bus stops) at known times. Thus, the following information is relevant for each scheduled trip:

        -   The day of the week and time of the departure from the line-source and the day of the week and time of the arrival to the line-destination. No trip can last more than 24 hours, so the arrival day is redundant. (If a trip departs on Monday 10am and arrives at 3pm, then you know it's same Monday. If it arrives at 8am, then it's Tuesday.)

        -   The bus types that can be used for the trip.

        -   The locations and times of the stops. (Note that the list of locations of all the stops served by the company exists independently of particular trips and, thus, should be regarded as a separate abstract category.)

    ●   The company employs drivers and other personnel. For each employee, the name, address, phone, hourly wage, and social security number are relevant. Additionally, for each driver, the expiration date of her/his license, the number of driving violation tickets, and the types of buses he/she is able to drive are recorded.

    ●   The company keeps track of the actual trips performed. The actual trips are instances of the scheduled trips. Since the trips are scheduled on the weekly basis, there are 52 actual trips per year per one scheduled trip. For every actual trip it is known who was the driver and what bus was used.

2.  Currently, there is the following instantaneous information. The company owns three buses, maintains four lines, ten stops totally, employs six drivers. (Complete this for a full instantaneous information.) Specify (in any formalism you wish) the corresponding binary instantaneous data base.

Solution on page 290.

*Problem 1-15.*

Design a binary schema for a car dealer. The car dealer is interested in information about his cars, their makers, models, submodels, specifications (description of all the price-affecting qualities of a car, several cars of the same submodel can share one specification), "extras" (non-standard equipment appearing in a car specification, such as a stereo system, air-conditioner), colors, prices, deals, customers, selling agents, maker's sales contacts.

Solution on page 292.

*Problem 1-16.*

Design a binary schema for the billing matters of a medical clinic.

Solution on page 293.

*Problem 1-17.*

Design a binary data base schema for a newspaper distribution department, covering the relevant information about customers and deliverers. No financial aspects need be covered.

For every customer we know:

- his name,
- his address,
- his deliverer,
- his subscription commencing day,
- his subscription end day,
- his telephone number.

Solution on page 294.

*Problem 1-18.*

Design a binary schema for an owner of many apartment buildings. The database shall contain all of the following information:

- The names of all tenants along with their lease information.
- For each apartment, its size: 1BR, 2BR and so on.
- Reserved parking information for each tenant. Each apartment building has a small parking lot and spaces are assigned to some apartments.
- Employee information for each building: the manager's name, his/her telephone number, and salary.

You may make reasonable assumptions. The schema shall include all graphically representable integrity constraints.

*Problem 1-19.*

Design a binary schema for a book store. Your schema shall have at least five relations between abstract categories. Specify integrity constraints (not shown in the schema) in English using the terminology of your schema.

Your database shall contain for each title ever sold by the store:

> authors, title, number of pages, bestseller rating; price; temporary discount price and its end-date; stock quantity; maximal desirable stock quantity; minimal desirable stock quantity; daily sales.

(None of the above items *needs* to appear in the schema explicitly, but the information should be derivable.)

Your database shall contain additional information usable for deciding when to change the price of a book.

*Problem 1-20.*

Design a binary schema for a department store. Your schema shall have at least five relations between abstract categories. Specify integrity constraints (not shown in the schema) in English using the terminology of your schema.

Your database shall contain for every product:

> brand name; manufacturer; supplier; store department; units of size/measure; price; temporary discount price and its end-date; stock quantity; maximal desirable stock quantity; minimal desirable stock quantity; employees who have expertise in the product; department manager.

Your data base shall contain additional information usable for deciding when to change the price of the product.

*Problem 1-21.*

Design a binary schema for a kindergarten. Your schema shall have at least 10 relations between abstract categories. Specify integrity constraints (not shown in the schema) in English using the terminology of your schema.

*Problem 1-22.*

Design a binary schema for a video rental store. The schema shall contain 7-12 abstract categories (including subcategories), 7-12 attributes (relations whose range is a concrete category), 7-15 other relations. Specify as many integrity constraints as are reasonable. Constraints which will not be shown in the schema itself shall be specified in English. The schema shall contain enough information so that the following query would make sense:

> "For every month, what was the most profitable title?"

# 2

# DATABASE LANGUAGES

Two abstracted languages or rather language models, for comprehending specific languages, are presented here:

- a fourth-generation structured extension of a structured third-generation programming language (*Pascal* taken as an example) and

- a non-procedural predicate-calculus language.

The languages are defined here for the Binary Model. Since all the other major database models will be defined as subsets of the Binary Model, these languages will be used for all the models.

Many languages, similar to one of the two languages studied here, with some syntactic variations, are in use in different database models and different database management systems. The purpose of the presentation here is to delineate the common denominators of the classes of languages, while avoiding the technical details specific to particular systems.

## 2.1. Notation

The following **syntactic notation** is used in the program fragments and in the definitions of syntactic constructs:

- Language keywords are set in **boldface**.
- The names of the relations and categories from the database are set in *UPPER-CASE ITALICS*.
- In syntax description templates, items to be substituted are set in *lower-case italics*.

---

*Example 2-1.*

- **procedure** — a language keyword
- *LAST-NAME* — a database relation
- *expression* — in a syntax template, substitute for an actual expression, for example, "(7+8*x)"

---

Gender: the pronoun *he* includes *she* and the pronoun *she* includes *he*.

## 2.2. Fourth-generation Extension of Programming Language

### 2.2.1. Preview

Programming languages which exhibit well-structured flow of control, elaborate typing, and a high degree of machine independence are called **third-generation programming languages**. An example of such a language is *Pascal*. In this section, we shall use the example of Pascal to introduce the principles of **fourth**-*generation* database manipulation *extensions* of third-generation programming languages.

The essence of the fourth-generation data manipulation languages is the **structured access to the database**. This is contrasted with earlier data manipulation languages, which provided no automatic loops to process bulks of information in the database, but only single commands to access one item at a time. As a result, the programmer was left with the responsibility of "navigating" between different data items in the database.

The principal instruction of the language extension to be introduced is the **for** loop, whose body is executed for every object which is present in the instantaneous database (when the program is run) and satisfies conditions given in the **for** statement.

---

*Example 2-2.*

(* Print the name of every instructor, that is, of every object in the category *INSTRUCTOR.* *)

> **for** instructor **in** *INSTRUCTOR* **do**
>
>> (* Print the name of the current instructor, that is, of the object referred to by the variable instructor. Separate the current name by a blank ' ' from the name printed in the previous iteration of this loop. *)
>>
>>> write (' ', instructor.*LAST-NAME*)

---

*Example 2-3.*

(* Print the name of every Computer Science instructor, that is, of every object in the category *INSTRUCTOR* that *WORKS-IN* the department whose name is 'Computer Science'. *)

> **for** department **in** *DEPARTMENT*
>
>> **where** (department *NAME* 'Computer Science')
>
> **do**
>
>> **for** instructor **in** *INSTRUCTOR*
>>
>>> **where** (instructor *WORKS-IN* department)
>>
>> **do**
>>
>>> (* Print the name of the current instructor, that is, of the object referred to by the variable instructor *)
>>>
>>> write (' ', instructor.*LAST-NAME*)

---

## 2.2.2. Specification

The following is a fourth-generation extension of Pascal for structured access to databases.

1.  **Global parameters** — among the global parameters of a program, such as INPUT and OUTPUT, there are the names of the database and of the userview. The database will be accessed through the userview during the execution of the program. The userview will also be accessed during the

compilation of the program, in order to check for the correct usage of the names of the categories and relations and to correctly interpret the program's commands.

---

*Example 2-4.*

Let *UNIVERSITY-MASTER-VIEW* be the userview identical to the whole schema. The following may be an Extended Pascal heading for a program using the whole schema of the University database. We assume that the name of the database is *UNIVERSITY-DB*. This name will be used by the DBMS to locate all the files comprising the database.

   **program** My-program (Input, Output, UNIVERSITY-DB,
      UNIVERSITY-MASTER-VIEW);

---

2.  **Data type** *ABSTRACT* — a new *basic* data type, in addition to *INTEGER, BOOL, REAL, CHAR,* enumerated types , and *STRING*. (The type *STRING* is not defined in the standard Pascal, but is used, sometimes with a different name, in most practical versions of Pascal.)

The variables of type *ABSTRACT* will contain abstract objects. (Practically, these variables will contain logical references to abstract objects. The referencing, however, is transparent to the user.)  The variables of this type are called **abstract variables**.

The abstract variables cannot be printed. They cannot receive a value through a *read* instruction. There are no constants of type *ABSTRACT*.

Assignment to the abstract variables can be done from other abstract variables, or from the data base, or by the instruction *create* as discussed later.

In expressions, the only meaningful operation on arguments of type *ABSTRACT* is the test for their equality. The equality test, "=", produces TRUE if the two arguments are one and the same object in the database.

---

*Example 2-5.*

**var** jackson: ABSTRACT   (* The abstract variable *jackson* may be used to retrieve from the database a reference to Professor Jackson, that is, to the abstract object of the category *INSTRUCTOR* related by the relation *LAST-NAME* to the string 'Jackson'. *)

---

3.  **Extended expressions.** There are new operators which can be used in Pascal expressions:

    (i)   (*expression-of-type-ABSTRACT*   **is a**   *category-from-the-userview*)

    This Boolean expression gives TRUE when the left-side sub-expression is evaluated into an object which is a member of the category on the right side. The membership test is done according to the information in the instantaneous database at the run time of the program.

    ---

    *Example 2-6.*

    •   (jackson **is a** *STUDENT*)

    If the variable *jackson* is uninitialized, then a run-time error results. If this variable contains an abstract object, then the result of the expression is TRUE if that object is a student. If this object is simultaneously a student and an instructor, the result is still TRUE.

    ---

    (ii)  (*expression    relation-from-the-userview    expression*)

    This Boolean expression gives TRUE when the two sub-expressions yield objects participating in the relation in the instantaneous database. The types of the sub-expressions must be consistent with the relation. For example, if the relation is between abstract objects and real numbers, then the type of the left sub-expression must be *ABSTRACT* and the type of the right sub-expression must be *REAL*.)

    ---

    *Example 2-7.*

    •   (jackson *FIRST-NAME* 'Roberta')
    •   (jackson *BIRTH-YEAR* 1960)

    ---

    Instead of one of the sub-expressions, the keyword **null** may appear. Then the Boolean expression would give TRUE if the object yielded by the remaining sub-expression is related by the relation to *no* object in the instantaneous database.

*Example 2-8.*

- (jackson *WORKS-IN* **null**)

This expression yields TRUE when the person referred to by the variable *jackson* does not work in any department.

*Example 2-9.*

- (jackson *BIRTH-YEAR* **null**)

This expression yields TRUE if, for the person referred to by the variable *jackson*, no birth-year was recorded in the database.

(iii) (*expression. functional-relation-from-the-userview*)

Reminder: a functional relation is an m:1 relation. It relates every object of its domain to at most *one* object of its range.

The expression *x.R* produces the object related by the relation *R* to *x*, that is, the result is the object *y* from the instantaneous database such that (*x R y*) is TRUE.

If no such object *y* exists, then a *null* object results, which can cause a subsequent execution-time error.

*Example 2-10.*

- (jackson. BIRTH-YEAR)

*Example 2-11.*

Here is a program fragment to print the age of the person referred to by the variable *jackson*. We assume that the current year is available in the variable *current-year*.

> write (' Professor ', jackson.*FIRST-NAME*, ' ', jackson. *LAST-NAME*, ' is approximately ', (current-year − jackson.*BIRTH-YEAR*), ' years old.')

4. **Atomic database manipulations**.

(i) **create new** *abstract-variable* **in** *abstract-category-from-the-userview*

- A new abstract object is *created* in the database;

- this object is placed into the specified category (the database is updated to reflect this fact);

- [a reference to] this object is *assigned* to the specified variable.

---

*Example 2-12.*

   **var** department: ABSTRACT; ...

   **create new** department **in** *DEPARTMENT*

This instruction has two effects:

- A new abstract object is created in the category *DEPARTMENT* in the database.

- A reference to this object is assigned to the variable *department* in the program's memory.

---

(ii) **categorize**: *expression-of-type-ABSTRACT* **is a** *category*

The expression is evaluated to produce an *existing* instantaneous data base object, and this object is inserted into the specified category (in addition to other categories the object may be a member of).

---

*Example 2-13.*

Let the variable *jackson* refer to an existing instructor Professor Jackson. The following instruction will place Professor Jackson also into the category *STUDENT* (in addition to the category *INSTRUCTOR*).

   **categorize**: jackson **is a** *STUDENT*

This instruction has only one effect: a change in the instantaneous database. It produces no change in the program's working space, that is, it does not change the contents of any variable.

---

(iii) **decategorize**: *expression-of-type-ABSTRACT* **is no longer a** *category*

The object is removed from the category.

The object is also automatically removed from the subcategories of the category. (Otherwise the database would become inconsistent.)

The object is also automatically removed from the relations whose domains or ranges are categories of which the object is no longer a member. (This automatic removal saves programming effort. This removal is also necessary to maintain the consistency of the database.)

If after the decategorization the object would not belong to any category in the database, then the object is removed from the database.

---

*Example 2-14.*

**decategorize**: jackson **is no longer a** *STUDENT*

The person referred to by the the variable *jackson* will no longer be a student. She will no longer participate in any relation whose domain or range is the category *STUDENT*. For example, she will be disconnected from her major and minor departments.

---

*Example 2-15.*

The following instruction removes the object referred to by the variable *jackson* from the database:

**decategorize**: jackson **is no longer a** *PERSON*

---

(iv) **relate**: *expression    relation    expression*

A new fact is added to the database: a relationship between the objects yielded by the two expressions.

---

*Example 2-16.*

Assuming that the variable *jackson* refers to an instructor whose birth-year was not known until now, the following instruction will set the birth-year:

**relate**: jackson *BIRTH-YEAR* 1961

---

*Example 2-17.*

Assuming that the variable *jackson* refers to an instructor who is also a student having a major department, the following instruction will make Jackson *work* in her major department. If she was working also in some other department, she will continue working there too.

**relate**: jackson *WORKS-IN* jackson.*MAJOR*

---

(v)  **unrelate**: *expression    relation    expression*

This has the reverse effect of the instruction **relate**.

---

*Example 2-18.*

Assuming that the variable *jackson* refers to an instructor whose birth-year has been incorrectly recorded, the following instructions will change the birth-year to 1961:

**unrelate**:  jackson  *BIRTH-YEAR*  jackson.*BIRTH-YEAR*

(* The expression "jackson.*BIRTH-YEAR*" gives the previously recorded birth-year.*);

**relate**: jackson *BIRTH-YEAR* 1961

---

(vi)  *expression.relation := expression*

The assignment statement

$x.R := y$

means:

- For every z, unrelate $x$ $R$ $z$;
- then relate $x$ $R$ $y$.

---

*Example 2-19.*

Assuming that the variable *jackson* refers to an instructor whose birth-year has not been recorded yet, or has been incorrectly recorded, the following instruction will make the birth-year be

1961:

jackson.*BIRTH-YEAR* := 1961

---

*Example 2-20.*

Assume that the variable *math* refers to the Mathematics department, and the variable *miller* refers to an instructor. What is the effect of the following instruction?

miller.*WORKS-IN* := math

Miller will be working *only* in the Mathematics department.

- If Miller was not working in any department, he will be working in Mathematics.
- If Miller was working in the Management Science and Physics departments, he is hereby fired from Management Science and Physics, and hired in Mathematics.

---

5. The **for** statement.

**for** *variable* **in** *category*
        **where** *boolean-expression*
        **do** *statement*

The *statement* after **do**, which may be a compound statement, will be performed once for every object which belongs to the *category* and satisfies the *boolean-expression*.

---

*Example 2-21.*

Print the last names of all the students born in 1964.

**for** s **in** *STUDENT*
      **where** s *BIRTH-YEAR* 1964
   **do** writeln(s.*LAST-NAME*)

---

*Example 2-22.*

Print the last names of all the students.

```
for s in STUDENT
        where true
      do writeln(s.LAST-NAME)
```

The **for** statement is *functionally* equivalent to the following algorithm.

Let *VEC* of length *L* be the vector of all the *category*'s objects in the instantaneous database. The vector is arranged in an arbitrary order, transparent to the user. Then the equivalent algorithm for the **for** statement is:

```
for i := 1 to L do
    begin
    variable := VEC [i];
    if boolean-expression
    then statement
    end
```

*Abbreviation:*

In the **for** statement, the "**in** *category*" part may be omitted. In this case, by default the category is assumed to be a special category *OBJECT* which is regarded as the union of all the abstract categories in the database. Thus, the body of the loop will be executed for every abstract object (in the instantaneous database) satisfying the condition of the loop. Practically, the condition may explicitly or implicitly restrict the loop to one category.

---

*Example 2-23.*

Print the last names of all the persons born in 1964.

```
for s where s BIRTH-YEAR 1964 do

    writeln (s.LAST-NAME)
```

---

*Example 2-24.*

A larger program fragment:
    Who are the persons that taught persons that taught persons that taught persons that taught Mary?

```
for mary in STUDENT where (mary FIRST-NAME 'Mary') do
```

> **for** enrl1 **in** *COURSE-ENROLLMENT* **where** (enrl1 *THE-STUDENT* mary) **do**
>
> > **for** enrl2 **in** *COURSE-ENROLLMENT* **where** (enrl2 *THE-STUDENT* enrl1.THE-OFFERING.THE-INSTRUCTOR*) **do**
> >
> > > **for** enrl3 **in** *COURSE-ENROLLMENT* **where** (enrl3 *THE-STUDENT* enrl2.THE-OFFERING.THE-INSTRUCTOR*) **do**
> > >
> > > > **for** enrl4 **in** *COURSE-ENROLLMENT* **where** (enrl4 *THE-STUDENT* enrl3.THE-OFFERING.THE-INSTRUCTOR*) **do**
> > > >
> > > > > writeln (enrl4.*THE-OFFERING.THE-INSTRUCTOR.LAST-NAME*)

6. The transaction statement.

**transaction** *compound-statement*

The effects of "**transaction** *S*" are:

(i) While *S* is being executed, the program containing the transaction statement and all the other concurrent programs see the database in its instantaneous state just before *S*.

(ii) All the updates are logically performed instantly when *S* is completed, provided the new instantaneous database would not violate the integrity constraints and no error-condition is raised.

*Note*:

Among the advantages of this statement is the following:

At an intermediate state, the instantaneous information could be incomplete, which could bring failure of an integrity constraint and incorrect comprehension of the data base by concurrent programs.

---

*Example 2-25.*

Assume that the relation *LAST-NAME* is *total*. We wish to create a new person and give her the last name 'Chen'.

The following is a *wrong* program fragment to perform the task:

**create new** chen in *PERSON*;

chen.*LAST-NAME* := 'Chen'

The above program would violate the integrity of the database when the instruction **create** is performed: there would be a person with no last name, contrary to the totality of the relation *LAST-NAME*. The program would probably be aborted before it reached the assignment statement. To prevent the integrity validation between the two statements, we enclose them in a transaction statement:

> **transaction begin**
>
> > **create new** chen in *PERSON*;
> >
> > chen.*LAST-NAME* := 'Chen'
>
> **end**

Also, we would not have to worry that concurrent queries see the database half-updated: a person without a last name.

---

*Example 2-26.*

The database needs to be changed to pretend that the person referred to by the variable *jackson* is not, nor has ever been, a student. Thus, the object has to be decategorized from *STUDENT*, and all the relevant enrollments have to be erased.

**transaction**

> **begin**
>
> **for** e **in** *COURSE-ENROLLMENT* **where** (e *THE-STUDENT* jackson) **do**
>
> > **decategorize**: e **is no longer a** *COURSE-ENROLLMENT*;
>
> **decategorize**: jackson **is no longer a** *STUDENT*
>
> **end**

---

A database update statement which is not embedded in a transaction statement is regarded as one transaction.

7.  **Error exit.**

When the system fails to perform a transaction due to an error, such as a violation of an integrity constraint, it notifies the program by invoking

**procedure** Transaction-error-handler (error-description: String)

The body of this procedure can be specified in the program by the user. This allows the programmer to decide what to do in case of error. If the procedure is not defined by the user in the program, then, by default, the system will insert the following specification of the body of this procedure:

**procedure** Transaction-error-handler (error-description: String);

    **begin**

        writeln ('The program was terminated by the default transaction error handler when a transaction failed with the following error condition: ', error-description);

    **stop**

    **end**

---

*Example 2-27.*

The user can specify the following handler, which prints a message and then allows the program to continue.

    **procedure** Transaction-error-handler (error-description: String);

    **begin**

        writeln ('A transaction failed with the following error condition: ', error-description);

    **end**

---

## 2.2.3. A comprehensive example

---

*Example 2-28.*

The university has decided to expel all the students whose average grade is below 60 (out of 100). To prevent this wrong-doing to computer science students, the department offered a fictitious course, Computer-Pass, by Prof. Good, in which all computer science students are to receive a sufficient grade so as to not to be expelled, if possible.

---

The following program fabricates Prof. Good and the Computer-Pass course, enrolls students in this course, grades them accordingly, and prints the names of those computer science students whom this measure cannot help.

---

**program** Pass (Input, Output, UNIVERSITY-DB, UNIVERSITY-MASTER-VIEW);

**var** Computer-Pass-Course, Prof-Good, Good-Offer, comp-science, this-quarter, cs-student, her-enrollment, fictitious-enrollment: *ABSTRACT*;

desired-grade, number-of-grades, total-of-grades, current-year: *INTEGER*;

**begin**

(* Get the current year from the standard input file.  *)

read (current-year);

(* Fabricate the course.  *)

**create new** Computer-Pass-Course **in** *COURSE*;

Computer-Pass-Course.*NAME* **:=** 'Computer Pass';

(* Fabricate the instructor.  *)

**create new** Prof-Good **in** *INSTRUCTOR*;

Prof-Good.*LAST-NAME* **:=** 'Good';

(* Fabricate the offering.  *)

**create new** Good-Offer **in** *COURSE-OFFERING*;

Good-Offer.*THE-COURSE* **:=** Computer-Pass-Course;

Good-Offer.*THE-INSTRUCTOR* **:=** Prof-Good;

(* Find the relevant quarter and connect it to the offering Good-Offer.  *)

**for** this-quarter **in** *QUARTER*

**where** (this-quarter.*YEAR* = current-year **and** this-quarter. *SEASON* = 'Winter')

**do** Good-Offer.*THE-QUARTER* **:=**  this-quarter;

(* The following loop will be performed only once. Inside the body of the loop, the variable *comp-science* will refer to the Computer Science Department.  *)

```
for comp-science in DEPARTMENT
        where (comp-science NAME 'COMPUTER SCIENCE') do
    begin
    (* Make believe that Prof. Good works in Computer Science. *)
        relate: Prof-Good WORKS-IN comp-science;
    for cs-student in STUDENT
            where (cs-student MAJOR comp-science) do
        begin (* the current computer science student *)
        (* Calculate this student's current statistics: number-of-grades and
            total-of-grades *)
            number-of-grades := 0;
            total-of-grades := 0;
            for her-enrollment in COURSE-ENROLLMENT
                    where (her-enrollment THE-STUDENT cs-student) do
                if not (her-enrollment FINAL-GRADE null) then
                    begin
                    number-of-grades := number-of-grades + 1;
                    total-of-grades := total-of-grades + her-
                        enrollment.FINAL-GRADE
                    end;
        (* calculate the minimal desired grade in computer-pass course, by
            solving the equation (total+x)/(number+1)=60 *)
            desired-grade := 60 * (number-of-grades + 1) — total-of-grades;
    if desired-grade > 100 then
            (* the student cannot be helped. Print a message *)
                writeln (' The student ', cs-student.LAST-NAME, ' cannot be
                    helped. Sorry!')
    else if desired-grade ≤ 60 then
            (* No need to help. *)
    else (* 100 ≥ desired-grade > 60 *)
```

```
transaction begin
        create new fictitious-enrollment in COURSE-ENROLLMENT;
        fictitious-enrollment.THE-OFFERING := Good-Offer;
        fictitious-enrollment.THE-STUDENT := cs-student;
        fictitious-enrollment.FINAL-GRADE := desired-grade
        end (* transaction *)
    end (* current student *)
  end (* Computer Science Department *)
end.
```

*Problem 2-1.*

Use the university/binary reference schema at the end of this book. Write an Extended Pascal program for the following specification. The program reads the standard input file until the end of file. It interprets every line as composed of the last name and first name of a student and a name of the student's proposed major department to be recorded in the database.

   If the request cannot be performed, the program prints an error message and proceeds to the next line. The possible errors are: 'student does not exist', 'more than one student exist for the given first and last names', 'department does not exist', 'the student already has a major'.

*Problem 2-2.*

Use the university/binary reference schema at the end of this book. Write programs or program fragments for the following requirements.
1.  Find the first and last names of the persons born in 1967.
2.  For every student, list the instructors of the student's major department.
3.  What instructors work in every department? (Each relevant instructor shares her time between all the departments.)
4.  What instructors taught every student?
5.  Who took Prof. Smith's courses?
6.  Check whether every student took at least one course.
7.  Print a table with two columns, which associates students to their teachers. Only last names have to be printed.
8.  Find the number of pairs (instructor, department) where the instructor works in the department.
9.  Find the average of grades of student Jane Howard.
10. Print the average of grades for every computer science student (as a table with two columns: the student's name and her average).

11. Print the average of all grades given by Prof. Brown.
12. How many students are there in the university?
13. What students have their average grade above 90?
14. When was Student Russel born?
15. What courses has Prof. Graham taught?
16. Print the names of the pairs of students who live together.
17. Print the names (last and first), the id-s, the birth-years, the major and minor departments, and the addresses of all computer science students.
18. What is the average grade in the *Databases* course?
19. List the distinct addresses of the students. (Do not list the same address twice.)
20. How many departments have minor students?
21. Find the names of the students who took at least one course.

*Problem 2-3.*

Use the university/binary reference schema at the end of this book. Write an extended Pascal program to

a) remove the student Jack Johnson, born in 1960, from the university database. (Do not forget to remove from the database all the information which will become meaningless when Mr. Johnson is removed.)

b) print the average number of courses taken last quarter by computer science majors.

*Problem 2-4.*

Use the university/binary reference schema at the end of this book. Write an Extended Pascal program to normalize the grades of every course offering. (Consistently change the grades so that the average grade would be 75/100.) Computer science majors shall be excluded from the normalization. (Their grades will neither be normalized nor will affect normalization of grades of other students.) The students who have not yet received a grade in a course offering shall be, of course, excluded from the normalization of that offering.

Solution on page 295.

*Problem 2-5.*

Use the medical/binary schema (Figure 8-6 on page 287). An illness is *probable* if, when the illness commenced, the patient had all the symptoms he is expected to have with probability of 0.9 at least. Write an extended Pascal program to find out what percentage of the illnesses diagnosed by Dr. Jack Smith are *probable* .

*Problem 2-6.*

Use the medical/binary schema (Figure 8-6 on page 287). Write an extended Pascal program to remove from the database the patients who have not been sick for the last 30 years.

## 2.3.  A Non-procedural Language Based on Predicate Calculus

### 2.3.1.  Preview

**Non-procedural language** — a language in which the user specifies *what* is to be done without specifying *how* it is to be done.

---

*Example 2-29.*

In a non-procedural language, the user might say:

> "Let no student be enrolled twice in the same offering of a course"

The user would probably use a more precise and formal statement, which still would be non-procedural:

> "If enrl1 is an enrollment, and enrl2 is an enrollment, and
> enrl1.*THE-STUDENT* = enrl2.*THE-STUDENT*, and
> enrl1.*THE-OFFERING* = enrl2.*THE-OFFERING*,
> then enrl1 = enrl2."

This statement contains no indication as to how the constraint is to be enforced: this is left to the system.  The system might enforce the constraint as follows:

Whenever a transaction like

> **transaction begin** ...
>
>> **create new** enrl **in** *COURSE-ENROLLMENT*;
>>
>> enrl.*THE-STUDENT* := s;
>>
>> enrl.*THE-OFFERING* := of;
>>
>> ...
>
> **end**

is being completed, perform automatically the following:

> (* If there is another enrollment with the same student and offering, then give an error message and stop.  *)
>
> **for** other-enrl **in** *COURSE-ENROLLMENT*
>
>> **where** ( other-enrl.*THE-STUDENT* = s **and** other-enrl.-
>> *THE-OFFERING* = of)
>
> **do begin**

> writeln (' In violation of an integrity constraint, the
> program has attempted to generate a duplicate
> enrollment'); **stop**
>
> **end**

---

*Example 2-30.*

In a non-procedural language, the user might request the following information:

"What instructors give the grade 100 (sometimes)?"

The user would probably use a more precise and formal statement, which still would be non-procedural:

"Get instructor.*LAST-NAME* where
exists enrollment s.t.
enrollment.*THE-OFFERING.THE-INSTRUCTOR* = instructor
and
enrollment.*FINAL-GRADE* = 100"

The statement would contain no indication as to *how* this query is to be performed: this is left to the system. The system might use the following algorithm:

**for** instructor **in** *INSTRUCTOR*

  **do begin**

    ok := false

    **for** enrl **in** *COURSE-ENROLLMENT*

      **where** (enrl.*THE-OFFERING.THE-INSTRUCTOR*
        = instructor **and**

      enrl *FINAL-GRADE* 100)

      **do** ok := true

    **if** ok **then** write (' ', instructor.*LAST-NAME*)

  **end**

---

Many non-procedural database languages are based on Predicate Calculus, borrowed from Mathematical Logic. The language of Predicate Calculus will be defined in the following subsection.

*Uses*:   non-procedural specification of queries, integrity constraints, inference of userviews, and update transactions.

Predicate Calculus is based on Boolean expressions involving variables.

> *Example 2-31.*
>
> - instructor.*LAST-NAME* = 'Einstein'
> - d *NAME* 'Geology'
> - student.*BIRTH-YEAR* > 1970 **or** student.*BIRTH-YEAR* = 1960

Such Boolean expressions can be used to specify queries similarly to the specification of sets in mathematics:

- a set of objects is found which make a Boolean expression to be true;
- these objects or their functions are displayed.

> *Example 2-32.*
>
> A query to find the names of the persons born in 1967:
>
> **get** person.*LAST-NAME*
>
> **where** (person.*BIRTH-YEAR* = 1967)

A query can display several columns of output, in a table form.

> *Example 2-33.*
>
> A query to find the first and last names of the persons born in 1967:
>
> **get** person.*FIRST-NAME*, person.*LAST-NAME*
>
> **where** (person.*BIRTH-YEAR* = 1967)

Several different objects, referred to by different variables, may be used in one row of the output tables.

> *Example 2-34.*
>
> For every student, list the instructors of the student's major department.
>
> **get** student.*FIRST-NAME*, student.*LAST-NAME*, instructor.-
> *FIRST-NAME*, instructor.*LAST-NAME*

**where**

> (instructor
>
> *WORKS-IN*
>
> student.*MAJOR*)

Very powerful constructs of Predicate Calculus are the **quantifiers** "for every" and "exists". They are used to form nontrivial Boolean expressions.

---

*Example 2-35.*

What instructors work in every department? (Each relevant instructor shares her time between all the departments.)

get instructor.*LAST-NAME* **where**

    (**for every** d **in** *DEPARTMENT*:

        instructor *WORKS-IN* d)

---

*Example 2-36.*

What instructors taught every student?

get instructor.*LAST-NAME* **where**

    (**for every** s **in** *STUDENT*:

        **exists** enrl **in** *COURSE-ENROLLMENT*:

            ((enrl *THE-STUDENT* s) **and**

            (enrl.*THE-OFFERING. THE-INSTRUCTOR* = instructor)))

---

## 2.3.2. First-order predicate calculus expressions

The First-order Predicate Calculus is well known to those who have studied some Mathematical Logic. This Calculus can be applied to databases, if we regard the instantaneous database as a finite structure with binary relations, unary relations (categories), and functions (functional relations). This text, however, does not require a prior knowledge of the Predicate Calculus.

**Expression** — a combination of *constants, variables, operators,* and parentheses. The syntax and semantics are given below.

An expression may depend on some variables. When the variables are interpreted as some fixed objects, the expression can be evaluated with respect to a given instantaneous database, and will yield an object, abstract or concrete. The following are syntactic forms of expressions:

1. *constant*

    a. *number*

    b. *character-string* (in quotes)

    c. *Boolean value* (TRUE and FALSE)

    > *Example 2-37.*
    >
    > 7, 16.5, 'Mary', '87/05/31', TRUE

2. *variable*

    A variable is a sequence of letters, digits, and hyphens. The first character must be a letter.

3. ( *expression* )

    Parentheses in expressions may be omitted when no ambiguity results.

4. (*expression    basic-binary-operator    expression*)

    The basic binary operators are: **+, −, \*, /, >, <, ≥, ≤, =, ≠, and, or.**

    Each operator may be used only when the expressions yield values of types appropriate for the operator. The only basic binary operators defined for abstract objects are '=' and '≠', which produce TRUE or FALSE as results.

    > *Example 2-38.*
    >
    > - 5+6\*7
    > - x ≠ y
    > - ('Abc' > 'Bcc') **or** (1+2 > 2)

5. (**if** *expression* **then** *expression*)

    Both component expressions must yield Boolean values. When the right expression yields TRUE, the result is TRUE regardless of the left expression. When the left expression yields TRUE and the right expression yields FALSE, the result is FALSE. When the left expression yields FALSE, the result is TRUE regardless of the right expression.

---

*Example 2-39.*

The following expressions are TRUE:

- **if** 1=1 **then** 2=2
- **if** 1=3 **then** 2=2
- **if** 1=3 **then** 2=4

The following is FALSE:

- **if** 1=1 **then** 2=4

---

*Note*:

    **if** $e_1$ **then** $e_2$

is equivalent to

    (**not** $e_1$) **or** $e_2$

6.   (*expression   relation   expression*)

The *relation* is a relation from the userview. The result is TRUE if the two objects are related by the *relation* in the instantaneous database.

---

*Example 2-40.*

(x *BIRTH-YEAR* 1960)

The value of this Boolean expression depends on the variable *x*.

---

7.   (*basic-unary-operator   expression*)

The basic unary operators are: **−**, **not**.

---

*Example 2-41.*

(**not** (1>1)) = TRUE

---

8.   (*expression* **is a** *category*)

This Boolean expression yields TRUE when the object is in the *category* in the instantaneous database.

> *Example 2-42.*
>
> x **is a** *STUDENT*

9.  (*expression* **.** *functional-relation*)

    *x*.*R* is the object related by the relation *R* to *x*, it is the object *y* from the instantaneous database s.t. (*x R y*) gives *true*.  Such an expression is called **dot-application.**

> *Example 2-43.*
>
> •    *x*.*BIRTH-YEAR*
> •    *e*.*THE-OFFERING.THE-INSTRUCTOR.LAST-NAME*

The dot-application is well-defined only for total functional relations. The case of non-total functional relations will be discussed later.

10.  (**exists** *variable* **in** *category* **:** *expression*)

    The ':' may be pronounced 'so that the following is true:'.

    The contained *expression* must be Boolean.

    The result is also Boolean.

    It is TRUE when there exists at least one object in the category which satisfies the Boolean *expression*.

    The *expression* usually depends on the *variable*, but may also depend on additional variables.  The resulting expression no longer depends on the *variable*.

    *Interpretation*:

    Let $a_1, a_2, ..., a_n$ be all the objects in the *category* in the instantaneous database.

    Let $e_1, e_2, ..., e_n$ be obtained from the *expression* by substituting each of $a_1, a_2, ..., a_n$ for all the occurrences of the *variable* in the *expression*.

    Then

    **exists** variable **in** *category* **:** *expression*

    is equivalent to

$e_1$ **or** $e_2$ **or** ... **or** $e_n$

---

*Example 2-44.*

(**exists** x **in** *INSTRUCTOR* :

    x.*BIRTH-YEAR* = 1960)

This expression is TRUE if there is at least one instructor who was born in 1960. The whole expression does not depend on the variable *x*, although its sub-expression "x.*BIRTH-YEAR* = 1960" does depend on this variable.

---

*Example 2-45.*

(**exists** x **in** *INSTRUCTOR* :

    x.*BIRTH-YEAR* = y)

This is TRUE if there is at least one instructor who was born in the year *y*. The whole expression depends only on the variable *y*.

---

The keyword '**exists**' is often called 'the **existential quantifier**'. It may be abbreviated by the symbol ∃.

11. (**for every** *variable* **in** *category* : *expression*)

The ':' is pronounced 'the following is true:'.

The *expression* must be Boolean. The result is also Boolean. It is TRUE when all the objects of the *category* satisfy the Boolean *expression*. The *expression* usually depends on the *variable*, and may also depend on additional variables. The resulting expression no longer depends on the *variable*.

*Interpretation*:

Let $a_1, a_2, ..., a_n$ be all the objects in the *category* in the instantaneous database.

Let $e_1, e_2, ..., e_n$ be obtained from the *expression* by substituting each of $a_1, a_2, ..., a_n$ for all the occurrences of the *variable* in the *expression*.

Then

**for every** variable **in** *category* **:** *expression*

is equivalent to

$e_1$ **and** $e_2$ **and** ... **and** $e_n$

---

*Example 2-46.*

(**for every** x **in** *INSTRUCTOR* **:**

    x.*BIRTH-YEAR* = 1960)

This expression is TRUE if all the instructors were born in 1960.

Notice, that the result is TRUE even if there are no instructors at all in the instantaneous database. (Isn't it true that every *presently living* dinosaur knows Predicate Calculus, or that every American monarch is a republican?)

The whole expression does not depend on the variable *x*, although its sub-expression "x.*BIRTH-YEAR* = 1960" does depend on this variable.

---

*Example 2-47.*

(**for every** x **in** *INSTRUCTOR* **:**

    x.*BIRTH-YEAR* = y)

This is TRUE if all the instructors were born in the year *y*. The whole expression depends only on the variable *y*.

---

The keyword '**for every**' is often called 'the **universal quantifier**'. It may be abbreviated by the symbol ∀.

*Note:*

    **for every** *variable* **in** *category* **:** *expression*

is equivalent to

    **not** (**exists** *variable* **in** *category* **:** **not** *expression*)

*Usage of variables:*

The variable after a quantifier in a subexpression should not be used outside that subexpression. Although many versions of Predicate Calculus do not have this requirement, this requirement does not decrease the power of the calculus, but improves readability, prevents some typical errors in query specification, and simplifies the semantics.

---

*Example 2-48.*

WRONG:

    (**exists** x **in** *PERSON*: x **is a** *STUDENT*) **and** (x *BIRTH-YEAR* 1970)

Here, *x* appears in the quantifier of the left sub-expression, but also appears in the right subexpression. Logically, these are two distinct variables, and they should not be called by the same name 'x'.

---

To use the expressions correctly, we shall need to know what variables are *quantified* in an expression, and on what variables an expression depends.

**Quantified variable**: variable *v* is quantified in expression *e* if *v* has an appearance in *e* immediately after a quantifier.

---

*Example 2-49.*

The variable *v* is quantified in:

    ((z > 0) **or** (**exists** v **in** *STUDENT*: v **is an** *INSTRUCTOR*))

---

Expression *e* **depends on** variable *v* if *v* appears in *e* and is not quantified.

---

*Example 2-50.*

The following expression depends on *z* and *x*, but not on *y*.

    ((z > 0) **or** (**exists** y **in** *STUDENT*: x = y.*BIRTH-YEAR*))

---

*Notation*: when an expression *e* depending on variables $x_1$, $x_2$, ..., $x_k$ is referred to (not in the actual syntax of the language), it may be denoted as

$$e(x_1, x_2, ..., x_k)$$

---

*Example 2-51.*

The expression of the previous example may be referred to as

$$e(z,x)$$

---

(In many texts, a variable on which an expression depends is called a **free variable** in that expression. An expression which depends on no variables is called a **closed expression**.)

**Condition** on variables $x_1$, $x_2$, ..., $x_k$ — a Boolean expression which depends on $x_1$, $x_2$, ..., $x_k$.

> *Example 2-52.*
>
> "(x+y>3)" is a condition on *x* and *y*.

**Assertion** — a Boolean expression which does not depend on any variable, that is, every variable is restricted by a quantifier.

*Interpretation*:   for a given instantaneous database, the assertion produces *true* or *false*.

> *Example 2-53.*
>
> Assertion that every student took at least one course in 1987:
>
> **for every** st **in** *STUDENT*:
>     **exists** enrl **in** *COURSE-ENROLLMENT*:
>     ((enrl *THE-STUDENT* st ) **and**
>     (enrl.*THE-OFFERING. THE-QUARTER. THE-YEAR*=1987))

### Dot-application of non-total functional relations

If *f* is not total then *e.f* may be amiguous. The concerned user might wish to avoid such expressions. However, a smart DBMS may be able to follow the user's intuition in using such expressions. In order to provide a meaningful result, the dot-application '*e.f*' of a non-total functional relation *f* to an expression *e* is interpreted by the smart DBMS by analyzing the whole condition or assertion containing the dot-application.

> *Example 2-54.*
>
> Consider the following assertion which contains a dot-application of the non-total relation *BIRTH-YEAR*.
>
>         **for every** y **in** *STUDENT*:
>
>             y.*BIRTH-YEAR* > 1980
>
> This assertion will be interpreted by a smart DBMS as
>
>         **for every** y **in** *STUDENT*:

> **exists** x **in** *Integer.*
>
> y *BIRTH-YEAR* x **and** x > 1980

This interpretation of the dot-application of non-total functional relations can be defined formally.*

## 2.3.3. Queries

**Specification of a query to retrieve a table,** that is, a set of rows of values:

**get** *expression, ..., expression*

**where**

   (*condition-on-the-variables-on-which-the-expressions-depend*)

*Interpretation* of

$$\textbf{get } e_1, \ldots, e_n \textbf{ where } (\phi(x_1, \ldots, x_k))$$

The variables $x_1, \ldots, x_k$ are assigned all the possible tuples of objects from the instantaneous database which make $\phi(x_1, \ldots, x_n)$ *true;* the expressions $e_1, \ldots, e_n$ are evaluated for these tuples and the corresponding results are output. (The output is not printable if any of the expressions produces an abstract object.)

---

  * Formally, an expression $e.f$, where $e$ is an expression and $f$ is a database functional relation, is regarded as a syntactic abbreviation. Let $x_1, \ldots, x_k$ be the variables on which the expression $e$ depends. For the above example, the only such variable is $y$.

Let $\phi$ be the largest subformula (within the whole assertion or condition) containing $e.f$ and still depending on all the variables $x_1, \ldots, x_k$, that is, none of these variables is quantified in the subformula $\phi$. ($\phi$ may depend also on additional variables.)   For the above example,

$$\phi = (y.BIRTH\text{-}YEAR > 1980)$$

Let $C$ be the range of $f$.

Let $\psi = \phi|_{e.f}^{x}$, that is, $\psi$ is obtained from $\phi$ by substitution of a new variable $x$ for all the occurrences of $(e.f)$ in $\psi$. For the above example,

$$\psi = (x > 1980)$$

Then $\phi$ stands for:

$$\textbf{(exists } x \textbf{ in } C: ((e \ f \ x) \textbf{ and } \psi))$$

---

*Example 2-55.*

Who took Prof. Smith's courses?

**get** student.*LAST-NAME* **where**
   **exists** enrl **in** *COURSE-ENROLLMENT*:
    (enrl.*THE-STUDENT*=student **and**
      enrl.*THE-OFFERING. THE-INSTRUCTOR. LAST-NAME*='Smith')

---

*Abbreviation*:

The following abbreviation is used in some literature for the query syntax. It is akin to the mathematical notation for sets.

$$\{e_1, \ldots, e_n \mid \phi(x_1, \ldots, x_k)\}$$

*Abbreviation*:

*Queries which output only one value* may be specified without the "**where condition**" part, as:

$$\textbf{get } expression$$

(provided the *expression* depends on no variables).

---

*Example 2-56.*

The following is a yes-or-no query which displays 'TRUE' if every student took at least one course.

**get**

    (**for every** s **in** *STUDENT*:

        **exists** enrl **in** *COURSE-ENROLLMENT*:

           s=enrl.*THE-STUDENT*)

---

**Headings** of output columns:

The columns in a table which is an output of *get* can be labeled:

$$\textbf{get } heading_1 : e_1, \ldots, heading_n : e_n \textbf{ where } condition$$

---

*Example 2-57.*

Print a table with two columns, which associates students to their teachers. Only last names are printed.

> **get** Teacher: instructor.*LAST-NAME*, Student-taught: student.-*LAST-NAME* **where**
>
> **exists** enrl **in** *COURSE-ENROLLMENT*:
>
> enrl.*THE-STUDENT* = student **and**
>
> enrl.*THE-OFFER. THE-INSTRUCTOR* = instructor

When no heading for $e_i$ is specified, then, by default, the following heading is assumed:

- if $e_i$ ends in ".*relation*", then the heading is the *relation*;
- otherwise the heading is the number *i*.

---

*Example 2-58.*

The query

> **get** x.*LAST-NAME*, x.*BIRTH-YEAR*
>
> **where** x **is a** *STUDENT*

produces a table with two columns, whose heading are:

> *LAST-NAME, BIRTH-YEAR*

---

## 2.3.4. Calculus for integrity constraints

**Specification of static integrity constraints** — by assertions.

---

*Example 2-59.*

No student may be enrolled twice in the very same offering of a course.

**for every** enrl **in** *COURSE-ENROLLMENT*:

> **for every** enrl2 **in** *COURSE-ENROLLMENT*:
>
> **if** enrl.*THE-STUDENT*=enrl2.*THE-STUDENT* **and**
>
> enrl.*THE-OFFERING=enrl2.THE-OFFERING*
>
> **then** enrl=enrl2

**Specification of dynamic integrity constraints**:

A *dynamic* integrity constraint is syntaxed as a static integrity constraint, but categories and relations may be suffixed with *-old* to denote the concepts of the previous state of the data base.

---

*Example 2-60.*

The Student Council has secured, that from 1987, once a grade has been reported (and thus, probably has been made known to the student) it may not be retroactively decreased.

    **for every** enrl **in** *COURSE-ENROLLMENT*:
    **if** enrl.*FINAL-GRADE-old>*enrl.*FINAL-GRADE* **then**
    enrl.*THE-OFFERING.THE-QUARTER.THE-YEAR*<1987

---

Dynamic integrity constraints are rarely dictated by the logic of a user's world, since their existence may cause irreversibility of some users' errors.

---

*Example 2-61.*

In the previous example, if a data-entry clerk erroneously enters the grade of 80 instead of the correct grade of 70, he may not be able to correct the typo.

---

(*The remainder of this chapter is optional.*)

## 2.3.5. *Calculus with aggregate operations: sum, count, average

Defined here is a second-order extension to enable set operations, such as summation, counting, etc. This is done by extending the syntax of *expression* with the **summation quantifier**:

$$\sum_{\substack{variables \\ \textbf{where} \\ condition}} expression_1$$

---

*Example 2-62.*

The sum of the birth-years of all students =

$$\sum s.BIRTH\text{-}YEAR$$

s **where** s **is a** STUDENT

---

*Example 2-63.*

The number of pairs (instructor, department) where the instructor works in the department.

$$\sum_{\substack{instructor,department \\ \textbf{where} \\ instructor\ WORKS\text{-}IN\ department}} 1$$

---

The *variables* under $\Sigma$ are quantified by the summation symbol. In addition to these *variables*, the *condition* and/or the *expression$_1$* may depend on other variables.

---

*Example 2-64.*

The sum of the grades of student *s*. The sum depends on the variable *s*, meaning *s* remains free in the sum.

$$\sum_{\substack{enrl \\ \textbf{where} \\ enrl\ \textbf{is a}\ COURSE\text{-}ENROLLMENT\ \textbf{and} \\ \textbf{not}\ (enrl\ FINAL\text{-}GRADE\ \textbf{null})\ \textbf{and} \\ enrl\ THE\text{-}STUDENT\ s}} enrl.FINAL\text{-}GRADE$$

---

*Interpretation:*

Let *e* be an expression, and let $\phi(x_1,...,x_n,y_1,\ldots,y_k)$ be a condition. Then the following is also an expression (it depends on the variables $y_1, ..., y_k$):

$$\sum_{\substack{x_1,\ldots,x_n \\ \textbf{where} \\ \phi(x_1,\ldots,x_n,y_1,\ldots,y_k)}} (\quad e(x_1,\ldots,x_n,y_1,\ldots,y_k))$$

When all the parameter-variables $y_1,\ldots,y_k$ are interpreted as some fixed objects, the **sum** yields a number. This number is the result of summation of the values of *e* computed for every tuple of objects $x_1,\ldots,x_n$ satisfying $\phi(x_1,\ldots,x_n,y_1,\ldots,y_k)$.

The $\Sigma$ acts like a quantifier for $x_1, \ldots, x_n$. The variables $y_1, \ldots, y_n$ remain unquantified.

*Alternative* (linear) notation (we would not use the two-dimensional notation of $\Sigma$ in a real computer language):

$$\textbf{sum } e$$
$$\textbf{for } x_1, \ldots, x_n$$
$$\textbf{where } \phi(x_1, \ldots, x_n, y_1, \ldots, y_k)$$

*Abbreviation.* When $x_1, \ldots, x_n$ are exactly the variables on which the expression $e$ depends (that is, all $x_i$ and none of $y_i$ appear free in the expression $e$), the **for** clause may be omitted:

$$\textbf{sum } e \textbf{ where } \phi(x_1, \ldots, x_n, y_1, \ldots, y_k)$$

---

*Example 2-65.*

For every information systems student, print his last name and the sum of his grades.

> **get**
>
> > student.*LAST-NAME,*
> >
> > (**sum** enrollment.*FINAL-GRADE*
> >
> > > **where** enrollment *THE-STUDENT* student)
>
> > **where**
> >
> > student **is a** *STUDENT* **and**
> >
> > (student.*MAJOR DEPARTMENT-NAME* 'Information Systems')

---

*Example 2-66.*

Print the sum of all the grades given by Prof. Smith. This query outputs only one value (the sum). There is no "**where** *condition*" for the "**get**" of the query.

**get** (**sum** enrollment.*FINAL-GRADE*

> **where**
> 'Smith'=enrollment.*THE-OFFERING.*
>        *THE-INSTRUCTOR.LAST-NAME*)

*Abbreviation* for **count**:

$$\textbf{count } x_1, \ldots, x_n \textbf{ where } \phi(x_1, \ldots, x_n, y_1, \ldots, y_k)$$

stands for:

$$\textbf{sum } 1 \textbf{ for } x_1, \ldots, x_n \textbf{ where } \phi(x_1, \ldots, x_n, y_1, \ldots, y_k).$$

---

*Example 2-67.*

How many students are there in the university?
   **get** (**count** std **where** std **is a** *STUDENT*)

---

*Abbreviation* for **average**:

$$\textbf{average } e \ldots$$

stands for:

$$(\textbf{sum } e \ldots) \ / \ (\textbf{count } e \ldots)$$

---

*Example 2-68.*

What students have their average grade below 60?

   **get** std.*LAST-NAME*
      **where** std **is a** *STUDENT* **and**
          60 > (**average** enrl.*FINAL-GRADE*
                 **where** enrl *THE-STUDENT* std)

Note: this query could *not* be formulated as follows, since only the distinct grades would be then taken into account:

   **get** std.*LAST-NAME*
      **where** 60 >
         **average** fgrade
            **where**
               **exists** enrl **in** *ENROLLMENT*:
               (enrl *FINAL-GRADE* fgrade **and**
               enrl *THE-STUDENT* std)

If a student has three enrollments with grades 100, 50, and 100, then the average calculated in the first version would be $\dfrac{250}{3}$

(correct), and in the second version $-\dfrac{150}{2}$ (incorrect).

## 2.3.6.  *Shorthand notation for n-ary relationships

*Example 2-69.*

Often we need to specify a condition like:

The instructor *i* offered course *c* in quarter *q*.

In calculus this can be stated as:

**exists** offer **in** *COURSE-OFFERING*:

offer *THE-INSTRUCTOR* i **and**

offer *THE-COURSE* c **and**

offer *THE-QUARTER* q

The above statement can be said in a shorthand notation as:

*COURSE-OFFERING*

(*THE-INSTRUCTOR*: i,

*THE-COURSE*: c,

*THE-QUARTER*: q)

*Abbreviation*:

category (relation$_1$: expression$_1$ , . . . , relation$_k$: expression$_k$)

stands for

**exists** x **in** *category*:

(x relation$_1$ expression$_1$ **and** $\cdots$ **and** x relation$_k$ expression$_k$)

*Example 2-70.*

Print the names of the courses taught by Prof. McFarland.

**get** c.*NAME*

**where**

**exists** i **in** *INSTRUCTOR*:

> i *LAST-NAME* 'McFarland' **and**
>
> *COURSE-OFFERING* (*THE-INSTRUCTOR*: i, *THE-COURSE*: c)

## 2.3.7. *Calculus for the inference rules of userviews

*Reminder:*

A userview consists of an alternative schema and inference rules. The inference rules specify the categories and relations of the alternative schema in terms of the categories and relations of the original schema.

**Specification of an inferred relation**

> **userview relation**:    *expression*₁    *new-relation*    *expression*₂
> **where** *condition*

---

*Example 2-71.*

The following is a specification of an inferred relation *TAUGHT* (between instructors and students) in terms of the the relations existing in the schema.

**userview relation**: instructor *TAUGHT* student

**where**

**exists** enrl **in** *COURSE-ENROLLMENT*:

enrl.*THE-STUDENT* = student **and**

enrl.*THE-OFFER. THE-INSTRUCTOR* = instructor

---

*Example 2-72.*

The following is a specification of an inferred relation

- Relation *average-grade* from *STUDENT* to the category of values *0..100*  (*m:1* )

**userview relation**: student *AVERAGE-GRADE*

(**average** e.*FINAL-GRADE*

**where**

e **is a** *COURSE-ENROLLMENT* **and**

> e *THE-STUDENT* student)
>
> **where** student is a *STUDENT*

## Specification of an inferred abstract category

Usually, but not always, an inferred abstract category is a new subcategory of an existing category. Its purpose is usually to restrict the userview user to a subset of objects which are relevant to that user's task. An inferred category can be specified as a set of objects which is derived from the categories and relations of the database. The specification is:

> **userview subcategory**: *expression* **is a** *new-subcategory*
> **where** *condition*

---

*Example 2-73.*

**userview subcategory**: s **is a** *COMPUTER-SCIENCE-MAJOR*

    **where**

        s **is a** *STUDENT* **and**

        s.*MAJOR    NAME*    'Computer Science'

---

## Specification of representation of relationships by a category

The definition is preceded by an example.

---

*Example 2-74.*

We wish to have (in the userview) a category of events of work of instructors in departments.

- Category *WORK*
- Relation **the-department** from *WORK* to *DEPARTMENT* (*m:1*)
- Relation **the-instructor** from *WORK* to *INSTRUCTOR* (*m:1*)

The user of the user-view will perceive the category *WORK* as containing objects (events) which are distinct from any other objects in the database. These new objects will be perceived only through the userview, without actually existing in the database. Thus, they are *virtual* objects.

This is done by specifying a category of virtual objects with relationships to existing objects. The syntax is:

**userview category**:
*new-category* (*relation*$_1$: *expression*$_1$ , . . . , *relation*$_k$: *expression*$_k$)
**where** *condition*

Let $x_1, . . . , x_n$ be the variables on which the *condition* and the *expessions* depend. (They must depend on the same variables.) For every tuple of values of variables satisfying the *condition*, one new virtual object is created. That object is related by the new relations *relation*$_1$, . . . , *relation*$_k$ to the values of the expressions *expression*$_1$, . . . , *expression*$_k$.

*Example 2-75.*

The following is a specification of an inferred category *WORK* and two inferred relations, *THE-DEPARTMENT* and *THE-INSTRUCTOR*, whose domain is *WORK*. The specification is in terms of the the relations existing in the schema.

**userview category**:

*WORK* (*THE-DEPARTMENT*: department, *THE-INSTRUCTOR*: instructor)

**where** instructor *WORKS-IN* department

## 2.3.8. *Calculus for transactions

This section shows how the calculus can be used to specify transactions — creation of sets of objects, categorization and decategorization of objects, relating and unrelating objects, and so on.

The operations in calculus are usually not atomic, but work on sets of objects. One single operation can create a *set* of new objects, place them in categories, and relate them to different existing objects by *several* relations.

**Creation** of new abstract objects and relating them to existing or concrete objects:

> **insert into** *category*
> (*relation*$_1$: *expression*$_1$ , . . . , *relation*$_k$: *expression*$_k$)
> **where** *condition*

- If no *where* clause is specified then only one new abstract object is created. This object is put into the *category* and related by the relations to the values of the expressions.

---

*Example 2-76.*

Create a new department named 'Computer Engineering'

**insert into** *DEPARTMENT* (*NAME*: 'Computer Engineering')

---

- Some of the names of the relations may be identical. This allows one object to be related to several objects by one relation (m:m or 1:m).

---

*Example 2-77.*

Create a new department named 'Computer Engineering' and 'CE'.

**insert into** *DEPARTMENT* (*NAME*: 'Computer Engineering', *NAME*: 'CE')

---

- If *where* clause is specified with a *condition* on variables $x_1, . . . ,x_n$, then for every tuple of values of the variables satisfying the *condition*, one new object is created and related accordingly.

---

*Example 2-78.*

Enroll the computer science student Jack Johnson into the *Databases* course given by Prof. Smith in Fall 1987.

**insert into** *COURSE-ENROLLMENT* (*THE-STUDENT*: s, *THE-OFFERING*: offer) **where**

s.*MAJOR NAME* 'Computer Science' **and**

s.*LAST-NAME*='Johnson' **and**

s.*FIRST-NAME*='Jack' **and**

offer.*THE-QUARTER.YEAR*=1987 **and**

offer.*THE-QUARTER.SEASON*='Fall' **and**

> offer.*THE-COURSE.NAME*='Databases' **and**
>
> offer.*THE-INSTRUCTOR.LAST-NAME*='Smith'

- The variables on which the *condition* depends must be those on which the *expressions* depend.

> *Example 2-79.*
>
> Enroll all computer science students into the *Databases* course given by Prof. Smith in Fall 1987.
>
> **insert into** *COURSE-ENROLLMENT* (*THE-STUDENT:* s, *THE-OFFERING:* offer)
>
> **where**
>
> s.*MAJOR NAME* 'Computer Science' **and**
>
> offer.*THE_QUARTER.YEAR*=1987 **and**
>
> offer.*THE-QUARTER.SEASON*='Fall' **and**
>
> offer.*THE-COURSE.NAME*='Databases' **and**
>
> offer.*THE-INSTRUCTOR.LAST-NAME*='Smith'

- when the *insert* statement calls for an insertion of a new object while there is already an object having the same relationships as those of the new object, the new object is not inserted.

> *Example 2-80.*
>
> If the department named 'Management' already exists, then the following command produces no effect:
>
> **insert into** *DEPARTMENT* (*NAME:* 'Management')

**Connection** between existing abstract objects, between existing abstract objects and concrete objects, between existing abstract objects and categories:

$$\textbf{connect } fact_1, \ldots, fact_k \ [\textbf{where } condition\,]$$

Each *fact_i* is either

$$expression_i \ category_i$$

or

$$expression_i \ relation_i \ expression'_i$$

*Interpretation:*

- If no *where* clause is specified, the values of the expressions are related by the *relations* and/or categorized by the categories.

- If a *where* clause is specified with a condition $\phi$ on variables $x_1, \ldots, x_n$, then for every tuple of values of the variables satisfying $\phi$ the values of the expressions are related and categorized as above.

- The variables on which the condition $\phi$ depends must be those on which the expressions depend.

---

*Example 2-81.*

Let 'CS' be an alternative name for the department named 'Computer Science'.

    **connect** dept *NAME* 'CS'

    **where**

        dept **is a** *DEPARTMENT* **and**

        dept *NAME* 'Computer Science'

---

*Example 2-82.*

Give the grade 100 to the computer science student Jack Johnson enrolled in the *Databases* course given by Prof. Smith in Fall 1987.

    **connect** enrl *FINAL-GRADE* 100

    **where**

        enrl.*THE-STUDENT.MAJOR NAME* 'Computer Science' **and**

        enrl.*THE-STUDENT.LAST-NAME*='Johnson' **and**

        enrl.*THE-STUDENT.FIRST-NAME*='Jack' **and**

        enrl.*THE-OFFERING.THE_QUARTER.YEAR*=1987 **and**

        enrl.*THE-OFFERING.THE-QUARTER.SEASON*='Fall' **and**

  enrl.*THE-OFFERING.THE-COURSE.NAME*='Databases' **and**

  enrl.*THE-OFFERING.THE-INSTRUCTOR.LAST-NAME*='Smith'

---

*Example 2-83.*

Give the grade 100 to all computer science students enrolled in the *Databases* course given by Prof. Smith in Fall 1987.

 **connect** enrl *FINAL-GRADE* 100

 **where**

  enrl.*THE-STUDENT.MAJOR NAME* 'Computer Science' **and**

  enrl.*THE-OFFERING.THE_QUARTER.YEAR*=1987 **and**

  enrl.*THE-OFFERING.THE-QUARTER.SEASON*='Fall' **and**

  enrl.*THE-OFFERING.THE-COURSE.NAME*='Databases' **and**

  enrl.*THE-OFFERING.THE-INSTRUCTOR.LAST-NAME*='Smith'

---

**Removal of connections** and **removal of objects**:

$$\textbf{disconnect } fact_1, \ldots, fact_k \ [\textbf{where } condition]$$

*Interpretation:*

- If no *where* clause is specified, the values of the expressions are unrelated and/or decategorized. Objects that are removed from all their categories, are removed from the database.

- If a *where* clause is specified with a condition $\phi$ on variables $x_1, \ldots, x_n$, then for every tuple of values of the variables satisfying $\phi$ the values of the expressions are unrelated and decategorized as above.

- The variables on which the *condition* depends must be those on which the expressions of the *facts* depend.

---

*Example 2-84.*

Let 'CS' no longer be an alternative name of a department.

 **disconnect** dept *NAME* 'CS'

**where**

> dept **is a** *DEPARTMENT* **and** dept *NAME* 'CS'

---

*Example 2-85.*

The computer science student Jack Johnson has dropped the *Databases* course given by Prof. Smith in Fall 1987.

**disconnect** enrl *ENROLLMENT*

**where**

> enrl.*THE-STUDENT.MAJOR  NAME* 'Computer  Science' **and**
>
> enrl.*THE-STUDENT.LAST-NAME*='Johnson' **and**
>
> enrl.*THE-STUDENT.FIRST-NAME*='Jack' **and**
>
> enrl.*THE-OFFERING.THE_QUARTER.YEAR*=1987 **and**
>
> enrl.*THE-OFFERING.THE-QUARTER.SEASON*='Fall' **and**
>
> enrl.*THE-OFFERING.THE-COURSE.NAME*='Databases' **and**
>
> enrl.*THE-OFFERING.THE-INSTRUCTOR.LAST-NAME*='Smith'

---

*Example 2-86.*

Void all the grades in the *Databases* course given by Prof. Smith in Fall 1987.

**disconnect** enrl *FINAL-GRADE* enrl.*FINAL-GRADE*

**where**

> enrl.*THE-OFFERING.THE_QUARTER.YEAR*=1987 **and**
>
> enrl.*THE-OFFERING.THE-QUARTER.SEASON*='Fall' **and**
>
> enrl.*THE-OFFERING.THE-COURSE.NAME*='Databases' **and**
>
> enrl.*THE-OFFERING.THE-INSTRUCTOR.LAST-NAME*='Smith'

---

**Correction of facts**:

$$\text{update } fact_1, \ldots, fact_k \text{ [\textbf{where} } condition]$$

This is a combination of *disconnect* and *connect*. Before a connection *aRb* is made, the relationships *aRx* are removed for every *x*.

---

*Example 2-87.*

Let 'CS' be the new name instead of 'Computer Science'.

**update** dept *NAME* 'CS'

**where**

      dept **is a** *DEPARTMENT* **and**

      dept *NAME* 'Computer Science'

---

*Example 2-88.*

Give the grade 100 to the computer science student Jack Johnson enrolled in the *Databases* course given by Prof. Smith in Fall 1987. If a grade has been previously given, replace it by the new grade.

    **update** enrl *FINAL-GRADE* 100

    **where**

        enrl.*THE-STUDENT.MAJOR NAME* 'Computer Science' **and**

        enrl.*THE-STUDENT.LAST-NAME*='Johnson' **and**

        enrl.*THE-STUDENT.FIRST-NAME*='Jack' **and**

        enrl.*THE-OFFERING.THE_QUARTER.YEAR*=1987 **and**

        enrl.*THE-OFFERING.THE-QUARTER.SEASON*='Fall' **and**

        enrl.*THE-OFFERING.THE-COURSE.NAME*='Databases' **and**

        enrl.*THE-OFFERING.THE-INSTRUCTOR.LAST-NAME*='Smith'

---

*Example 2-89.*

Increase by 10% the grades of all computer science students enrolled in the *Databases* course given by Prof. Smith in Fall 1987.

    **update** enrl *FINAL-GRADE* $1.1 \times$ enrl.*FINAL-GRADE*

    **where**

        enrl.*THE-STUDENT.MAJOR NAME* 'Computer Science' **and**

        enrl.*THE-OFFERING.THE_QUARTER.YEAR*=1987 **and**

> enrl. *THE-OFFERING.THE-QUARTER.SEASON*='Fall' **and**
>
> enrl. *THE-OFFERING.THE-COURSE.NAME*='Databases' **and**
>
> enrl. *THE-OFFERING.THE-INSTRUCTOR.LAST-NAME*='Smith'

## 2.3.9.  *Query forms

Often the users ask similar queries which differ only in the values of some parameters.

---

*Example 2-90.*

1.   What are the grades of the student whose name is 'Jackson'?
2.   What are the grades of the student whose name is 'Smith'?

---

It is desirable that such queries are predefined in parametric form, and the users would supply only the values of the parameters.

---

*Example 2-91.*

What are the grades of the student whose name is $x$, where $x$ is supplied by the end-user when the query runs?

---

Such a predefinition is called a **'query in parametric form'** or **'query form'**. It saves time on specification of similar queries, and allows the less-sophisticated end-users to use queries which can be specified only by more sophisticated users, such as programmers and analysts.

In calculus, query forms are specified by the following syntax:

**depending on** *parameters*

**get** *expressions*

**where** *condition*

The condition and the expressions may depend on the parameters.

---

*Example 2-92.*

What are the grades of the student whose name is $x$, where $x$ is supplied by the end-user when the query runs?

**depending on** $x$

---

> **get** e.*THE-OFFERING.THE-COURSE.NAME*, e.*FINAL-GRADE*
> **where**
> > e **is an** *ENROLLMENT* **and**
> > e.*THE-STUDENT.LAST-NAME* = x

*Problem 2-7.*

Use the medical/binary schema (Figure 8-6 on page 287). A patient's illness is *improbable* if when the illness commenced the patient did not have a symptom he would be expected to have with a probability of 0.9 at least. Write a calculus query to print the names of the patients and the names of the diseases for all those improbable cases.

You may assume that the userview you are using contains the whole schema and, additionally, the inverses of all the schema relations. For example, in addition to

- Relation **occurred** from *DISEASE* to *SICKNESS*   (*1:m*)

there is the inverse relation

- Relation **the-disease** from *SICKNESS* to *DISEASE*   (*m:1*)

Solution on page 297.

*Problem 2-8.*

Use the medical/binary schema (Figure 8-6 on page 287). Specify the following integrity constraints in calculus:

- A patient could not have suffered from any disease or suffered any symptom before he was born.

- In the catalog of symptoms for each disease, a symptom can have at most one probability value for that disease.

- Any other integrity constraint involving at least 2 abstract categories.

*Problem 2-9.*

1. Design a binary data base schema for a theater ticket reservation office. The following information must be covered (or be deducible from your data base):
   - telephone number and name of the customer, his credit card information, his charge, his seats, and the performance;
   - seats available for different performances and their prices.

   You may explicitly make reasonable assumptions.

2. Write a calculus expression to find the customers each of which reserved all the seats for an entire performance ("bought the performance").

*Problem 2-10.*

Use the university/binary reference schema at the end of this book. Write query to print the names of the students who took course/s with instructor/s not working in the student's major or minor department.

> For example,
> > if Jack Benson took a course offered by Prof. King, where
> > > Benson's major and minor are CS and Mathematics,
> > > but King works only in the departments of History and Music,
> > then 'Benson' will appear in the output.

Write this query in

a.    Calculus

b.    Extended Pascal

# 3
# THE RELATIONAL MODEL

## 3.1. Definitions

**Attribute** — A functional relation whose range is a concrete category.

> *Example 3-1.*
>
> - Relation *last-name* from *PERSON* to the category of values *String* (*m:1*)
>
> - Relation *first-name* from *PERSON* to the category of values *String* (*m:1*)
>
> - Relation *birth-year* from *PERSON* to the category of values *1870..1990* (*m:1*)
>
> - Relation *address* from *PERSON* to the category of values *String* (*m:1*)
>
> - Relation *year* from *QUARTER* to the category of values *1980..1995* (*m:1*)
>
> - Relation *season* from *QUARTER* to the category of values *String* (*m:1*)

- Relation *name* from *COURSE* to the category of values *String* (*m:1* )

- Relation *final-grade* from *COURSE-ENROLLMENT* to the category of values *0..100* (*m:1* )

The phrase '*a* is an **attribute of** *C*' means:
*a* is an attribute, and its domain is the category *C*.

> *Example 3-2.*
>
> *Last-name, first-name,* and *birth-year* are attributes of *PERSON*.

**Time-invariant attribute** — An attribute *A* is *time-invariant* if once an object *x* becomes related by *A* to a value *y*, the object *x* will forever be related by *A* to *y*, as long as *x* exists.

There are no time-invariant attributes in the natural user world. Even if the laws of physics or society do not allow for an attribute to change in time, the attribute may change in the perceived real world due to discoveries of errors in earlier perception. For example, a social security number could be wrongly reported and then corrected. Thus, *time-invariance* is defined only in implementational restrictions. Such restrictions are unavoidable in the relational database design. The methodology of relational schema design that is presented below has among its goals the minimization of the negative effect of such implementational restrictions.

> *Example 3-3.*
>
> None of the attributes given in the previous examples is truly time-invariant. The following attributes are the next closest thing: they change only when an error is discovered.
>
> > *birth-year* of *PERSON*;
> > *year* and *season* of *QUARTER*.
>
> The following attributes may sometimes change in time "in the real world". Thus, declaring them as time-invariant would be a stronger implementational restriction.
>
> > *last-name* and *first-name* of *PERSON*;
> > *name* of *COURSE*.
>
> The following attributes have a high probability of change in time;

no reasonable database design would restrict them as time-invariant.

> *address* of *PERSON*;
> *final-grade* of *ENROLLMENT*.

## Keys

1.  ### Single-attribute key

A time invariant attribute of a category is called its *key* if it is *1:1* and *total*. That means that the values of the attribute can be used to identify the objects of the category.

> *Example 3-4.*
>
> If we assume that the attribute *name* of *COURSE* is time-invariant, then it is probably also a key since:
>
> a.  it is *total*, provided we do not want our database to contain courses without names;
>
> b.  it is 1:1, that is, no two courses have the same name, and no course has two names.

Due to the *time-invariance* requirement, no attribute is really a key in the natural user's world. Thus, the property of a *key* is defined only in implementational restrictions, which are unavoidable in the relational database design. Also, the requirement of *totality* is very rarely an integrity constraint imposed by the logic of the user world, but rather is an implementational restriction.

> *Example 3-5.*
>
> Would the attribute *social-security-number* of the category *PERSON* be its key? Let us assume that we have already imposed an implementational restriction of *time-invariance* on this attribute (thus making it very hard and dangerous for our users to correct errors).
>
> To be a key, this attribute must be *one-to-one* and *total*. It is indeed one-to-one. But in the real world it is not really total: there are some persons who do not have social security numbers before they are reported to our database. The totality can be imposed as an implementational restriction with one of the following practical

provisions:

a.  Persons who do not have social security numbers would be assigned the dummy default number 0, which would be called a "social security number" for the purposes of the database. But then this attribute would no longer be *one-to-one* since two persons may have the same number 0.

b.  For persons who do not have real social security numbers, generate dummy temporary numbers in such a way that all these numbers are different and not in the range of possible real social security numbers. For example, if the real s.s. numbers may never begin with the digit 9, then begin all the dummy numbers with this digit.

Apart from the unnaturalness and "cheating" which are bound to result in misinterpretation of the computer's reports, there is a serious technical problem: What if a person did not have a real s.s. number at first, but later received one, and this new number is a valuable piece of information which the user wants to keep in the database? If we allow replacement of the old dummy number by the new real one, then the *time-invariance* requirement is violated.

c.  Yet another possibility is to disallow recording of information about persons who do not have s.s. numbers. I am afraid that our client might be unhappy with such a restriction.

*Example 3-6.*

We can generate a new artificial attribute to serve as a key. Let *id#* be a new artificial attribute of the category *PERSON*, generated in such a way that when a new person enters the database, he is assigned an arbitrary meaningless number which has not been used before. (When the person is deleted from the database, the number is not reused.)  This attribute would be a key.

*Convention:*  In this text, we shall name the attributes constrained to be keys with the suffix *-key*.

> *Example 3-7.*
>
> ### name-key of COURSE
>
> The name of the attribute *name-key* implicitly defines a constraint or implementational restriction "This attribute is a key of its domain, the category *COURSE*."

2. **Multi-attribute key**

The following definition extends the concept *key* to a collection of attributes.

**Key** of a category — a *collection* of total time-invariant attributes $f_1, f_2, \ldots, f_n$ whose domain is that category s.t.

(i)    For any collection of values, $x_1, \ldots, x_n$ there is no more than one object $y$ of the category s.t.

$$x_1 = y.f_1 \text{ and } x_2 = y.f_2 \text{ and } \cdots \text{ and } x_n = y.f_n$$

(ii)    No proper subcollection of these attributes *always* satisfies (i).

Practically, requirement (i) means that the collection of attributes is sufficient to identify every object of the category. Requirement (ii) means that the collection is minimal: if one of the attributes is not known then the remaining attributes might not provide sufficient information to identify every object of the category.

> *Example 3-8.*
>
> (*the-year, the-season*) is the only key of the category *QUARTER*.
>
> Either attribute alone does not identify each object. Together they do.

*Convention*:    in this text, when a category is constrained to have exactly one key, and the key is composed of several attributes, we shall name these attributes with the suffix *-in-key*.

> *Example 3-9.*
>
> *the-year-in-key* and *the-season-in-key* of *QUARTER*

*Note*:

(i)   In the real world a category usually has *no* key. Thus, the existence of a key is usually not an integrity constraint but rather an implementational restriction. This restriction will be imposed when unavoidable due to limitations of a DBMS or a database model, especially the relational model.

(ii)  Existence of a key makes every object of the category identifiable with the values of the key and eliminates the necessity to refer to abstract objects.

> *Example 3-10.*
>
> Courses can be identified with strings *name-key*. Quarters can be identified with pairs *(the-year-in-key, the-season-in-key)*.

(iii) A category which has no key may still have all its objects completely identifiable (using different relations and their combinations for different objects), but the identification would not be uniform.

> *Example 3-11.*
>
> The category *DEPARTMENT* does not have a key (it does not have any attribute at all; the relation *NAME* is not an attribute because it is 1:m). However, if the relation *department-name* is total, then, being 1:m, it distinguishes between every two departments according to their names.
>
> If the relation *department-name* is not total, then we might have a problem distinguishing between two departments having no names at all. In that case, it is possible that the "anonymous" departments can be distinguished by their relationships of *works-in* with instructors.

> *Example 3-12.*
>
> We have not defined any key for the category INSTRUCTOR. However, most instructors have unique names and can be identified by their names. Few instructors have common names, and their identification requires names of their departments in addition to their first and last names. Some of the instructors have non-unique names, but do not work for any department at all. These rare persons can be identifiable by their names in conjunction with their

birth years or with courses they teach or with their addresses (whichever of this information is available and sufficient for identification).

This identification is non-uniform because different instructors are identified by different relations.

The non-uniform identification is quite common and satisfactory in the real world and in the Binary Model, but the implementational restrictions of the Relational Model will necessitate a *uniform* identification of the objects of a category.

(iv) When a key is composed of several attributes it is still *one* key.

(v) A category may theoretically have several keys. However, since categories in the real world rarely have even one key, the existence of more than one key would be an unnecessarily strong implementational restriction, which is not required by database management systems. Thus, the possibility of multiple keys will be ignored in this text.

A binary schema is called **table-oriented**, or a **relational schema** if

(i) all the abstract categories of the schema have keys

(ii) all the abstract categories are pairwise disjoint

(iii) the only relations are attributes.

Thus, all the information in a relational schema is represented by attributes of categories.

*Example 3-13.*

Figure Ref-2 could be a relational schema for the university application, provided

- all the categories are restricted to having keys as shown,
- there are no persons but students and instructors, and
- the categories *INSTRUCTOR* and *STUDENT* are disjoint.

We shall see later that this schema can be used even without imposing the severe restriction of disjointness.

*Example 3-14.*

Consider the category *COURSE-ENROLLMENT*. In the relational schema it has no relations to the categories *STUDENT* and *COURSE-OFFERING*. Instead, it has attributes giving essentially the same information. Thus, instead

- Relation **the-student** from *COURSE-ENROLLMENT* to *STUDENT* (*m:1*)

it has the attribute

- Relation *student-id-in-key* from *COURSE-ENROLLMENT* to the category of values *Integer* (*m:1* )

**Table-declaration, relation-declaration** — any subschema of a relational schema having only one abstract category with all of its attributes and their ranges. The *name* of the *table* is the name of that category.

*Example 3-15.*

Here is the table-declaration *QUARTER*.

| QUARTER |
|---|
| *year-in-key: 1980..1995*<br>*season-in-key: String* |

**Instantaneous table, instantaneous relation** — an instantaneous database viewed under a table-declaration. This means that an instantaneous table is a part of an instantaneous relational database containing all the objects of one table and all their relationships (attributes).

**Representation of an instantaneous table** — a printable table whose title is the name of the category, the names of the columns are the attributes, and for every object in the category there is a row (called a **tuple**) composed of the values of the attributes of that object.

> *Example 3-16.*
>
> The following is an instantaneous table of *STUDENT*. (Of course, in this example the instantaneous table is unrealistically small. It would contain thousands of tuples for a normal university.)

### STUDENT

| id-key | last-name | first-name | birth-year | address | major-dept-main-name | minor-dept-main-name |
|--------|-----------|------------|------------|---------|----------------------|----------------------|
| 12345 | Victory | Elizabeth | 1966 | 100 Sun St. | Computer Science | Economics |
| 12348 | Howards | Jane | 1965 | 200 Dorms | Arts | Economics |
| 43532 | Wood | Michael | 1964 | 110 Dorms | Arts | Economics |

**Figure 3-1.** An instantaneous table.

*Note*:

(i)   There cannot be two identical rows in an instantaneous table, because this would imply that there are two objects with the same values of the key.

(ii)  The order of tuples (rows) is immaterial; the order of columns is immaterial.

> *Example 3-17.*
>
> The following figure represents the very same instantaneous table as the previous example.

### STUDENT

| birth-year | address | major-dept-main-name | id-key | last-name | first-name | minor-dept-main-name |
|------------|---------|----------------------|--------|-----------|------------|----------------------|
| 1964 | 110 Dorms | Arts | 43532 | Wood | Michael | Economics |
| 1965 | 200 Dorms | Arts | 12348 | Howards | Jane | Economics |
| 1966 | 100 Sun St. | Computer Science | 12345 | Victory | Elizabeth | Economics |

**Figure 3-2.** Some columns and rows have been moved in the representation without changing the instantaneous table.

**Representation of an instantaneous relational database** — a collection of instantaneous tables.

*Example 3-18.*

The following figure is a representation of an instantaneous database for the schema of Figure Ref-2. This instantaneous database represents the same state of the application's real world as the binary instantaneous database of Figure 1-1 on page 22.

## STUDENT

| id-key | last-name | first-name | birth-year | address | major-dept-main-name | minor-dept-main-name |
|--------|-----------|------------|------------|---------|----------------------|----------------------|
| 12345 | Victory | Elizabeth | 1966 | 100 Sun St. | Computer Science | Economics |
| 12348 | Howards | Jane | 1965 | 200 Dorms | Arts | Economics |
| 43532 | Wood | Michael | 1964 | 110 Dorms | Arts | Economics |

## INSTRUCTOR

| id-key | last-name | first-name | birth-year | address |
|--------|-----------|------------|------------|---------|
| 11332 | Brown | George | 1956 | 112 Lucky Dr. |
| 14352 | Whatson | Mary | 1953 | 231 Fortune Dr. |
| 24453 | Blue | John | 1950 | 536 Orange Dr. |

## DEPARTMENT

| main-name-key |
|---------------|
| Computer Science |
| Mathematics |
| Physics |
| Arts |
| Economics |

## DEPARTMENT NAMING

| name-key | main name |
|----------|-----------|
| CS | Computer Science |
| Math | Mathematics |
| Physics | Physics |
| Mathematics | Mathematics |
| Computer Science | Computer Science |
| Arts | Arts |
| Economics | Economics |

**WORK**

| instructor-id-in-key | department-main-name-in-key |
|---|---|
| 11332 | Computer Science |
| 11332 | Mathematics |
| 14352 | Physics |
| 24453 | Mathematics |

**COURSE**

| name-key |
|---|
| Databases |
| Football |
| Gastronomy |

**QUARTER**

| year-in-key | season-in-key |
|---|---|
| 1987 | Fall |
| 1987 | Winter |
| 1987 | Spring |

**COURSE OFFERING**

| instructor-id-in-key | course-name-in-key | year-in-key | season-in-key |
|---|---|---|---|
| 11332 | Databases | 1987 | Fall |
| 11332 | Football | 1987 | Fall |
| 11332 | Gastronomy | 1987 | Fall |

**COURSE ENROLLMENT**

| instructor-id-in-key | course-name-in-key | year-in-key | season-in-key | student-id-in-key | final-grade |
|---|---|---|---|---|---|
| 11332 | Gastronomy | 1987 | Fall | 12345 | 100 |
| 11332 | Gastronomy | 1987 | Fall | 12348 | 70 |
| 11332 | Databases | 1987 | Fall | 12348 | 80 |

**Figure 3-3.** An instantaneous database for the relational schema of the university application.

An alternative **representation of relational schemas (linear, non-graphic)**:

> *table name*     [ *attribute* : *range*, . . . , *attribute* : *range* ]
>
> . . .
>
> *table name*     [ *attribute* : *range*, . . . , *attribute* : *range* ]

---

*Example 3-19.*

Here is a linear representation of the schema of Figure Ref-2:

DEPARTMENT [ main-name-key: String]

DEPARTMENT-NAMING [ name-key: String, main-name: String]

STUDENT [ id-key: Integer, last-name: String, first-name: String, birth-year: 1870..1990, address: String, major-department-main-name: String, minor-department-main-name: String]

INSTRUCTOR [ id-key: Integer, last-name: String, first-name: String, birth-year: 1870..1990, address: String]

WORK [ instructor-id-in-key: Integer, department-main-name-in-key: String]

QUARTER [ year-in-key: 1980..1995, season-in-key: String]

COURSE [ name-key: String]

COURSE-OFFERING [ instructor-id-in-key: Integer, course-name-in-key: String, year-in-key: 1980..1995, season-in-key: String]

COURSE-ENROLLMENT [ instructor-id-in-key: Integer, course-name-in-key: String, year-in-key: 1980..1995, season-in-key: String, student-id-in-key: Integer, final-grade: 0..100]

---

*Problem 3-1.*

A small enterprise is described by the following binary schema:

- Category *EMPLOYEE*
- Relation **name** from *EMPLOYEE* to *Text*  (*m:1*)
- Relation **the-boss** from *EMPLOYEE* to *EMPLOYEE*  (*m:1*)
- Category *PROJECT*
- Relation **proj-name** from *PROJECT* to *Text*  (*1:1,total*)

- Relation **is-a-part-of** from *PROJECT* to *PROJECT*   (*m:m*)
- Relation **works-for** from *EMPLOYEE* to *PROJECT*   (*m:m*)

Design a relational schema for the enterprise.

Solution on page 298.

*Problem 3-2.*

Design a relational schema for a post office, covering the following information:

- The zip-code of every house in the U.S.A. (When a state, a city, a street and a street number are known, the zip-code can be found.)
- The names and addresses of the postmen employed by *this* post office.
- For every address in the post office's service area, the postmen serving the address.

Note: There are too many houses in the U.S.A. You cannot allot a row in a table for every house in the U.S.A. if the data is to be kept at a local post office.

## Consequences of implementational restrictions in the Relational Model:

- The schemas often deviate from the real world.
- The schemas are often unnatural, inflexible, and redundant.
- The integrity constraints are often under-represented in the schemas.
- The queries are usually harder to specify.

---

*Example 3-20.*

Instead of

$$(i\ WORKS\text{-}IN\ d)$$

we have to say:

   (**exists** w **in** *WORK*:

      i.*ID-key* = w.*INSTRUCTOR-ID-in-key* **and**

      d.*MAIN-NAME-key* = w.*DEPARTMENT-MAIN-NAME-in-key*)

---

## Purposes of implementational restrictions in the Relational Model:

- **Exclusion of non-attribute relations, exclusion of intersecting categories, exclusion of sub- and super-categories** — allow for readable and simple representation of the instantaneous database as every-day tables.

- **Totality and uniqueness of keys** — allow
  - a standard printable representation for every object,
  - readable reference to objects of one table from objects of another table,
  - unambiguous definition of simple updates.

- **Time-invariance of keys** — prevents inconsistent update of keys.

  If the values of the key of an object are updated, then all the references to this object throughout the instantaneous database become wrong. The human user cannot be relied upon to find and update all the references. The database management system is normally unaware of these references, and thus cannot update them automatically, unless it is a very advanced system having a high-level support for the so called **referential integrity**.

  Many database management systems do not explicitly require the time-invariance, but do not provide a high-level support for the referential integrity either. This does not mean that those systems do not need the time-invariance. Rather, this means that they do not check for the time-invariance, and, without warning to the user, they corrupt the database when the user modifies a value of a key.

  *Note*: It is hard to say whether the severe implementational restrictions can really be justified by the benefits of the model.

### Totality of non-key attributes

Many relational database management systems require a further implementational restriction: they require that all the attributes be total.

Relational DBMS that do not require the totality of attributes allow **null values of attributes**.

The restriction of the totality of the non-key attributes pragmatically requires a modification of the meaning of an attribute which is non-total in the real world. A special value is identified which can never be a value of the attribute in the real world. This value is assigned to the objects that do not have any real value of the attribute.

---

*Example 3-21.*

We can assign the dummy grade "−1" to the enrollments which do not have any real grade. Thus we convert

- Relation *final-grade* from *COURSE-ENROLLMENT* to the

> category of values  *0..100*  (*m:1* )
>
> into:
>
> - Relation *new-final-grade* from *COURSE-ENROLLMENT* to the category of values  *-1..100*  (*m:1* )
>
> so that:
>
> x.*NEW-FINAL-GRADE* = -1 **iff**
>
> x *FINAL-GRADE* **null**

Such "cheating" will, however, cause inconvenience and misinterpretation of queries of naive users.

> *Example 3-22.*
>
> The query
>
> **get** enrl.*STUDENT-ID* **where**
>
> enrl **is a** COURSE-ENROLLMENT **and**
>
> enrl.*new-FINAL-GRADE* < 60
>
> will retrieve also the students who have no grades at all. The system will also believe that two students who really have no grades have identical grades, and thus will mislead the user.

Some relational database management systems allow the analyst to define **default values of attributes**. These would be the values for the objects when the user has entered no value. The definition of default values enhances the convenience of updates, but it does not solve the problem of the misinterpretation of queries. A default value is still a regular value as far as the system is concerned.

> *Example 3-23.*
>
> We can define "-1" to be the default grade. This will be then the grade of all the enrollments for which the user has not provided a grade.

In many cases the default value is defined as 0 or the empty string.

---

*Example 3-24.*

We should not define 0 as the default for the grade if our intention is to use the default value as a substitute for *null*. This is because 0 might be a real grade of a poor student.

We can use the empty string " as the default for *last-name*.

---

## 3.2.  Database Design

The purpose of this section is to show how a high-quality relational database can be designed once we have a binary schema for the application.

## 3.2.1.  Objectives of schema conversion

**Schema-conversion** — replacement of a schema by another schema having the same information content. This means that each of the two schemas can be regarded as a userview of the other.

Schema-conversion is a means of database design: a schema is first designed in a higher-level database model and then translated into a lower-level model which is supported by the available DBMS (when a DBMS for a higher-level model is unavailable or inadequate).

*Note*:

    (i) Schema conversion is usually done in order to impose implementation restrictions needed because of the database model or the database management system. Thus, the latter schema is usually of lesser quality than the former.

---

*Example 3-25.*

We shall see in this section how the binary schema of the university application can be converted into the relational schema of Figure Ref-2.

---

    (ii) Although only the latter schema (or its descendents after more conversions) will be used by the DBMS software, after conversion the former schema *must* be kept and maintained as a documentation of the application's real world.

    (iii) After conversion, the former schema is called the **conceptual semantic schema** of the latter *physical* schema or its descendents.

(iv) When the concepts of the real world change, the conceptual semantic schema must be changed *first*, and only then the physical schema is *regenerated* from the conceptual semantic binary schema by conversion.

This section presents a conversion algorithm of an adequate binary schema into a relational schema whose quality is among the highest possible for the Relational Model.

This algorithm can be performed manually by the database designer. Alternatively, an automatic tool can be used to perform all the busy-work, while prompting the database designer for intelligent decisions (and using defaults when the designer fails to provide such a guidance). One such tool has been developed at the University of California by the Author and his students.

## 3.2.2.  Composition and split of relations

Two auxiliary definitions of terminology that will be used in the conversion algorithm follow.

**Composition of relations**

Let the range of Relation $R_1$ be the domain of Relation $R_2$.

Relation $R$ is the composition of $R_1$ on $R_2$ if

$$xRy \text{ iff exists } z \text{ such that } xR_1z \text{ and } zR_2y.$$

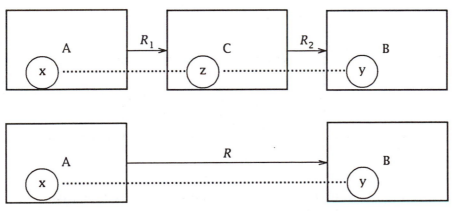

**Figure 3-4.** Relation $R$ is the composition of two relations, $R_1$ and $R_2$:    $xRy$ is whenever $xR_1z$ and $zR_2y$.

*Example 3-26.*

Consider two relations:

- Relation **the-course** from *COURSE-OFFERING* to *COURSE* (*m:1*)

- Relation **name** from *COURSE* to *String* (*1:1*)

The composition of *THE-COURSE* on *NAME* is:

- Relation *the-name-of-the-course* from *COURSE-OFFERING* to the category of values *String* (*m:1* )

**Relation-split** — conversion of a schema having a relation $R$ into another schema having, instead of $R$, a new abstract category $C$ and two total functional relations $R_1, R_2$, whose domain is $C$, s.t. $xRy$ *iff* exists an object $z$ in $C$ for which $zR_1x$ and $zR_2y$.

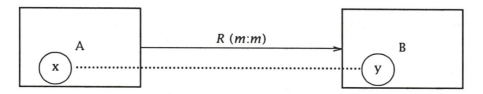

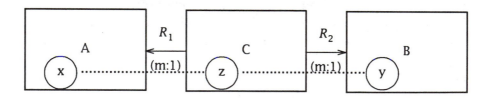

**Figure 3-5.** Relation $R$ is split into a category $C$ and two relations, $R_1$ and $R_2$. Every relationship $x-y$ is broken into $x-z$ and $z-y$.

*Example 3-27.*

If due to an implementational restriction we may not have a *m:m* relation:

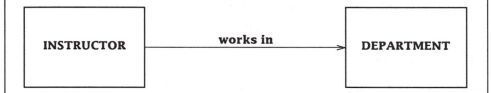

then we can split it into:

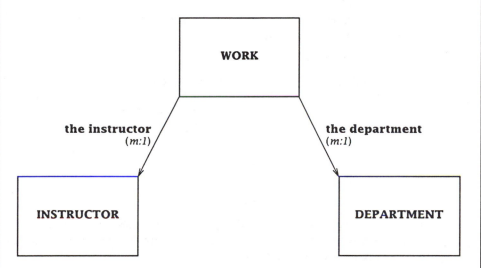

This split necessitates additional integrity constraints:

(i)    Both new relations are total.

(ii)   For any combination of an instructor and a department there is at most one object in work.

The latter constraint is more rigorously formulated in calculus, as follows.

**for every** w **in** *WORK:*

    **for every** v **in** *WORK:*

        **if** w.*the-instructor* = v.*the-instructor* **and**

> w.*the-department* = v.*the-department*
>
> **then** *w=v*.

The composition of relations and relation-split can be regarded as userviews.*

The following subsections present the conversion algorithm

## 3.2.3. Keys

**Step 1. Choose a key for every abstract category**, excluding subcategories of other categories, as follows.

   a.   **(single-attribute key)**

   *if* the category has an attribute which is *1:1*, time-invariant, and total, *then* let that attribute be the key;

   b.   **("forced" single-attribute key)**

   *else if* the category has an attribute which can be implementationally restricted to be *1:1*, time-invariant, and total, without very harmful alteration of the real world, *then* make that attribute into a key (declare the implementational restriction);

---

*Example 3-28.*

*name-key* of *COURSE*

It is not a very far reaching alteration of the real world to make this implementation restriction: "Every course has exactly one name, and this name may never be changed."

---

* The following is a formal definition of the *composition* in the predicate calculus for the inference rules of userviews. Here, the category $C$ is the range of $R_1$.

   **userview relation**: x $R$ y

      **where exists** z **in** $C$:

         (x $R_1$ z   **and**   z $R_2$ y)

The following is a formal definition of the *relation-spilt* in the predicate calculus for the inference rules of userviews.

      **userview category** $C$ ($R_1$: x, $R_2$: y)

         **where** x $R$ y

c.    **(multi-attribute key)**

*else if* the category has a collection of attributes which are time-invariant and total, and jointly identify all the objects in the category, *then* let a minimal such collection be the key;

---

*Example 3-29.*

(*season-in-key, year-in-key*) of *QUARTER*

---

d.    ("forced" **multi-attribute key**)

*else if* the category has a collection of attributes which can be implementationally restricted to be time-invariant and total, and to jointly identify all the objects of the category, without very harmful alteration of the real world, *then* make a minimal such collection of attributes into a key;

e.    **(inferred key)**

*else if* a collection of attributes can be inferred from the information existing in the schema and from keys of other categories, so that

- these attributes can be implementationally restricted, without very harmful alteration of the real world,

    (i)    to be time-invariant and total, and

    (ii)   to jointly identify all the objects of the category,

*then*

    (i)    choose a minimal such collection of inferable attributes;

    (ii)   add to the schema those attributes from the collection which are not already in the schema;

    (iii)  make this collection of attributes into a key (declare the implementational restrictions);

    (iv)   convert the inference rule of these attributes into constraints. (Since these will now be new attributes, their values will be updated by the users with possible inconsistency relative to the information from which these attributes are inferable.)

---

*Example 3-30.*

To obtain a key for *DEPARTMENT* we alter the real world slightly: we require every department to have at least one name; we shall call the first name ever given to a department the *"main-name"*, and we require that the *main-name* of a department may never be changed. We add the new attribute

- Relation *main-name-key* from *DEPARTMENT* to the category of values *String* (*m:1* )

and the constraint

**for every** d **in** *DEPARTMENT:*

d *NAME* d.*MAIN-NAME-key*

Note: In conjunction with the implicit constraint *-key*, the above constraint means that the main-name is the first name ever given to the department, and that it will remain the department's name forever.

---

*Example 3-31.*

More characteristic examples of inferred keys are for the categories *COURSE-OFFERING* and *COURSE-ENROLLMENT*. These will be given and generalized after we have a key for *PERSON*.

---

f.    (**enumerator id key**)

*else* create a new external enumeration for the objects in the category (thus altering the real world) and add it as an attribute, which will be the chosen key.

---

*Example 3-32.*

The key of *PERSON* will be a new attribute *id-key*.

---

Pragmatically, a program should be written to generate new values of an *enumerator id key*. These numbers will be assigned by the user to the new objects of the category. The numbers may not be reused when an object is removed. The numbers themselves should bear no correlation to the other information in the database, since the other information may change in time, while the key is time-invariant.

It is also advisable that the numbers be not assigned sequentially, but rather in an arbitrary sequence. Otherwise, the irrelevant information on the "seniority" of objects will be hidden in the id. Any hidden information will be abused by the application programmers. Since it is not always possible to update such hidden information correctly, the programs will not produce the expected results in some special cases.

*Note:* The step of finding keys is performed simultaneously for all the categories, since we might need to know the key of one category in order to find a key of a related category.

---

*Example 3-33.*

An *inferred key* of *COURSE-OFFERING* can be obtained when keys for *QUARTER*, *COURSE*, and *PERSON* have been chosen. The inferred key of *COURSE-OFFERING* will be

> {the name of the course, the year of the quarter, the season of the quarter, id of the instructor}

Hence, we add 4 new attributes to *COURSE-OFFERING*. The *inferred* key of *COURSE-ENROLLMENT* will be 5 new attributes

> {id of the student, the key of the offering}.

(The "key of the offering" consists of four attributes. Thus, there is a total of five attributes in the key of *COURSE-ENROLLMENT.*)

---

*Example 3-34.*

The category *COURSE-OFFERING* is now:

**COURSE OFFERING**

*instructor-id-in-key: Integer*
*course-name-in-key: String*
*year-in-key: 1980..1995*
*season-in-key: String*

---

The above is an example of the prevalent case of an *inferred key*. The following is a generalization of this example.

Assume that a category $C$ is the domain of total functional relations $f_1, \ldots, f_n$ which jointly identify all the objects of the category.

*Example 3-35.*

Every course offering is uniquely identified by its instructor, course, and quarter. Thus, the total functional relations

*THE-INSTRUCTOR, THE-COURSE, THE-QUARTER*

jointly identify all the objects of their domain, the category *COURSE-OFFERING*.

The above assumption means that there is an integrity constraint

**for every** x **in** $C$:

  **for every** y **in** $C$:

   **if** $x.f_1=y.f_1$ **and** $\cdots$ **and** $x.f_n=y.f_n$

    **then** $x=y$

*Example 3-36.*

**for every** x **in** *COURSE-OFFERING*:

  **for every** y **in** *COURSE-OFFERING*:

   **if**

      $x.THE\text{-}INSTRUCTOR=y.THE\text{-}INSTRUCTOR$ **and**

      $x.THE\text{-}COURSE=y.THE\text{-}COURSE$ **and**

      $x.THE\text{-}QUARTER=y.THE\text{-}QUARTER$

      **then** $x=y$

In this case, once the keys of the ranges of the functional relations $f_1, \ldots, f_n$ are known, a key of $C$ can be inferred from them. Let the keys of the ranges be $k_1, \ldots, k_n$. Let $k_i\text{-of-}f_i$ be the set of inferred attributes obtained by the composition of the attributes comprising the key $k_i$ and the relation $f_i$.

*Example 3-37.*

There are three such sets of inferred attributes for the category *COURSE-OFFERING*:

• id-of-the-instructor

- the-name-of-the-course
- the-year-of-the-quarter, the-season-of-the-quarter

The key of $C$ is contained in the union of compositions of the relations $f_i$ onto the keys of their ranges, that is,

$$\{(k_1 \text{ of } f_1), \cdots, (k_n \text{ of } f_n)\}$$

Notice that the key of $C$ is *contained* in the above union of compositions. Usually the key of $C$ is equal to that union of compositions, but sometimes it is *properly* contained.

---

*Example 3-38.*

Let us change the meaning of *COURSE-OFFERING*. Now, it does not have to occur in one particular quarter, but can last several quarters, as long as the quarters are within one academic year. There are two relations between offerings and quarters:

- Relation **beginning-quarter** from *COURSE-OFFERING* to *QUARTER* (*m:1,total*)
- Relation **ending-quarter** from *COURSE-OFFERING* to *QUARTER* (*m:1,total*)

The key of *COURSE-OFFERING* is properly contained in

{the name of the course;
the year and season of the beginning quarter;
the year and season of the ending quarter;
id of the instructor}

The attribute *THE-YEAR-OF-THE-ENDING-QUARTER* is not a part of the key, since this attribute is not needed for identification of the offerings. For given beginning quarter and the season of the ending quarter, we can deduce the year of the ending quarter, since we know that the offering is within one academic year.

---

*Example 3-39.*

The binary schema of the university application has been converted so far into the schema on the following page.

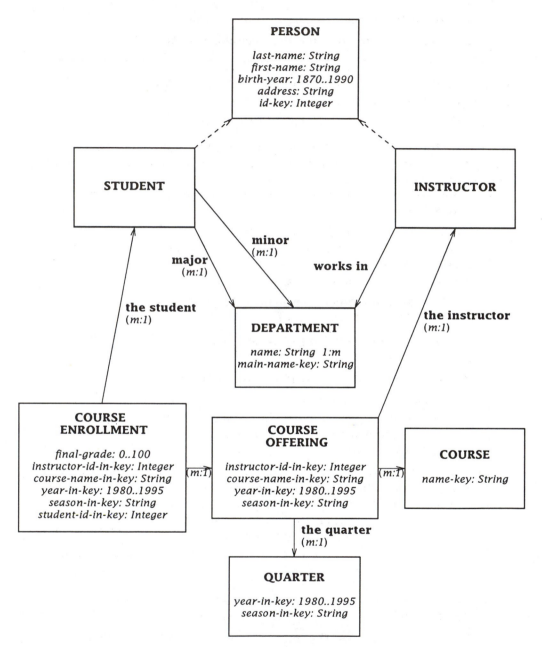

**Figure 3-6.** The university schema with keys.

## 3.2.4. **Disjointness of categories**

**Step 2. Convert the intersecting abstract categories into disjoint** categories by the following procedure for every group of intersecting categories.

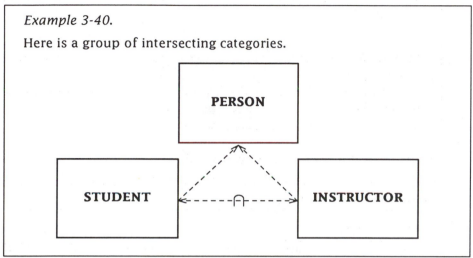

*Example 3-40.*

Here is a group of intersecting categories.

A. Consider a **complete group of categories** so that every category outside the group is disjoint from every category in the group.

Let *C* denote the union of all the categories in the group. If such a category *C* does not already exist in the schema, then add it.

Let $S_1, S_2, \ldots, S_n$ be the other categories in the group. (All of them are direct or indirect subcategories of *C*.)

*Example 3-41.*

$C=PERSON, S_1=INSTRUCTOR, S_2=STUDENT.$

Let

$$S_0 = C - \bigcup_{i=1}^{n} S_i$$

$S_0$ is the hypothetical category consisting of the objects of *C* which do not belong to any of the subcategories. The category $S_0$ is considered in order to ensure that no information is lost during the conversion. It is not added to the schema at this time. It may or may not be added to the schema at a later step, depending on decisions made at that step.

---

*Example 3-42.*

If there may be other persons in addition to instructors and students, then

$$S_0 = OTHER\text{-}PERSON$$

Otherwise, $S_0 = \varnothing$, and it would not have to be added to the schema at any step.

In the continuation of this case study in the examples we will assume the latter case: no "other persons".

---

B.   Estimate the **intersection factors** $\pi$ and $\rho$.

In order to chose the best way of conversion, we shall need to estimate the following quantities.

---

*Example 3-43.*

For the above group of intersecting categories, the choice of the method to eliminate the intersection of the categories will depend on the correlation of two parameters:

- the percentage of people who are both students and instructors, $\pi$, and

- the percentage of relations specific to students or instructors among all the relations which can be relevant to persons, $\rho$.

---

$$\rho = \frac{number\ of\ relations\ whose\ domain\ or\ range\ is\ S_1\ or\ \cdots\ or\ S_n}{number\ of\ relations\ whose\ domain\ or\ range\ is\ C\ or\ S_1\ or\ \cdots\ or\ S_n}$$

---

*Example 3-44.*

For the group of the previous examples, $\rho = \dfrac{5}{10}$.

---

$$\pi = \frac{expected\ total\ number\ of\ objects\ in\ the\ intersections}{expected\ total\ number\ of\ objects\ in\ C}$$

The above formula is rather informal.*

---

*Example 3-45.*

To estimate $\pi$, we have to predict the future of our database. It is reasonable to assume that about 5% percent of all persons would be simultaneously students and instructors, so $\pi$=0.05.

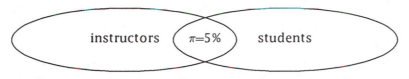

---

*Example 3-46.*

If we had several intersecting categories, we would count all the intersections:

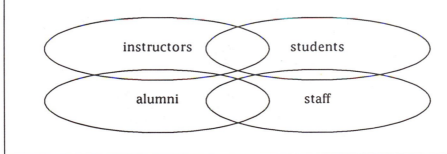

---

C.   Select the best conversion into disjoint categories.

---

* More formally:

$$\pi = \frac{expected\ cardinality\ of\ \bigcup_{i \neq j} (S_i \cap S_j)}{expected\ cardinality\ of\ C}$$

*Example 3-47.*

Consider the non-disjoint categories *INSTRUCTOR* and *STUDENT*, which are subcategories of the category *PERSON=INSTRUCTOR* ∪ *STUDENT*. The following are several possibilities of conversion. We will later select the best of the possibilities, depending on the circumstances.

a. *Conversion into one category (Union)*

*Example 3-48.*

Substitute the whole group of categories by their union, the category *PERSON*. This category will serve as the domain or the range for all the relations whose domain or range was one of the original categories. In addition, this category will have two Boolean attributes, *IS-AN-INSTRUCTOR* and *IS-A-STUDENT*, associating the value *true* with objects representing instructors and students respectively.

**PERSON**

*id-key: Integer*
*last-name: String*
*first-name: String*
*birth-year: 1870..1990*
*address: String*
*is-a-student: Boolean*
*is-an-instructor: Boolean*

- Relation **major** from *PERSON* to *DEPARTMENT* (*m:1*)

- Relation **minor** from *PERSON* to *DEPARTMENT* (*m:1*)

- Relation **the-instructor** from *COURSE-OFFERING* to *PERSON* (*m:1*)

- Relation **the-student** from *COURSE-ENROLLMENT* to *PERSON* (*m:1*)

- Relation **works-in** from *PERSON* to *DEPARTMENT* (*m:m*)

b.    *Conversion into artificially disjoint categories of **Events***

> *Example 3-49.*
>
> Substitute these categories by two disjoint categories of events: *Event-of-being-a-STUDENT* and *Event-of-being-an-INSTRUCTOR* (usually abbreviated just *STUDENT* and *INSTRUCTOR*, but the meaning of the full names is intended).
>
> An instructor who is also a student will be represented by two distinct objects of the aforementioned categories.
>
> The objects of the new categories are not persons, but rather their "hats" — a person may have two "hats", one as an instructor and one as a student. The two categories of "hats" are disjoint.
>
> The relations whose domain or range is the category *PERSON*, for example the relation *ADDRESS*, will be replaced by two relations having the new categories as their domains or ranges, such as the relations *STUDENT'S-ADDRESS* and *INSTRUCTOR'S-ADDRESS*.
>
> | **STUDENT** | **INSTRUCTOR** |
> |---|---|
> | *id-key: Integer*<br>*last-name: String*<br>*first-name: String*<br>*birth-year: 1870..1990*<br>*address: String* | *id-key: Integer*<br>*last-name: String*<br>*first-name: String*<br>*birth-year: 1870..1990*<br>*address: String* |

It may appear that by introducing the categories of "hats" we have succeeded in fooling the system. Actually, we have fooled ourselves. Without understanding the relationship between two hats of one person, the system will not be able to correctly interpret some queries of naive users, and may cause inconsistency in the stored information and other problems:

-    When the address of a person is updated, it may get updated in one category, but not in the other. The database will become inconsistent.

-    A naive query like "How many people are there?" will involve double count of persons who are instructors and students simultaneously.

c. *Conversion into **Union+Events***

*Example 3-50.*

We can retain the category *PERSON* with all its relationships and define two categories of events which will inherit all the relationships of *STUDENT* and *INSTRUCTOR*, and additionally will have keys and special 1:1 relationships with the category *PERSON*:

```
                    ┌─────────────────────┐
                    │      PERSON         │
                    │  id-key: Integer    │
                    │  last-name: String  │
                    │    (and other       │
                    │      relations      │
                    │     of PERSON)      │
                    └─────────────────────┘
                              ↑
                        /          \
          ┌───────────────┐   1:1   1:1  ┌───────────────┐
          │   Event of    │               │   Event of    │
          │   being a     │               │   being an    │
          │   STUDENT     │               │   INSTRUCTOR  │
          │ id-key: Integer│              │ id-key: Integer│
          │               │               │               │
          │    other      │               │    other      │
          │   relations   │               │   relations   │
          │  of STUDENT   │               │ of INSTRUCTOR │
          └───────────────┘               └───────────────┘
```

- Category *PERSON* (retains its relations from the binary schema)

- Category *Event-of-being-a-STUDENT* (inherits all the relations of *STUDENT*)

- Category *Event-of-being-an-INSTRUCTOR* (inherits all the relations of *INSTRUCTOR*)

- Relation **student-person** from *Event-of-being-a-STUDENT* to *PERSON* (*1:1,total*)

- Relation **instructor-person** from *Event-of-being-an-INSTRUCTOR* to *PERSON* (*1:1,total*)

*Example 3-51.*

To further explore the differences between the three approaches, consider the formulation of the query "Print the names of all the students."

*Events*:

>    **get** s.*LAST-NAME*
>
>>    **where** s **is a** *STUDENT*

*Union*:

>    **get** s.*LAST-NAME*
>
>>    **where**
>>
>>>    s **is a** *PERSON* **and**
>>>
>>>    s.*IS-A-STUDENT*

*Union+Events*:

>    **get** p.*LAST-NAME*
>
>>    **where**
>>
>>>    p **is a** *PERSON* **and**
>>>
>>>    **exists** s **in** *STUDENT*:
>>>
>>>>    s.*ID-key* = p.*ID-key*

*Relative disadvantages of each approach*

The principal disadvantage of *Events* is the *redundancy*. For example, the birth-year of an instructor who is also a student has to be logically represented twice in the database, which can cause inconsistency and other problems.

The principal disadvantages of *Union* are the *unnaturalness* of the schema and the *under-coverage of integrity constraints*. For example, an additional integrity constraint has to be defined to prevent association of a non-student instructor with *a major department of studies*. Another important deficiency is the *null-values*, causing significant problems in formulation of queries. (We say that "*p.MAJOR* is **null**" if the person *p* is not related to any department by the relation *MAJOR*.)

The principal disadvantages of *Union+Events* are the *unnaturalness* of the schema and significant difficulties in the formulation of queries and other operations. These difficulties, however, can be overcome by the use of userviews which would conveniently redefine the concepts of the schema. This requires that the DBMS provide a high level support for userviews, including the capability to specify updates through userviews. Most relational DBMS, however, do not provide sufficient support of userviews.

*Conclusion*

Unless the DBMS provides sufficient support for userviews as discussed above, we have to exclude the *Union+Events* approach.

Both other approaches, *Union* and *Events*, would result in low-quality schemas, but the relational database designer has to choose the better of the two.

---

*Example 3-52.*

The choice should usually depend on the correlation of two parameters: the percentage of people who are both students and instructors, $\pi$, and the percentage of relations specific to students or instructors among all the relations which can be relevant to persons, $\rho$.

---

The relative redundancy in *Events* increases when $\pi$ increases and when $\rho$ decreases. The unnaturalness and the undercoverage of constraints in *Union* increase when $\pi$ decreases and when $\rho$ increases.

The following provides a decision criteria for an arbitrary group of categories. The decision is made according to the $\pi{:}\rho$ ratio. A comparison quotient of 0.6 is suggested, which is quite often reasonable, as has been shown by analysis of a class of databases. If $\pi/\rho > 0.6$ then the *Union* approach would usually be preferable. In some special cases, however, the database designer should consider a different comparison quotient. The number 0.6 is only a "rule of thumb."

When there is chain of sub-sub-categories, the approach *Events* becomes too complicated, and is not recommended. It is however the most natural approach in the majority of situations, because in the majority of cases $\pi$ is small, the subcategory hierarchy is rather flat (no sub-sub-categories), and the DBMS does not provide a sufficient support for userviews.

D.   Convert the group of categories into disjoint categories.

   a.   *if* the DBMS provides a high level support for userviews, including specification of updates, *then (Union+Events)*:

      (i)   Substitute every direct or indirect subcategory $S$ of $C$ in the schema being converted by the category **Event-of-being-a[n]-$S$.**

Each object in this new category is an event of membership in the category $S$, that is, if $x$ is an $S$ then "$x$ is an $S$" is one element in Event-of-being-an-$S$. (The categories of events are disjoint. For simplicity, the former names $S$ may be kept but the new meaning is assumed.)

---

*Example 3-53.*

- Category *[Event-of-being-a-]STUDENT*
- Category *[Event-of-being-an-]INSTRUCTOR*

---

*Example 3-54.*

If we also had

- Subcategory    *TENURED-FACULTY*    of    the    category    *INSTRUCTOR*

then we would convert it into

- Category *Event-of-being-TENURED-FACULTY*

---

(ii)  Retain the category $C$.

---

*Example 3-55.*

- Category *PERSON*

---

(iii) Connect every new category of events $S$ to each immediate supercategory of $S$ by a new relation. Specify integrity constraints that these new relations are one-to-one and total.

---

*Example 3-56.*

- Relation **student-person** from *Event-of-being-a-STUDENT* to *PERSON* (*1:1,total*)

---

(iv)  Let every new category of events $S$ have all the relations that the former category $S$ had.

---

*Example 3-57.*

- Relation **major** from *Event-of-being-a-STUDENT* to *DEPARTMENT* (*m:1*)

---

(v) Specify and add a key for every category of events *S*. The simplest way to do this is to inherit the key of *C*.

---

*Example 3-58.*

- Relation *id-key* from *Event-of-being-a-STUDENT* to the category of values *Integer* (*1:1,total*)

---

b.   *else if $\pi/\rho > 0.6$ or* there is a chain of sub-sub-categories *then* (*Union*):

(i)  Replace the whole group of categories by one category *C*.

---

*Example 3-59.*

- Category *PERSON*

---

(ii) Bring all the relations exiting or entering the former subcategories to *C*.

---

*Example 3-60.*

- Relation **the-student** from *COURSE-ENROLLMENT* to *PERSON* (*m:1*)

---

(iii) Add to *C* total Boolean attributes named **is-a**[n]-*S* for every direct and indirect subcategory *S* of *C* in the schema being converted.

---

*Example 3-61.*

- Relation *is-a-student* from *PERSON* to the category of values *Boolean* (*m:1,total*)

> - Relation *is-an-instructor* from *PERSON* to the category of values *Boolean*  (*m:1,total*)

(iv) Add an integrity constraint stating that any object of *C* may participate in a former *S*'s corresponding relation only if the respective function is-an-*S* gives *true*.

---

*Example 3-62.*

**for every** p **in** *PERSON*:

    **if**   **exists** d **in** *DEPARTMENT*:   p *WORKS-IN* d

**then** p.*IS-AN-INSTRUCTOR*

---

*Example 3-63.*

**for every** p **in** *PERSON*:

    **if not** (p *MAJOR* **null**)

    **then** p.*IS-A-STUDENT*

---

(v) Whenever there are attributes is-an-$S_1$ and is-an-$S_2$, where $S_1$ is a subcategory of $S_2$ in the original schema, add a constraint enforcing that in terms of the new attributes.

---

*Example 3-64.*

If we had:

- Subcategory *UNDERGRADUATE* of the category *STUDENT*

then we would add a constraint:

    **for every** s **in** *PERSON*:

        **if** s.*IS-AN-UNDERGRADUATE*

            **then** s.*IS-A-STUDENT*

---

(vi) Whenever there are attributes is-an-$S_1$ and is-an-$S_2$, where $S_1$ and $S_2$ are disjoint in the original schema, add a constraint enforcing that in terms of the new attributes.

*Example 3-65.*

If the category *UNDERGRADUATE* was disjoint from the category *INSTRUCTOR*, then we would add a constraint:

**for every** s **in** *PERSON*:

**if** s.*IS-AN-UNDERGRADUATE*

**then not** (s.*IS-AN-INSTRUCTOR*)

c.   *else* (*Events*):

(i)   Substitute the categories $S_1, \ldots, S_n$ by the corresponding $n$ categories **Event-of-being-a-**$S_1, \ldots,$ **Event-of-being-a-**$S_n$ of the events of membership in categories, that is, if $x$ is an $S_i$ then "$x$ is an $S_i$" is one element in the category Event-of-being-an-$S_i$. (The categories $S_i$ are disjoint. For simplicity, former names $S_i$ may be kept but the new meaning is assumed.)

*Example 3-66.*

   •   Category *Event-of-being-a-STUDENT*

disjoint from

   •   Category *Event-of-being-an-Instructor*

(ii)   If there are, or *may* be in the future, objects in $C$ that do not belong to any of the subcategories $S_1, \ldots, S_n$, then add a new category $S_0$ to the schema. This will be the category of the objects that do not belong to any of the subcategories. This category is usually called **other-**$C$.

*Example 3-67.*

   •   Category *OTHER-PERSON*

(iii)   Replace every relation $R$ whose domain or range is $C$, by a relation of the same name, but having the categories $S_i$ as their domains or ranges. (The relation $R$ is partitioned into several relations according to the restricted domains or ranges $S_i$.)

---

*Example 3-68.*

- Relation *birth-year* from *Event-of-being-a-STUDENT* to the category of values *1870..1990*  (*m:1* )

---

(iv)  Eliminate the category *C*.

(v)  Specify integrity constraints to prevent inconsistency of the redundant information:

> key values as an object *y* of the category Event-of-being-an-$S_j$, then the other relations of *C* (inherited by the categories of events) must be equal for *x* and *y*."

---

*Example 3-69.*

We choose this alternative (*Events*) for the intersecting group of the subcategories of *PERSON* in the case-study database.

The schema now has redundancy, which should be controlled by an integrity constraint, if possible.  The integrity constraint is

**for every** s **in** *Event-of-being-a-STUDENT*:

**for every** i **in** *Event-of-being-an-INSTRUCTOR*:

  **if**

>  (s.*ADDRESS* $\neq$ i.*ADDRESS* **or**
>
>  s.*LAST-NAME* $\neq$ i.*LAST-NAME* **or**
>
>  s.*FIRST-NAME* $\neq$ i.*FIRST-NAME* **or**
>
>  s.*BIRTH-YEAR* $\neq$ i.*BIRTH-YEAR*)

  **then** s.*ID-key* $\neq$ i.*ID-key*

(Note:  The constraint could have been written without negations, "in a positive spirit", but then the meaning of the absent values could be misinterpreted.)

---

*Example 3-70.*

The binary schema of the university application has been converted so far (by *Events*) into the schema on the following page.

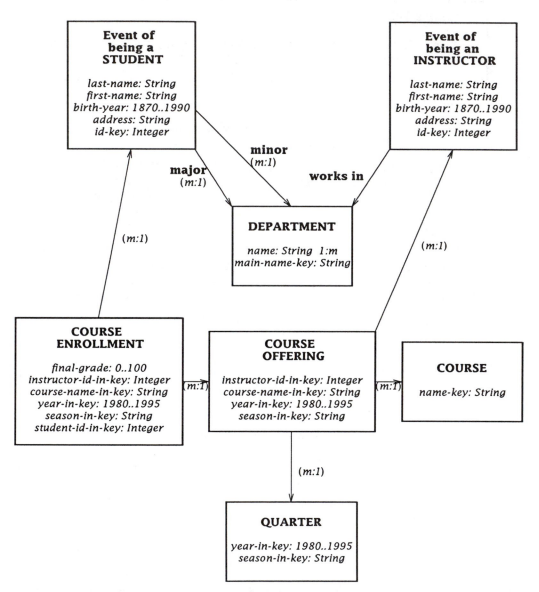

**Figure 3-7.** The university schema with the categories made artificially disjoint.

## 3.2.5. **Removal of relations**

**Step 3. Convert** every proper **1:m** or **m:m** relation whose **range is a concrete category** into a new abstract category with its two functional relations through a relation-split.

---

*Example 3-71.*

Instead of the relation

- Relation **name** from *DEPARTMENT* to *String*   *(1:m)*

we shall have

- Category *DEPARTMENT-NAMING*

- Relation **the-department** from *DEPARTMENT-NAMING* to *DEPARTMENT*   *(m:1,total)*

- Relation **the-name** from *DEPARTMENT-NAMING* to *String* *(1:1,total)*

---

**Step 4. Convert** every **1:m** relation into an m:1 relation by changing its direction and its name.

---

*Example 3-72.*

We do not have such relations in the university schema. If we assume we have the relation

- Relation **provides** from *DEPARTMENT* to *COURSE*   *(1:m)*

then we would change it into

- Relation **the-department-providing-the-course** from *COURSE* to *DEPARTMENT*   *(m:1)*

---

**Step 5. Convert** every proper **many-to-many** relation into a category and two functional relations through a relation-split.

---

*Example 3-73.*

We split the relation *WORKS-IN* into a new category *WORK* and its two functional relations *THE-DEPARTMENT* and *THE-INSTRUCTOR.*

---

*Example 3-74.*

If we had the following m:m relation

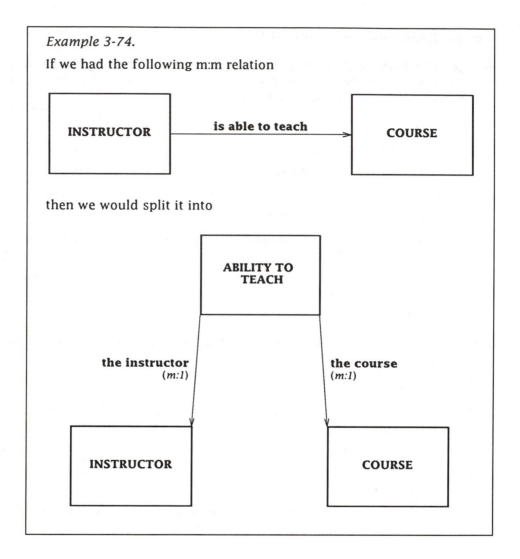

then we would split it into

*Example 3-75.*

The binary schema of the university application has been converted so far into the schema on the following page.

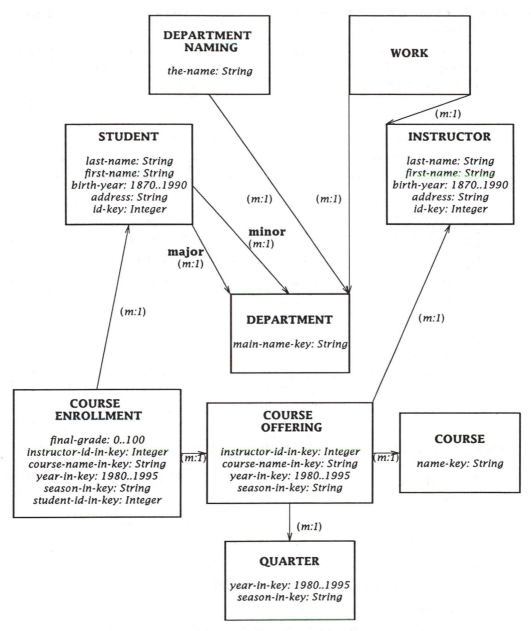

**Figure 3-8.** The university schema after all the relation splits have been performed.

**Step 6. Choose a key** for every category produced through a **relation-split** as follows.

For every category which was obtained through a relation-split, a key is contained in the union of the compositions of its two functional relations on the keys of their ranges.

> *Example 3-76.*
>
> The key of *WORK* is 2 new attributes of this category:
>
> {main-name of the department, instructor-id of the instructor}

> *Example 3-77.*
>
> The key of *DEPARTMENT-NAMING* is contained in
>
> {the-name, main-name of the department}
>
> Since *the-name* is 1:1, the key of *DEPARTMENT-NAMING* is {*the-name*}.

> *Example 3-78.*
>
> The binary schema of the university application has been converted so far into the schema on the following page.

**Step 7. Replace** every **m:1 relation** $f$ whose **range is an abstract category** by the composition of $f$ on the chosen key of its range, that is, by attributes $b_1, \ldots, b_n$, where $x.b_i = (x.f).a_i$, and $a_1, \ldots, a_n$ is the chosen key of $f$'s range.

> *Example 3-79.*
>
> Instead of
>
> • Relation **major** from *STUDENT* to *DEPARTMENT* (m:1)
>
> we shall have
>
> • Relation *major-dept-main-name* from *STUDENT* to the category of values *String* (m:1)

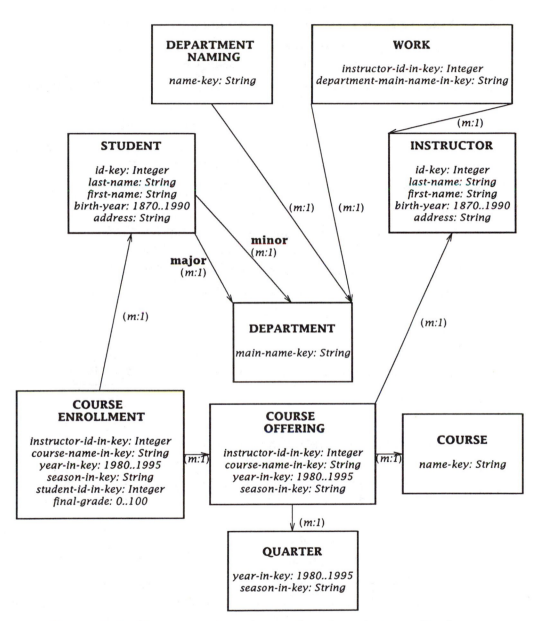

**Figure 3-9.** The university schema after the relation splits have been performed and keys have been chosen for every category.

**Step 8.  Remove redundant non-key attributes**.

From every category **remove attributes** which are not in the key, but are **inferable** from other attributes of the same category.

These attributes would usually have resulted from a "blind" application of this algorithm, particularly

a.   A non-key attribute which is always equal to an attribute in the key.

   *Note:*  It is possible that step (7) brought to a category $C$ an attribute $b$ which is always equal to an attribute in the key of $C$.

b.   A redundant Boolean attribute brought in step (1):

   Suppose

   - We were converting intersecting categories $C, S_1, \ldots, S_n$ into disjoint categories,

   - we replaced them by one *Union* category $C$, and

   - one of the categories $S_i$ was disjoint from all of the rest $S_j$'s.

   Then the new attribute is-an-$S_i$ is inferable from the rest of the attributes is-an-$S_j$.

   This attribute should be removed from the schema. (It may be present in a userview, where it would be an inferred attribute.)

---

*Example 3-80.*

If we had

- Subcategory *ILLITERATE* of the category *PERSON*  (disjoint from INSTRUCTOR and from STUDENT)

and furthermore, there were no other persons but students, instructors, and illiterate persons, then the attribute *is-illiterate* would be derivable:

for every p in PERSON:

p.*IS-ILLITERATE* =

(not p.*IS-A-STUDENT* and not p. *IS-AN-INSTRUCTOR*)

---

*Note:*  The removal of several attributes should *not* be performed simultaneously. Otherwise, two attributes mutually inferable, but not inferable from the rest, might be removed.

**Step 9. Translate the integrity constraints** into the terms of the new schema:

a.   The constraints of the original schema.

b.   The additional constraints accumulated during the conversion process.

> *Example 3-81.*
>
> The binary schema of the university application has been converted into the relational schema of Figure Ref-2.

*Problem 3-3.*

Use the university/relational reference schema at the end of this book. Specify in calculus all the integrity constraints which are not covered by this relational schema but are covered by the binary schema, that is, the constraints generated during the conversion from the binary schema.

*Problem 3-4.*

Use the university/binary reference schema at the end of this book. Convert this schema into a relational schema, assuming

- 50% of the instructors are students and 40% of students are instructors
- an instructor can give the same course several times during one quarter
- every name of a department is subject to change
- the DBMS does not support userviews

Specify the integrity constraints which are not covered by your relational schema, but are covered by the binary schema.

*Problem 3-5.*

Use the university/binary reference schema at the end of this book. Solve the previous problem replacing the *userviews* assumption:

- the DBMS provides excellent support for userviews, including userview updates

**In the following problems**, design a relational schema equivalent to the appropriate binary schema. Specify the integrity constraints incident to the conversion from the binary schema to the relational schema.

*Problem 3-6.*

Use the clan/binary schema (Figure 8-3 on page 282).

*Problem 3-7.*

Use the wholesaler/binary schema (Figure 8-1 on page 280).

Solution on page 299.

*Problem 3-8.*

Use the studio/binary schema (Figure 8-2 on page 281). Design a relational schema for the Studio application. Specify in English the integrity constraints (besides the keys) which should accompany the above relational schema but are implied by the binary schema.

Solution on page 301.

*Problem 3-9.*

Use the circuit/binary schema (Figure 8-5 on page 283).

Solution on page 302.

*Problem 3-10.*

Use the sales/binary schema (Figure 8-4 on page 283).

Solution on page 303.

*Problem 3-11.*

Use the medical/binary schema (Figure 8-6 on page 287).

1. Design a relational schema for the medical world. Your data base shall be equivalent in the information content to the binary data base described by the above binary schema.

2. Specify in calculus all the integrity constraints that have to be added to the schema during conversion.

3. Whenever the conversion algorithm allows a selection between alternatives, discuss the alternatives, show briefly every alternative way and justify your selection.

Solution on page 304.

*Problem 3-12.*

Use the busstop/binary schema (Figure 8-11 on page 291).

Solution on page 307.

*Problem 3-13.*

Use the carsale/binary schema (Figure 8-12 on page 292).

*Problem 3-14.*

Use the newspaper/binary schema (Figure 8-27 on page 310).

Solution on page 310.

*Problem 3-15.*

Use the clinic/binary schema (Figure 8-13 on page 293).

Solution on page 311.

*Problem 3-16.*

Use the library/binary schema (Figure 8-7 on page 288).

Solution on page 312.

## 3.3. Relational Languages

## 3.3.1. A structured extension of Pascal

This language is the same as the binary extension of Pascal, but used for the relational schema. (Every relational schema is a binary schema. Thus, every language used for the Binary Model can be used for the Relational Model.)

---

*Example 3-82.*

The university has decided to expel all the students whose average grade is below 60 (out of 100). To prevent this wrong-doing to computer science students, the department offered a fictitious course, Computer-Pass, by Prof. Good, in which all computer science students are to receive a sufficient grade so as to not to be expelled, if possible.

 The following program fabricates Prof. Good and the Computer-Pass course, enrolls students in this course, grades them accordingly, and prints the names of those computer science students whom this measure cannot help.

---

**program** Pass (Input, Output, UNIVERSITY-DB, UNIVERSITY-MASTER-VIEW);

**var** Computer-Pass-Course, Prof-Good, Good-Offer, computer-science-name, comp-science, cs-student, her-enrollment, fictitious-enrollment: *ABSTRACT*;

 the-grade, desired-grade, number-of-grades, total-of-grades, current-year: *INTEGER*;

**begin**

(* Get the current year from the standard input file. *)

 read (current-year);

**transaction begin**

 (* Fabricate the course. *)

   **create new** Computer-Pass-Course **in** *COURSE*;

   Computer-Pass-Course.*NAME-key* := 'Computer Pass';

 (* Fabricate the Prof. Good. *)

    **create new** Prof-Good **in** *INSTRUCTOR*;

    Prof-Good.*LAST-NAME* **:=** 'Good';

    Prof-Good.*ID-key* **:=** 1234; (* Let's hope that this fabricated id number does not already belong to a legitimate instructor. Otherwise, an error will result. *)

(* Fabricate the offering. *)

    **create new** Good-Offer **in** *COURSE-OFFERING*;

    Good-Offer.*COURSE-NAME-in-key* **:=** 'Computer Pass';

    Good-Offer.*INSTRUCTOR-ID-in-key* **:=** 1234;

    Good-Offer.*YEAR* **:=** current-year;

    Good-Offer.*SEASON* **:=** 'Winter'

**end**;


(* The following two nested loops will be performed only once. Inside the body of the second loop, the variable *comp-science* will refer to the Computer Science Department. *)

**for** computer-science-name **in** *DEPARTMENT-NAMING*

    **where** (computer-science-name.*NAME-key* = 'COMPUTER SCIENCE') **do**

**for** comp-science **in** *DEPARTMENT*

    **where** (comp-science.*MAIN-NAME-key* = comp-science-name.-*MAIN-NAME*) **do begin**

(* Make believe that Prof. Good works in Computer Science. *)

    (* In terms of the binary schema, **relate**: Prof-Good *WORKS-IN* comp-science *)

    **transaction begin**

        **create new** work **in** *WORK*;

        work.*INSTRUCTOR-ID-in-key* **:=** 1234;

        work.*DEPARTMENT-MAIN-NAME-in-key* **:=** comp-science.*MAIN-NAME-key*

        **end**;

```
for cs-student in STUDENT
        where (cs-student.MAJOR-DEPARTMENT-MAIN-NAME
            = comp-science.MAIN-NAME-key) do
    begin (* the current computer science student *)
    (* calculate this student's current statistics: number-of-grades
        and total-of-grades *)
    number-of-grades := 0;
    total-of-grades := 0;
        for her-enrollment in COURSE-ENROLLMENT where (her-
            enrollment.STUDENT-ID-in-key = cs-student.ID-key and
            not her-enrollment FINAL-GRADE null) do begin
        the_grade := her-enrollment.FINAL-GRADE;
        number-of-grades := number-of-grades + 1;
        total-of-grades := total-of-grades + the-grade
        end;
    (* calculate the minimal desired grade in computer-pass course,
        solving the equation
```

$$(total+x)/(number+1)=60 \quad *)$$

```
    desired-grade := 60 * (number-of-grades + 1) — total-of-
        grades;
    if desired-grade > 100 then
        (* the student cannot be helped. Print a message *)
            writeln (' The student ', cs-student.LAST-NAME, ' cannot
                be helped. Sorry!')
    else if desired-grade > 60 then
        transaction begin
            create new fictitious-enrollment in COURSE-
                ENROLLMENT;
            fictitious-enrollment.STUDENT-ID-in-key := cs-student.-
                ID-key;
            fictitious-enrollment.COURSE-NAME-in-key := 'Computer
                Pass';
```

fictitious-enrollment.*INSTRUCTOR-ID-in-key* := 1234;

fictitious-enrollment.*YEAR* := 1987;

fictitious-enrollment.*SEASON* := 'Winter';

fictitious-enrollment.*FINAL-GRADE* := desired-grade

**end** (* transaction *)

**end** (* current student *)

**end** (* computer science department *)

**end**.

## 3.3.1.1. Transaction processing

Many application programs process a continuous sequence of end-users' requests for transactions. In each cycle, such a program accepts a request from an end-user, translates it from the data-entry form into the terms of the database, determines the validity of the request, and performs it.

Most relational DBMS are unable to automatically enforce the integrity constraints, particularly the *referential integrity*. In this case, the busy-work of **manual integrity validation** must be performed by the application programs processing the user transactions.

---

*Example 3-83.*

The following program reads from the standard input a series of requests for enrolling students in classes. For every request, the program checks its integrity against the database. If the request is integral, the program performs the update. Otherwise, an error message is printed.

It is assumed that the DBMS is unable to automatically enforce the referential integrity.

---

**program** Enroll (Input, Output, University-database, University-master-userview);

**var**

student-id, instructor-id, year: Integer;

course-name, season: String;

student, instructor, course, quarter, offering, enrollment: ABSTARCT;

student-ok, instructor-ok, course-ok, quarter-ok, offering-ok, enrollment-ok: Boolean;

**procedure** Erroneous-transaction (explanation: String);

(* This procedure is called

- from Transaction-error-handler, when an error is detected by the DBMS

- from the program, when an error is detected by the program. *)

**begin**

writeln ('The enrollment request listed in the following line could not be granted for the reason: ', explanation);

writeln (student-id, instructor-id, course-name, year, season)

**end**

**procedure** Transaction-error-handler (error-description: String);

**begin**

Erroneous-transaction (concatenate('System error: ', error-description);

**end**

**begin**

**while not** eof(Input) **do**

**transaction begin**

(* Get a request for the next enrollment transaction *)

readln (student-id, instructor-id, course-name, year, season)

(* Check student id *)

student-ok := false;

**for** student **in** *STUDENT*

**where** (student.*ID-key* = student-id)

**do** student-ok := true;

**if not** student-ok **then**

Erroneous-transaction ('No student known by the student-id submitted in the first field of the enrollment request');

(* Check instructor id *)

instructor-ok := false;

**for** instructor **in** *INSTRUCTOR*

>   **where** (instructor.*ID-key* = instructor-id)

>   **do** instructor-ok := true;

**if not** instructor-ok **then**

>   Erroneous-transaction ('No instructor known by the instructor-id submitted in the second field of the enrollment request');

(* Check course name  *)

course-ok := false;

**for** course **in** *COURSE*

>   **where** (course.*NAME-key* = course-name)

>   **do** course-ok := true;

**if not** course-ok **then**

>   Erroneous-transaction ('No course known by the course-name submitted in the third field of the enrollment request');

(* Check quarter  *)

quarter-ok := false;

**for** quarter **in** *QUARTER*

>   **where** (quarter.*YEAR-in-key* = year **and** quarter.*SEASON-in-key* = season)

>   **do** quarter-ok := true;

**if not** quarter-ok **then**

>   Erroneous-transaction ('No quarter known by the year and season submitted in the fourth and fifth fields of the enrollment request');

(* Check the offering  *)

offering-ok := false;

**for** offering **in** *COURSE-OFFERING*

>   **where** (offering. INSTRUCTOR-ID-in-key = instructor-id **and** offering.*COURSE-NAME-in-key* = course-name **and** offering.-*YEAR-in-key* = year **and** offering.*SEASON-in-key* = season)

**do** offering-ok := true;

**if** instructor-ok **and** course-ok **and** quarter-ok **and not** offering-ok **then**

Erroneous-transaction ('No offering known by the instructor-id, course, year and season submitted in the second through fifth fields of the enrollment request');

(* The following check of non-duplicate enrollment is not strictly necessary, since it can be performed automatically by the DBMS, which knows to enforce the uniqueness of the keys. Thus, the only practical reason for this test is to produce a better message than what would be produced by the system by default. *)

(* Check that student is not already enrolled in the offering *)

enrollment-ok := true;

**for** enrollment **in** *COURSE-ENROLLMENT*

**where** (enrollment.*STUDENT-ID-in-key* = student-id **and** enrollment.*INSTRUCTOR-ID-in-key* = instructor-id **and** enrollment.*COURSE-NAME-in-key* = course-name **and** enrollment.*YEAR-in-key* = year **and** enrollment.*SEASON-in-key* = season)

**do** enrollment-ok := false;

**if not** enrollment-ok **then**

Erroneous-transaction ('The requested enrollment of the student already exists')

**if** student-ok **and** instructor-ok **and** course-ok **and** quarter-ok **and** offering-ok **and** enrollment-ok

**then**

(* Insert the new enrollment *)

**begin**

**create new** enrollment **in** *COURSE-ENROLLMENT*;

enrollment.*STUDENT-ID-in-key* := student-id;

enrollment.*INSTRUCTOR-ID-in-key* := instructor-id;

enrollment.*COURSE-NAME-in-key* := course-name;

enrollment.*YEAR-in-key* := year;

enrollment.*SEASON-in-key* := season

**end**

**end** (* transaction *)

**end**.

*Problem 3-17.*

Use the studio/relational schema (Figure 8-20 on page 301). Write a relational data manipulation program in the structured extension of Pascal for the following task:

Create a new film 'Memories of Actress Jane Smith'. For every scene that Jane Smith has played, this film shall contain a scene to be shot at Jane's home.

Solution on page 315.

*Problem 3-18.*

Use the projects/relational schema (Figure 8-15 on page 298). Write a program in Extended Pascal for the following task:

Let employee id#555 work for all the projects for which his immediate subordinates work. You may assume that the employee is already known in the data base.

Solution on page 316.

## 3.3.2. Calculus

**RELATIONAL CALCULUS** — the Predicate Calculus, when used for the relational schema. (Since every relational schema is a binary schema, we already know the Relational Calculus.)

---

*Example 3-84.*

What are the last names of all the students?

**get** s.*LAST-NAME*

   **where** s **is a** STUDENT

---

*Example 3-85.*

What are the distinct last names of the students? (No name may be printed twice.)

**get** n

**where**

> **exists** s **in** *STUDENT*:
>> n = s.*LAST-NAME*

**Tuple-oriented RELATIONAL CALCULUS** — Relational calculus with the following restriction: the quantification is done only on abstract categories, *i.e.*, tables.

Among the languages of the Relational Model, more languages are based on the tuple-oriented predicate calculus than on the more general form of predicate calculus.

---

*Example 3-86.*

The previous example was not in the tuple-oriented form because the variable *n* was implicitly quantified over the concrete category *String*.

The following examples *are* in tuple-oriented form.

---

*Example 3-87.*

Has every student enrolled in at least one course in 1987?

> **for every** st **in** *STUDENT*:
>> **exists** enrl **in** *COURSE-ENROLLMENT*:
>>> ((enrl.*STUDENT-ID-in-key* = st.*ID-key* ) **and** (enrl.-*YEAR*=1987))

---

*Example 3-88.*

Who took Prof. Smith's courses?

> **get** student.*LAST-NAME* **where**
>> (student **is a** *STUDENT* **and**
>> **exists** enrl **in** *COURSE-ENROLLMENT*:
>>> (enrl.*STUDENT-ID-in-key*=student.*ID-key* **and**

**exists** inst **in** *INSTRUCTOR*:

(inst.*LAST-NAME* = 'Smith' **and**

enrl.*INSTRUCTOR-ID-in-key*=inst.*ID-key*)))

---

*Example 3-89.*

Print the average grade of every computer science student.

**get** student.*LAST-NAME*,

(**average** enrollment.*FINAL-GRADE*

**where**

enrollment.*STUDENT-ID-in-key* = student.*ID-key*)

**where**

student **is a** *STUDENT* and

(student.*MAJOR-DEPT-MAIN-NAME* = 'Computer Science')

---

*Example 3-90.*

How many students are there in the university?

**get** (**count** std **where** std **is a** *STUDENT*)

---

*Example 3-91.*

What students have their average grade below 60?

**get** std.*LAST-NAME*

**where** std **is a** *STUDENT* and

60 >

**average** enrl.*FINAL-GRADE*

**where**

> enrl **is a** *COURSE-ENROLLMENT* **and**
>
> enrl.*STUDENT-ID-in-key* = std.*ID-key*

*Problem 3-19.*

Use the studio/relational schema (Figure 8-20 on page 301). Write a query in Calculus to find the following information from the above relational data base:

> The names of the actors who assisted in or directed the same *film* in which they acted.

Solution on page 317.

*Problem 3-20.*

Use the projects/relational schema (Figure 8-15 on page 298). Write a query in the relational predicate calculus to find the following information from the database:

> The names of the employees who do not work for any project but do supervise somebody.

Solution on page 317.

*Problem 3-21.*

Use the projects/relational schema (Figure 8-15 on page 298). Specify in English a meaningful integrity constraint (not necessarily one of the above) which cannot be specified in the Relational Calculus even if aggregate functions are used.

*Problem 3-22.*

An attribute $A$ of table $T$ is said to be **functionally dependent** on a set of attributes $\{B_1, \ldots, B_k\}$ of $T$ if for no tuple of values $(b_1, \ldots, b_k)$ of these attributes there may be two different values of $A$ in the table at the same time.

Let $T$ be a table with four attributes $A, B, C$ and $D$. Specify in the Relational Calculus the constraint:

> "$D$ is functionally dependent on $\{A, B\}$"

Solution on page 317.

### 3.3.3.  *Relational Alebra

Relational Algebra is an algebraic language in which new tables are defined by applying operators to other tables.

This is a language of expressions. In it, a new table is defined as an expression involving original tables and operators.

The most important operators are:

- **Projection operator** creates a new table containing some of the columns of another table.

- **Join operator** combines the rows of the first table with "related" rows of the second table.

- **Selection operator** extracts some rows from a table according to a given condition on the values of the row.

> *Example 3-92.*
>
> {The last names of the students born in 1975} =
>
> (*project*-the-column-*LAST-NAME*
>
> (*select*-the-rows-where-the-*BIRTH-YEAR*-is-1975
>
> (the table *STUDENT*)))

In this section, the operators of Relational Algebra are defined by inference laws in Predicate Calculus.

Consider two tables:

table $T$, whose attributes are $A_1, \ldots, A_n$

table $T'$, whose attributes are $A'_1, \ldots, A'_{n'}$

1. **Projection operator** creates a new table containing some of the columns of another table.

    Let $F_1, \ldots, F_k$ be some of the attributes (columns) of table $T$. Then

    $T [F_1, \ldots, F_k] =$

    > **get** $F_1: v_1, \ldots, F_k: v_k$
    >
    > > **where**
    > >
    > > > **exists** x **in** $T$:
    > > >
    > > > > $x.F_1 = v_1$ **and** $\cdots$ **and** $x.F_k = v_k$

*Note:*   When several tuples of *T* have the same values in the columns being projected, only one row will appear in the result. Thus, the resulting table may have fewer tuples than *T*.

---

*Example 3-93.*

A list of the distinct last names of the students =

    *STUDENT*[*LAST-NAME*]=

    **get** *LAST-NAME*: name

        **where**

            **exists** x **in** *STUDENT*:

                x.*LAST-NAME* = name

---

*Example 3-94.*

Last names and majors of all the students =

    *STUDENT*[*LAST-NAME, MAJOR-DEPARTMENT-MAIN-NAME*] =

    **get** *LAST-NAME*: name, *MAJOR-DEPARTMENT-MAIN-NAME* : major

        **where**

            **exists** x **in** *STUDENT*:

                x.*LAST-NAME* = name **and**

                x.*MAJOR-DEPARTMENT-MAIN-NAME* = major

---

*Example 3-95.*

We can define an inferred table *STUDENT-BASIC* containing all the information from the table *STUDENT* except the departments:

    *STUDENT-BASIC = STUDENT* [*ID-key, LAST-NAME, FIRST-NAME, BIRTH-YEAR, ADDRESS*]

---

2.   **Renaming operator** changes the name of a column in a table.

    $T[A_i \ / \ \overline{A}_i] =$

(* Copy the attributes $A_1, \ldots, A_{i-1}, A_{i+1}, \ldots, A_n$; rename the attribute $A_i$. *)

**get** $A_1$: x.$A_1, \cdots, A_{i-1}$: x.$A_{i-1}, \overline{A}_i$: x.$A_i, A_{i+1}$: x.$A_{i+1}, \cdots, A_n$: x.$A_n$

**where** x **is a** $T$

---

*Example 3-96.*

A table just like *STUDENT*, with 'FAMILY-NAME' column title instead of 'LAST-NAME':

$$STUDENT \ [LAST\text{-}NAME/FAMILY\text{-}NAME]$$

---

3. **Cartesian product operator**

For every row of the first operand and for every row of the second operand, the product operator produces the concatenation of the two rows.

The number of rows in the result =

(the number of rows in the first operand $\times$

the number of rows in the second operand)

The number of columns in the result =

(the number of columns in the first operand $+$

the number of columns in the second operand)

This operation is syntactically erroneous when the two tables have a common attribute.

Cartesian product =

$T \times T' =$

**get** $A_1$:x.$A_1, \cdots, A_n$:x.$A_n, A'_1$:y.$A'_1, \cdots, A_{n'}$:y.$A_{n'}$

**where** x **is a** $T$ **and** y **is a** $T'$

4. **Set operators**

The following operators are defined only when the two tables have the same attributes.

a.    **Union of tables** produces all the rows of the first table and all the rows of the second table.

$T \bigcup T' =$

    **get** $A_1{:}v_1, \cdots, A_n{:}v_n$

        **where**

            **exists** x **in** $T$:

                $x.A_1{=}v_1$ **and** $\cdots$ **and** $x.A_n{=}v_n$

            **or exists** x **in** $T'$:

                $x.A_1{=}v_1$ **and** $\cdots$ **and** $x.A_n{=}v_n$

---

*Example 3-97.*

All the persons =

    *STUDENT-BASIC* $\bigcup$ *INSTRUCTOR* =

        **get** *ID-key* : id, $\cdots$, *ADDRESS* : addr

            **where**

                **exists** x **in** *STUDENT-BASIC*:

                    $x.ID\text{-}key$ = id **and** $\cdots$ **and** $x.ADDRESS$ = addr

                **or exists** x **in** *INSTRUCTOR*:

                    $x.ID\text{-}key$ = id **and** $\cdots$ **and** $x.ADDRESS$ = addr

---

b.  **Intersection of tables** produces the rows which appear in both tables.

    $T \bigcap T' =$

        **get** $A_1{:}v_1, \cdots, A_n{:}v_n$

            **where**

                **exists** x **in** $T$:

                    $x.A_1{=}v_1$ **and** $\cdots$ **and** $x.A_n{=}v_n$

                **and exists** x **in** $T'$:

                    $x.A_1{=}v_1$ **and** $\cdots$ **and** $x.A_n{=}v_n$

> *Example 3-98.*
>
> Instructors who are students =
>
>     *INSTRUCTOR* $\cap$ *STUDENT-BASIC*

c.  **Difference of tables** produces the rows of the first table which do not appear in the second table.

$T-T' =$

>    **get** $A_1{:}v_1, \cdots, A_n{:}v_n$
>
>       **where**
>
>          **exists** x **in** $T$:
>
>             $x.A_1{=}v_1$ **and** $\cdots$ **and** $x.A_n{=}v_n$
>
>          **and not exists** x **in** $T'$:
>
>             $x.A_1{=}v_1$ **and** $\cdots$ **and** $x.A_n{=}v_n$

> *Example 3-99.*
>
> Instructors who are not students =
>
>     *INSTRUCTOR* $-$ *STUDENT-BASIC*

5.  **Selection operator** extracts some rows from a table according to a given condition for the values of the row.

Let $F_1, \ldots, F_k$ be some of the attributes of $T$.

Let $boolexp(v_1, \ldots, v_{k)}$ be a Boolean expression with k variables.

Then

$T\,[boolexp(F_1, \ldots, F_k)] =$

>    **get** $x.A_1, \cdots, x.A_n$
>
>       **where**
>
>          x **is a** $T$ **and**
>
>             $boolexp(x.F_1, \cdots, x.F_k)$

*Example 3-100.*

The student whose first name is Mary=

> *STUDENT [FIRST-NAME=*'Mary'*]*

---

*Example 3-101.*

The instructor whose name is Chung and who is not a student (as distinguished from another Chung who is both an instructor and a student.)

All the instructors whose name is 'Chung' =

> *INSTRUCTOR [LAST-NAME=*'Chung'*]*

The non-student instructor/s whose name is 'Chung' =

> *INSTRUCTOR [LAST-NAME=*'Chung'*] − STUDENT-BASIC*

---

*Example 3-102.*

Names of the instructors teaching databases.

> All combinations of instructors and offerings (including the unrelated ones) =
>
> > *(INSTRUCTOR × COURSE-OFFERING)*
> >
> > > (*product*)
>
> All combinations of instructors and their offerings =
>
> > *(INSTRUCTOR × COURSE-OFFERING)*
> > *[ID-key=INSTRUCTOR-ID-in-key]*
> >
> > > (*selection*)
>
> All combinations of instructors and their offerings of *Databases* =
>
> > *(INSTRUCTOR × COURSE-OFFERING)*
> > *[ID-key=INSTRUCTOR-ID-in-key]*
> > *[COURSE-NAME-in-key=*'Databases'*]*
> >
> > > (*selection*)
>
> The last names of the instructors offering *Databases* =
>
> > *(INSTRUCTOR × COURSE-OFFERING)*
> > *[ID-key=INSTRUCTOR-ID-in-key]*

---

[*COURSE-NAME-in-key*=‘Databases’]
[*LAST-NAME*]

(*projection*)

---

6. **Join operator** combines the rows of the first table with "related" rows of the second table. It is equivalent to a selection from the Cartesian product.

   $T[boolexp(attributes)]T' =$

   $(T \times T')[boolexp(attributes)]$

   ---

   *Example 3-103.*

   Names of instructors teaching databases.

   All combinations of instructors and their offerings =

   (*INSTRUCTOR* [*ID-key*=*INSTRUCTOR-ID-in-key*] *COURSE-OFFERING*)

   (*join*)

   The last names of the instructors offering databases =

   (*INSTRUCTOR* [*ID-key*=*INSTRUCTOR-ID-in-key*] *COURSE-OFFERING*)
   [*COURSE-NAME-in-key*=‘Databases’]
   [*LAST-NAME*]

   ---

7. **Natural join operator** combines two tables according to the equal values of the common attributes (column names) of the two tables.

   Let the table $T$ have $k$ attributes with names identical to the names of $k$ attributes of the table $T'$, that is,

   the attributes of $T$ are: $A_1, \ldots, A_k, A_{k+1}, \ldots, A_n$
   the attributes of $T'$ are: $A_1, \ldots, A_k, A'_{k+1}, \ldots, A'_{n'}$

   Then

   $T \square T' =$

   **get** $A_1{:}v_1, \cdots, A_n{:}v_n, A'_{k+1}{:}w_{k+1}, \cdots, A'_{n'}{:}w_{n'}$

   **where**

**exists** x **in** $T$:

$x.A_1=v_1$ **and** $\cdots$ **and** $x.A_n=v_n$

**and exists** x **in** $T'$:

$x.A_1=v_1$ **and** $\cdots$ **and** $x.A_k=v_k$ **and** $x.A'_{k+1}=v_{k+1}$
**and** $\cdots$ **and** $x.A'_{n'}=w_{n'}$

---

*Example 3-104.*

Names of instructors teaching databases.

The table *INSTRUCTOR* with the column *ID-key* renamed in order to be naturally joinable with the table *COURSE-OFFERING* =

(*INSTRUCTOR* [*ID-key/INSTRUCTOR-ID-in-key*]

(*rename*)

All combinations of instructors and their offerings =

(*INSTRUCTOR* [*ID-key/INSTRUCTOR-ID-in-key*] □
*COURSE-OFFERING*)

(*natural join*)

The last names of the instructors offering databases =

(*INSTRUCTOR* [*ID-key/INSTRUCTOR-ID-in-key*] □
*COURSE-OFFERING*)
[*COURSE-NAME-in-key*='Databases']
[*LAST-NAME*]

---

**Uses of Relational Algebra**:

1.   Specification of userviews (inference rules).

2.   Specification of queries. Albeit, the language is not friendly enough to be used for specification of complex queries.

3.   An intermediate language, because it is easy to implement Relational Algebra. Other, more friendly languages, can be translated into Relational Algebra.

4.   A tool to evaluate and compare different languages. We can estimate the expressive power of an arbitrary language by checking whether it is

   •   able to specify every query expressible in Relational Algebra

   •   able to specify every query expressible in Relational Algebra and more

- able to specify a subset of the queries expressible in Relational Algebra, where the subset is defined by weakening the Algebra through eliminating some of its operators. The list of the eliminated operators shows the weakness of the language. The list of the remaining operators shows the power of the language:

  (i) Many simple query languages can express *projection* and *selection*, but not *join* or *difference*.

  (ii) More powerful languages can express *join*.

  (iii) Languages which are even more powerful can also express *difference*.

*Problem 3-23.*

Use the studio/relational schema (Figure 8-20 on page 301). Write a relational algebra expression to find the names of the directors of the films using helicopters.

Solution on page 318.

*Problem 3-24.*

Use the projects/relational schema (Figure 8-15 on page 298). Write a relational algebra expression to find the names of the projects beginning with the letter 'Z' in which Smith works.

Solution on page 318.

## 3.3.4.  *SQL

## 3.3.4.1. Preview

SQL has become a very popular language of commercial relational database management systems.

The acronym *SQL* stands for 'Structured Query Language.'

A basic query in SQL      **select**s the values of some attributes

**from** some rows of a table or tables,

**where** the rows satisfy a condition.

---

*Example 3-105.*

When was Student Russel born?

**select** *BIRTH-YEAR*

**from** *STUDENT*

**where** *LAST-NAME*='Russel'

---

*Example 3-105.*

List the names of all students.

**select** *FIRST-NAME, LAST-NAME*

**from** *STUDENT*

**where** true

---

*Example 3-106.*

What courses has Prof. Graham taught?

**select** *COURSE-NAME*

**from** *COURSE-OFFERING, INSTRUCTOR*

**where** *INSTRUCTOR.NAME* = 'Graham' **and** *INSTRUCTOR.ID* = *COURSE-OFFERING.  INSTRUCTOR-ID*

---

## 3.3.4.2.  Basic queries

Syntax:

**select** $expression_1, \ldots, expression_n$

**from** $table_1\ var_1, \ldots, table_n\ var_n$

**where** *condition*

The *condition* is a Boolean expression without quantifiers.  It may depend on the variables $var_1, \ldots, var_n$.

Meaning:

**get** $expression_1, \ldots, expression_n$

**where**

$var_1$ **is a** $table_1$ **and** $\cdots$ $var_n$ **is a** $table_n$ **and**

*condition*

*Example 3-107.*

Print the names of the pairs of students who live together.

> **select** s1.*LAST-NAME*, s2.*LAST-NAME*
>
> **from** *STUDENT* s1, *STUDENT* s2
>
> **where** s1.*ADDRESS* = s2.*ADDRESS*

*Abbreviation:*

If a table $T_i$ appears exactly once in the *from* list, then it does not have to be explicitly accompanied by a variable. Implicitly, the name of the variable is identical to the name of the table.

> **select** *expression*$_1$, . . . , *expression*$_n$
>
> **from** *table*$_1$ , . . . , *table*$_n$
>
> **where** *condition*

*Example 3-108.*

Print the names of the pairs of a student and an instructor who live together. (This includes an instructor who is also a student and lives with himself only.)

> **select** *STUDENT.LAST-NAME, INSTRUCTOR.LAST-NAME*
>
> **from** *STUDENT, INSTRUCTOR*
>
> **where** *STUDENT.ADDRESS* = *INSTRUCTOR.ADDRESS*

> *Abbreviation:* When there is only one table in the *from* list, then whenever "*T.attribute*" appears in the query, it may be shortened to "*attribute*" without the prefix "*T.*" .

*Example 3-109.*

Print the names and the addresses of all computer science students.

> **select** *LAST-NAME, ADDRESS*
>
> **from** *STUDENT*
>
> **where** *MAJOR-DEPARTMENT-MAIN-NAME* = 'Computer Science'

*Abbreviation:* When the *select* list consists of all the attributes of the *from* tables, the select list may be abbreviated by "**select** ✳".

---

*Example 3-110.*

Print the names (last and first), the id-s, the birth-years, the major and minor departments, and the addresses of all computer science students.

> **select** ✳
>
> **from** *STUDENT*
>
> **where** *MAJOR-DEPARTMENT-MAIN-NAME* = 'Computer Science'

---

*Note:*

- The output of a query is a partial instantaneous binary database. It can be printed as a "table" (in the common sense of the word *table*).

- Often, but not always, the output of a query is an instantaneous table in the sense of the Relational Model. This is not always true since the output of a query may contain identical rows, while a relational instantaneous table may not contain identical rows.

## 3.3.4.3. Basic aggregates

Basic aggregates are predefined functions which are applied to the whole output of a query. Syntactically, the functions are applied to the expression/s in the *select* list.

1. **count** — when this function is applied to the *select* list, it replaces the output of the query by the number of rows in the output.

---

*Example 3-111.*

How many computer science students are there?

> **select count(✳)**
>
> **from** *STUDENT*
>
> **where** *MAJOR-DEPARTMENT-MAIN-NAME* = 'Computer Science'

---

2.  **avg** — when the *select* list consists of only one expression, and the expression produces numerical values, the function **avg** replaces the output by the average of the values in the output.

> *Example 3-112.*
>
> What is the average grade in the *Databases* course?
>
>    **select avg**(*FINAL-GRADE*)
>
>    **from** *COURSE-ENROLLMENT*
>
>    **where** *COURSE-NAME-IN-KEY* = 'Databases'

3.  **sum** — when the *select* list consists of only one expression, and the expression produces numerical values, the function **sum** replaces the output by the sum of the values in the output.

4.  **max** — when the *select* list consists of only one expression, and the expression produces numerical values, the function **max** replaces the output by the maximum of the values in the output.

5.  **min** — when the *select* list consists of only one expression, and the expression produces numerical values, the function **min** replaces the output by the minimum of the values in the output.

6.  **distinct** — eliminates duplicate rows in the output. This function must be applied on the whole *select* list. (In many implementations, this function is called "**unique**".)

> *Example 3-113.*
>
> List the distinct addresses of the students. (Do not list the same address twice.)
>
>    **select distinct**(*ADDRESS*)
>
>    **from** *STUDENT*
>
>    **where** TRUE

7.  The function **distinct** can can be combined with any other aggregate function. The function **distinct** is applied first, and then another function is applied on the result. Thus,

**select count** (**distinct** ✳)

produces the number of the distinct rows in the output.

> *Example 3-114.*
>
> How many departments have minor students?
>
> > **select count** (**distinct** *MINOR-DEPARTMENT-MAIN-NAME*)
> >
> > **from** *STUDENT*
> >
> > **where** TRUE

## 3.3.4.4. Nested queries

Query forms are represented in SQL by allowing some expressions to contain variables which are not defined (either explicitly or implicitly) in the *from* list. A query form would become a query if the expressions with undefined variables were replaced by constants. Query forms are used in SQL primarily in order to construct nested queries.

> *Example 3-115.*
>
> The following is not a query because it contains an undefined variable "s". It is a query form, which would become a query if the expression "s.*ID-KEY*" were replaced by a constant, such as "345466".
>
> > **select** *
> >
> > **from** *COURSE-ENROLLMENT*
> >
> > **where** s.*ID-KEY* = *COURSE-ENROLLMENT.STUDENT-ID-IN-KEY*

The nested queries are obtained in SQL by extending the syntax of the "**where condition**" by allowing the following subconditions within the *condition*:

1.  **exists**   *query-form*

    This subcondition gives *true* when the result of the query form is not empty — when it contains at least one row. (This subcondition is evaluated when all the variables on which the query form depends are interpreted.)

> *Example 3-116.*
>
> Find the names of the students who never took a course.
>
> > **select** *LAST-NAME*

> **from** *STUDENT*
>
> **where**
>
> > **not exists**
> >
> > > **(select** *
> > >
> > > **from** *COURSE-ENROLLMENT*
> > >
> > > **where** *STUDENT.ID-KEY = COURSE-*
> > > *ENROLLMENT.STUDENT-ID-IN-KEY)*

2.  *expression*    **in**    *query-form-producing-only-one-value-per-row*

    This subcondition gives *true* when the value of the *expression* constitutes a row in the output of the *query-form*

> *Example 3-117.*
>
> Find the names of the students who took at least one course.
>
> > **select** *LAST-NAME*
> >
> > **from** *STUDENT*
> >
> > **where**
> >
> > > *(ID-KEY* **in**
> > >
> > > > **select** *STUDENT-ID-IN-KEY*
> > > >
> > > > **from** *COURSE-ENROLLMENT*
> > > >
> > > > **where** TRUE)

3.  *expression*    **not in**    *query-form-producing-only-one-value-per-row*

    This subcondition gives *true* when the value of the *expression* does not constitute a row in the output of the *query-form*

> *Example 3-118.*
>
> Find the names of the students who never took a course.
>
> > **select** *LAST-NAME*
> >
> > **from** *STUDENT*
> >
> > **where**
> >
> > > *(ID-KEY* **not in**

> **select** *STUDENT-ID-IN-KEY*
>
> **from** *COURSE-ENROLLMENT*
>
> **where** TRUE)

4.   *<expressions>*     **in**     *query-form*

This subcondition gives *true* when the values of the *expressions* constitute a row in the output of the *query-form*

> *Example 3-119.*
>
> Find the names of the students who may be spouses of instructors — those who have the same last name and address as an instructor.
>
>> **select** *LAST-NAME, FIRST-NAME*
>>
>> **from** *STUDENT*
>>
>> **where**
>>
>>> *<LAST-NAME, ADDRESS>* **in**
>>>
>>>> **select** *LAST-NAME, ADDRESS*
>>>>
>>>> **from** *INSTRUCTOR*
>>>>
>>>> **where** TRUE

5.   *<expressions>*     **not in**     *query-form*

This subcondition gives *true* when the values of the *expressions* do not constitute a row in the output of the *query-form*

> *Example 3-120.*
>
> Find the names of some students who are certainly not spouses of instructors.
>
>> **select** *LAST-NAME, FIRST-NAME*
>>
>> **from** *STUDENT*
>>
>> **where**
>>
>>> *<LAST-NAME, ADDRESS>* **not in**
>>>
>>>> **select** *LAST-NAME, ADDRESS*

> **from** *INSTRUCTOR*
>
> **where** TRUE

6.  *query-form*   **contains**   *query-form*

    This subcondition gives *true* when every row produced by the right query form is also produced by the left query form.

    ---

    *Example 3-121.*

    Find the names of the students who took all the courses.

    > **select** *LAST-NAME, FIRST-NAME*
    >
    > **from** *STUDENT*
    >
    > **where**
    >
    > > **select** COURSE-NAME-IN-KEY
    > >
    > > **from** *COURSE-ENROLLMENT*
    > >
    > > **where** *STUDENT.ID-KEY = COURSE-ENROLLMENT.STUDENT-ID-IN-KEY*
    >
    > **contains**
    >
    > > **select** *NAME-KEY*
    > >
    > > **from** *COURSE*
    > >
    > > **where** TRUE

    ---

7.  *expression*    *comparison*    *query-form-producing-only-one-value*

    The allowed comparisons are: =, <, >, >=, <=, <>.

    ---

    *Example 3-122.*

    Find the names of the students who took more than 1000 course offerings.

    > **select** *LAST-NAME, FIRST-NAME*
    >
    > **from** *STUDENT*
    >
    > **where**
    >
    > > 1000 <
    > >
    > > > **select count** (∗)

> **from** *COURSE-ENROLLMENT*
>
> **where** *STUDENT.ID-KEY = COURSE-*
> *ENROLLMENT.STUDENT-ID-IN-KEY*

8.   *expression    comparison*   **any**   *query-form*

This subcondition is *true* if the comparison with at least one row of the query-form's output is *true*.

> *Example 3-123.*
>
> Find the names of the students who studied something in the first 20 calendar years of their life.
>
> > **select** *LAST-NAME, FIRST-NAME*
> >
> > **from** *STUDENT*
> >
> > **where**
> >
> > > *BIRTH-YEAR + 20 >* **any**
> > >
> > > > **select** *YEAR*
> > > >
> > > > **from** *COURSE-ENROLLMENT*
> > > >
> > > > **where** *STUDENT.ID-KEY = COURSE-*
> > > > *ENROLLMENT.STUDENT-ID-IN-KEY*

9.   *expression    comparison*   **all**   *query-form*

This subcondition is *true* if the comparison with every one of the query-form's output rows is *true*.

> *Example 3-124.*
>
> Find the names of the students who studied nothing (as far as the database knows) in the first 20 calendar years of their life.
>
> > **select** *LAST-NAME, FIRST-NAME*
> >
> > **from** *STUDENT*
> >
> > **where**
> >
> > > *BIRTH-YEAR + 20 <=* **all**
> > >
> > > > **select** *YEAR*
> > > >
> > > > **from** *COURSE-ENROLLMENT*

> **where** *STUDENT.ID-KEY = COURSE-*
> *ENROLLMENT.STUDENT-ID-IN-KEY*

## 3.3.4.5.  Grouping of rows

The aggregate functions can by applied to subsets of rows produced by *select*. For this purpose, the rows resulting from *select* can be partitioned into groups according to the values of some attributes.

Syntax:

> **select** *expression*$_1$, . . . , *expression*$_n$
>
> **from** *table*$_1$ *var*$_1$, . . . , *table*$_n$ *var*$_n$
>
> **where** *condition*
>
> **group by** *attribute*$_1$, . . . , *attribute*$_k$

Each *attribute*$_i$ has the form

> *variable.attribute-name*

When no ambiguity arises, the table-name can be used instead of the variable:

> *table-name.attribute-name*

When no ambiguity further arises, the table-name can be omitted:

> *attribute-name*

Meaning:

> The rows satisfying the *condition* are combined into groups so that in each group the attributes of the grouping have constant values, that is, two rows $r_1$ and $r_2$ are in the same group if and only if
>
> $$r_1.attribute_1 = r_2.attribute_1 \text{ and}$$
> $$r_1.attribute_2 = r_2.attribute_2 \text{ and } \cdots$$
> $$r_1.attribute_k = r_2.attribute_k$$

For every group, only one cumulative row is produced in the result. The resulting cumulative row is obtained by evaluation of the *expressions* of the **select** clause. The aggregates in those expressions are interpreted as applying not to the whole output but only to the rows comprising one group.

*Example 3-125.*

For every department, list the number of instructors it employs.

> **select** *DEPARTMENT-MAIN-NAME-in-key*,
> **count**(*INSTRUCTOR-ID-in-key*)
>
> **from** *WORK*
>
> **group by** *DEPARTMENT-MAIN-NAME-in-key*

*Example 3-126.*

For every student who took classes in a summer, for every instructor who gave grades to the student in a summer, print the average of the summer grades given by the instructor to the student.

> **select** *STUDENT-ID-in-key, INSTRUCTOR-ID-in-key,* **avg**(*FINAL-GRADE*)
>
> **from** *COURSE-ENROLLMENT*
>
> **where** *SEASON* = 'Summer'
>
> **group by** *STUDENT-ID-in-key, INSTRUCTOR-ID-in-key*

Some of the groups produced by **group by** can be screened out according to the values of aggregate functions applied to the group. A group screening condition can be specified in a **having** clause as follows.

**select** *expressions*

**from** *tables*

**where** *condition-on-the-source-rows-of-the-tables*

**group by** *attributes*

**having** *condition-on-the-groups*

The *condition-on-the-groups* is a Boolean expression. The aggregate functions appearing in this condition apply to the rows comprising one group.

*Example 3-127.*

What departments employ more than 100 instructors each?

> **select** *DEPARTMENT-MAIN-NAME-in-key*

**from** *WORK*

**where** true

**group by** *DEPARTMENT-MAIN-NAME-in-key*

**having count**(*INSTRUCTOR-ID-in-key*) > 100

---

*Example 3-128.*

For every student who took classes in a summer, for every instructor who gave grades to the student in a summer, so that the average of the summer grades given by the instructor to the student is greater than 60, print the average of the summer grades given by the instructor to the student.

**select** *STUDENT-ID-in-key, INSTRUCTOR-ID-in-key*, **avg**(*FINAL-GRADE*)

**from** *COURSE-ENROLLMENT*

**where** *SEASON* = 'Summer'

**group by** *STUDENT-ID-in-key, INSTRUCTOR-ID-in-key*

**having avg**(*FINAL-GRADE*) > 60

## 3.3.4.6.  Sorting

The output of an SQL query can be sorted for the purpose of printing in any desired order or for delivery to an application program in a desired order. This is accomplished by an **order by** clause specifying one or more attributes to sort by:

*query*

**order by** *attributes*

When more than one sorting attribute is given, the output's primary order is according to the first attribute, then according to the second, and so on.

---

*Example 3-129.*

List all computer science majoring students sorted by their minors.

**select** *

**from** *STUDENT*

> **where**  *MAJOR-DEPARTMENT-MAIN-NAME* = 'Computer Science'
>
> **order by**  *MINOR-DEPARTMENT-MAIN-NAME*

### 3.3.4.7.  Update transactions

Update transactions can be specified in SQL.

1.    Deleting a set of rows from a table.

> **delete from** *table*
>
> **where** *condition-on-rows-to-be-deleted*

> *Example 3-130.*
>
> Delete the student whose id is 11111.
>
> > **delete from**  *STUDENT*
> >
> > **where**  *ID-key = 11111*

> *Example 3-131.*
>
> Delete all music majors.
>
> > **delete from**  *STUDENT*
> >
> > **where**  *MAJOR-DEPARTMENT-MAIN-NAME = 'Music'*

2.    Inserting a row into a table.

> **insert into** *table*
>
> $$attribute_1, \ldots, attribute_n$$
>
> **values**
>
> $$value_1, \ldots, value_n$$

The attributes of the table which are not specified in the *insert* command are set to *null* values for the row being inserted.

> *Example 3-132.*
>
> Let the instructor whose id is 22222 work in the department whose main name is *Arts*.

> **insert into**  WORK
>
> > INSTRUCTOR-ID-in-key, DEPARTMENT-MAIN-NAME-in-key
>
> **values**
>
> > 22222, 'Arts'

3.   Inserting a set of rows into a table.  A set of rows to be inserted can be defined as the result of a query.

> **insert into** *table*
>
> > $attribute_1, \ldots, attribute_n$
>
> *query*

> *Example 3-133.*
>
> Let all physics instructors work also in *Arts*.
>
> > **insert into**  WORK
> >
> > > INSTRUCTOR-ID-in-key, DEPARTMENT-MAIN-NAME-in-key
> > >
> > > **select**  *INSTRUCTOR-ID-in-key, 'Arts'*
> > >
> > > **from**  WORK
> > >
> > > **where**  *DEPARTMENT-MAIN-NAME-in-key = 'Physics'*

4.   Modifying the values of some attribute in a set of rows of a table.  The set of rows can be specified by a **where** condition.  The new values can be specified as constants or as expressions using the old values of the row being updated.

> **update**  *table*
>
> **set**
>
> > $attribute_1 = expression_1, \ldots, attribute_n = expression_n$
>
> **where**  *condition*

> *Example 3-134.*
>
> Decrease by 10% all grades above 90.
>
> > **update**  *COURSE-ENROLLMENT*

> **set** *FINAL-GRADE = FINAL-GRADE\*0.9*
>
> **where** *FINAL-GRADE > 90*

### 3.3.4.8. DDL

SQL has a data definition capability.

**Specification of a table**

> **create table** *table-name*
>
> *attribute$_1$ data-type$_1$, . . . , attribute$_n$ data-type$_n$*

> *Example 3-135.*
>
> **create table** *QUARTER*
>
> | *YEAR-in-key* | Integer |
> |---|---|
> | *SEASON-in-key* | String |

**Specification of a userview table**

> **create view** *new-table-name*
>
> *attribute$_1$, . . . , attribute$_n$*
>
> **as** *select-command*

> *Example 3-136.*
>
> **create view** *TAUGHT*
>
> *STUDENT-ID HIS-TEACHER-ID*
>
> **as**  **select** *STUDENT-ID-in-key, INSTRUCTOR-ID-in-key*
>
>     **from** *COURSE-ENROLLMENT*

### 3.3.4.9. SQL extension of Pascal

SQL can be used not only interactively, but also as a DML extension of a programming language. This section shows how SQL can be embedded in PASCAL. The embedding in other programming languages is similar.

## Host variables in SQL statements

Wherever a constant can appear in SQL, a host program variable can appear instead. Before the SQL statement is performed, the variable is evaluated to give a value. To distinguish between host program variables and SQL variables, the host variables are preceded by a colon (:).

---

*Example 3-137.*

Create a new course whose name is in the Pascal variable *course-name*.

**insert into**  *COURSE*

*NAME-key*

**values** :course-name

---

*Example 3-138.*

For each standard input line create a new course whose name is the string appearing in that line.

**var** course-name: String;

**begin**

**while not** eof(Input) **do begin**

    **readln** (course-name);

    **insert into**  *COURSE*

        *NAME-key* **values** :course-name

    **end**

**end**.

---

## Retrieving a row of values from the database

If we anticipate that a select command will retrieve exactly one row of data, we can have this data placed into variables of the host program by the following command.

*select-command* **into** *host-variables*

*Example 3-139.*

(* Get the total number students born in 1980 into the variable *myvar.* *)

> **select count** (✳)
>
> **from** *STUDENT*
>
> **where** *BIRTH-YEAR* = 1980
>
> **into** :myvar

## Processing of multi-row output of a query

The program can retrieve a set of rows of data from the database.

- Such a set of rows can be defined as the output of a *select* command. The program would then process the retrieved rows, one row at a time.

*Example 3-140.*

**select** *BIRTH-YEAR*

**from** *STUDENT*

**where** *MAJOR-DEPARTMENT-MAIN-NAME* = 'Management';

- To scan such rows in a program, SQL defines a **cursor,** a logical pointer to the current row. The declaration of a cursor defines a query.

*Example 3-141.*

**declare** current-student **cursor for**
> **select** *BIRTH-YEAR*
>
> **from** *STUDENT*
>
> **where** *MAJOR-DEPARTMENT-MAIN-NAME* =
> 'Management';

- The opening of the cursor performs the query.

> *Example 3-142.*
>
> **open** current-student;

- The **fetch** command then brings to the program one row each time and advances the cursor to point to the next row.

> *Example 3-143.*
>
> **fetch** current-student **into** :birth-year;

- When a *fetch* is attempted beyond the last row in the output of a query, the special variable **sqlstatus** is set to the value of the special constant **not-found**.

> *Example 3-144.*
>
> (* Print the logarithm of the birth year of every management student (major) *)
>
>     **declare** current-student **cursor for**
>
>         **select** *BIRTH-YEAR*
>
>         **from** *STUDENT*
>
>         **where** *MAJOR-DEPARTMENT-MAIN-NAME* =
>            'Management';
>
>     **open** current-student;
>
>     **repeat**
>
>         **fetch** current-student **into** :birth-year;
>
>         **if** sqlstatus $\neq$ not-found **then** writeln(log(birth-year))
>
>     **until** sqlstatus = not-found

The relevant commands are:

a.    **declare** *cursor-name* **cursor for** *select-command*

b.    **open** *cursor-name*

c.    **fetch** *cursor-name* **into** *host-variables*

**Update and deletion of fetched rows**

After a row has been *fetched*, it can be updated or deleted provided the row belongs to one table of the schema (and not to a join of tables).

a.  **update** *table-name*

   **set**

           $attribute_1 = expression_1, \ldots, attribute_n = expression_n$

   **where current of** *cursor-name*

---

*Example 3-145.*

(* Replace the birth year of every management student (major) by the logarithm of the birth year. *)

     **declare** current-student **cursor for**

         **select** *BIRTH-YEAR*

         **from** *STUDENT*

         **where** *MAJOR-DEPARTMENT-MAIN-NAME* = 'Management';

    **open** current-student;

    **repeat**

        **fetch** current-student **into** :birth-year;

        birth-year := log (birth-year);

        **if** sqlstatus $\neq$ not-found **then**

           **update** *STUDENT*

               **set** *BIRTH-YEAR* = :birth-year

               **where current of** current-student

    **until** sqlstatus = not-found

---

b.  **delete from** *table-name*

   **where current of** *cursor-name*

---

*Example 3-146.*

(* Display the name of every student; prompt the user whether the student should be deleted; if the user replies 'yes' — delete the

```
student. *)
    declare current-student cursor for
            select LAST-NAME, FIRST-NAME
            from  STUDENT
    open current-student;
    repeat
        fetch current-student into :last-name, :first-name;
        if sqlstatus ≠ not-found then begin
            writeln (' Would you like to delete ', last-name, ' ',
                first-name, '?');
            readln (answer);
            if answer='yes' then
                delete from STUDENT
                    where current of current-student
        end
    until sqlstatus = not-found
```

*Problem 3-25.*

Use the studio/relational schema (Figure 8-20 on page 301). Write an SQL query to find the titles of Fellini's films.

Solution on page 318.

*Problem 3-26.*

Use the projects/relational schema (Figure 8-15 on page 298). Write in SQL a query to find the names of the projects which have subprojects.

Solution on page 318.

**In the following problems,** translate the English specification into SQL.

*Problem 3-27.*

Use the sales/relational schema (Figure 8-22 on page 303).
What are the id numbers of all persons whose name is *Johnson*?

Solution on page 318.

*Problem 3-28.*

Use the sales/relational schema (Figure 8-22 on page 303).
What items has Johnson bought?

Solution on page 319.

*Problem 3-29.*

Use the sales/relational schema (Figure 8-22 on page 303).
What are the names of the persons who bought something from Rothschild?

Solution on page 319.

*Problem 3-30.*

Use the sales/relational schema (Figure 8-22 on page 303).
For what prices were nails sold?

Solution on page 319.

*Problem 3-31.*

Use the sales/relational schema (Figure 8-22 on page 303).
For all sale transactions above $100, list the price, the item type, and the id-s of the
seller and the buyer.

Solution on page 319.

*Problem 3-32.*

Use the sales/relational schema (Figure 8-22 on page 303).
Who sold an item for a lower price than he himself paid for the same (or identical)
item?

Solution on page 319.

*Problem 3-33.*

Use the sales/relational schema (Figure 8-22 on page 303).
How many sale transactions were there for the price of $1?

Solution on page 320.

*Problem 3-34.*

Use the sales/relational schema (Figure 8-22 on page 303).
What is the average price of one nail?

Solution on page 320.

*Problem 3-35.*

Use the sales/relational schema (Figure 8-22 on page 303). What are the *different* items that Tsai bought?

Solution on page 320.

*Problem 3-36.*

Use the sales/relational schema (Figure 8-22 on page 303). How many *different* items has Tsai bought?

Solution on page 320.

*Problem 3-37.*

Use the sales/relational schema (Figure 8-22 on page 303). For every item type, list its average price.

Solution on page 320.

*Problem 3-38.*

Use the sales/relational schema (Figure 8-22 on page 303). What items cost more than $1000 on the average?

Solution on page 320.

*Problem 3-39.*

Use the sales/relational schema (Figure 8-22 on page 303). What items cost more than $1000 on the average, ignoring the nominal transactions for a token price of $10 and less?

Solution on page 321.

*Problem 3-40.*

Use the sales/relational schema (Figure 8-22 on page 303). List all persons sorted by their names.

Solution on page 321.

*Problem 3-41.*

Use the sales/relational schema (Figure 8-22 on page 303). Delete the person whose id is 555.

Solution on page 321.

*Problem 3-42.*

Use the sales/relational schema (Figure 8-22 on page 303). Delete all car sale transactions.

*Problem 3-43.*

Use the sales/relational schema (Figure 8-22 on page 303).
Insert a new person whose id is 333 and whose name is Vasudha.

Solution on page 321.

*Problem 3-44.*

Use the sales/relational schema (Figure 8-22 on page 303).
For every hammer transaction, let there be a nail transaction between the same persons. The price of the nail will be 1% of the price of the hammer. The id of the nail transaction will be 100000 + the id of the hammer transaction.

Solution on page 322.

*Problem 3-45.*

Use the sales/relational schema (Figure 8-22 on page 303).
Decrease by 10% all prices above $90.

Solution on page 322.

*Problem 3-46.*

Use the sales/relational schema (Figure 8-22 on page 303).
Define the table *PERSON*.

Solution on page 322.

*Problem 3-47.*

Use the sales/relational schema (Figure 8-22 on page 303).
Define a userview table which contains *ID*'s of persons and descriptions of the items they bought.

Solution on page 322.

*Problem 3-48.*

Use the sales/relational schema (Figure 8-22 on page 303). Write an SQL/Pascal program fragment
(* Create a new item-type whose description is in the Pascal variable *item*. *)

Solution on page 322.

*Problem 3-49.*

Use the sales/relational schema (Figure 8-22 on page 303). Write an SQL/Pascal program
(* For each standard input line create a new item type whose description is the string appearing in that line. *)

*Problem 3-50.*

Use the sales/relational schema (Figure 8-22 on page 303). Write an SQL/Pascal program fragment
(* Get the total number of sale transactions below $10 into the variable *total.* *)

Solution on page 323.

*Problem 3-51.*

Use the sales/relational schema (Figure 8-22 on page 303). Write an SQL/Pascal program fragment
(* Print the item of every $20 transaction. *)

Solution on page 323.

*Problem 3-52.*

Use the sales/relational schema (Figure 8-22 on page 303). Write an SQL/Pascal program fragment
(* Modify the price of every sale transaction by applying to it the Pascal function *modify* (defined elsewhere in the program). *)

Solution on page 324.

*Problem 3-53.*

Use the sales/relational schema (Figure 8-22 on page 303). Write an SQL/Pascal program fragment
(* Display the description of every item type; prompt the user whether the item type should be deleted; if the user replies 'yes' — delete the item type. *)

Solution on page 324.

*Problem 3-54.*

Use the circuitboard/relational schema (Figure 8-21 on page 302). Write the following query in SQL.

For circuit name = databit01, list the function of each component to which the circuit is connected.

Solution on page 325.

*Problem 3-55.*

Use the circuitboard/relational schema (Figure 8-21 on page 302). Write the following query in SQL.

For each circuit name list the components and the pins sorted by circuit name, then by component id, then by pin number.

Solution on page 325.

*Problem 3-56.*

Use the circuitboard/relational schema (Figure 8-21 on page 302). Write the following query in SQL.

List the circuits that contain only one pin (this would be a design error).

Solution on page 325.

*Problem 3-57.*

Use the circuitboard/relational schema (Figure 8-21 on page 302). Write the following query in SQL.

List the distinct component type names of the components whose pin #14 is connected to a red-colored circuit.

Solution on page 325.

*Problem 3-58.*

Use the circuitboard/relational schema (Figure 8-21 on page 302). Write the following query in SQL.

Generate a list of types and functions of all the components.

Solution on page 325.

*Problem 3-59.*

Use the circuitboard/relational schema (Figure 8-21 on page 302). Write the following transaction in SQL.

Change the circuit name from *databit01* to *databit02*.

Solution on page 326.

## 3.3.5.  Power of relational query languages

Ignoring minor differences in expressiveness, such as the output of identical rows, the following languages have approximately equal power. A query that can be expressed in one language can also be expressed in the others:

-     the Tuple-oriented Relational Calculus without aggregate functions,

-     Relational Algebra, and

-     SQL without aggregate functions.

The aggregate extension of the Predicate Calculus and SQL with aggregate functions have a higher power.

   The structured extension of Pascal, being a general-purpose programming language, has a much higher power of expressiveness.

**Problems to compare the different relational languages.** For each of the following tasks write an appropriate statement or program in each of the following languages (excluding those languages in which the particular task cannot be specified).

- Relational Calculus
- Extended Pascal
- Relational Algebra
- SQL

Use the university/relational reference schema.

*Problem 3-60.*

Find the names of the persons born in 1967.

Solution on page 326.

*Problem 3-61.*

For every student, list the instructors of the student's major department.

Solution on page 327.

*Problem 3-62.*

What instructors work in every department? (Each relevant instructor shares her time between all the departments.)

Solution on page 329.

*Problem 3-63.*

What instructors taught every student?

Solution on page 331.

*Problem 3-64.*

Who took Prof. Smith's courses?

Solution on page 333.

*Problem 3-65.*

Display 'TRUE' if every student took at least one course.

Solution on page 334.

*Problem 3-66.*

Print a table with two columns, which associates students to their teachers. Only last names are printed.

*Problem 3-67.*

Find the average birth year of the students.

Solution on page 337.

*Problem 3-68.*

Find the number of pairs (*INSTRUCTOR, DEPARTMENT*) where the instructor works in the department.

Solution on page 338.

*Problem 3-69.*

Find the average of grades of student 'Jane Howard'.

Solution on page 338.

*Problem 3-70.*

Print the average of all grades given by Prof. Brown.

Solution on page 340.

*Problem 3-71.*

How many students are there in the university?

Solution on page 341.

*Problem 3-72.*

What students have their average grade above 90?

Solution on page 341.

*Problem 3-73.*

What are the last names of all the students?

Solution on page 342.

*Problem 3-74.*

When was Student Russel born?

Solution on page 343.

*Problem 3-75.*

What courses has Prof. Graham taught?

Solution on page 343.

*Problem 3-76.*

Print the names of the pairs of students who live together.

Solution on page 344.

*Problem 3-77.*

Print the names and the addresses of all computer science students.

Solution on page 345.

*Problem 3-78.*

How many computer science students are there in the database?

Solution on page 346.

*Problem 3-79.*

What is the average grade in the *Databases* course?

Solution on page 346.

*Problem 3-80.*

List the distinct addresses of the students. (Do not list the same address twice.)

Solution on page 347.

*Problem 3-81.*

Find the names of the students who never took a course.

Solution on page 347.

# 4

# SUMMARY OF DATABASE DESIGN METHODOLOGY

## 4.1. The Methodology of This Text

The following information flow diagram outlines the major steps of database application design, including the schema, integrity constraints, userviews, data manipulation programs, query forms, and ad-hoc queries. The design proceeds in the direction of the arrows from semantic descriptions to descriptions in the conventions and languages supported by the available DBMS. Nodes marked in brackets are omitted for some DBMS.

In the first step, a conceptual schema of an enterprise is designed using the semantic binary model. Then the schema is converted into the relational, network, or hierarchical model by manual algorithms. According to the criteria described in the text to assess the quality of data bases, these manual algorithms produce very high-quality results.

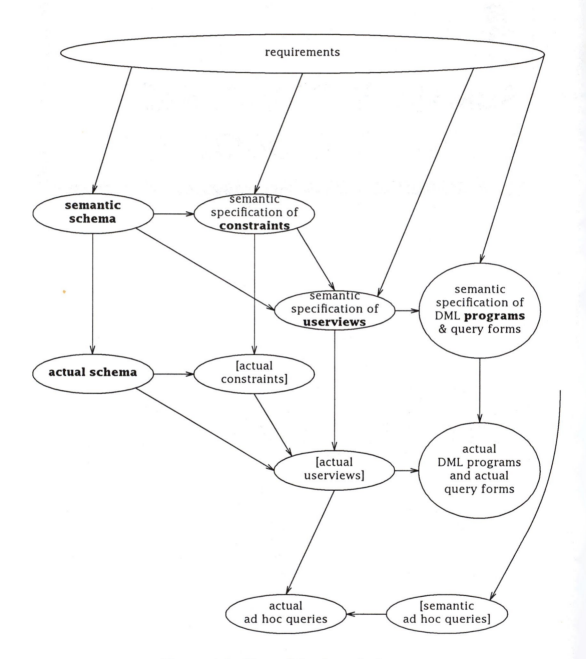

**Figure 4-1.** Flow of database design.

## 4.2.  An Alternative Methodology: Normalization

**Normalization** is a methodology for the design of relational databases. This methodology used to be quite popular in the academic world. However, it has been rarely used in the application industry. One of the reasons for the lack of popularity in the industry was mathematical sophistication of the normalization methodology.

This is a "bottom-up" methodology. The design proceeds as follows. First, a poor relational schema is designed directly from the requirements. Then, the schema is refined in steps by eliminating certain aspects of redundancy (and thus potential inconsistency and update anomalies). The schema at every step satisfies certain mathematically defined criteria of non-redundancy corresponding to the step. These criteria are called **normal forms** corresponding to the steps.

1.   The initial schema is called to be in the **first normal form**.

2.   The product of the first step, satisfying certain broad criteria, is in the **second normal form**.

3.   The product of the next step, satisfying certain stricter criteria, is in the **third normal form.**\*

------

\* An attribute $A$ of table $T$ is said to be **functionally dependent** on a set of attributes $\{B_1, \ldots, B_k\}$ of $T$ if for no tuple of values $(b_1, \ldots, b_k)$ of these attributes there may be two different values of $A$ in the table at the same time.

A table $T$ having exactly one key (possibly a multi-attribute key) is said to be in the **third normal form** if:

> no non-key attribute $A$ is functionally dependent on any set of attributes, unless the latter set of attributes contains $A$ or contains the whole key.

(The definition is more complex for the unlikely case that the table has more than one key.)

Let, for example, $T$ be a table with four attributes $A, B, C$ and $D$. Let the key of $T$ be $\{A, B\}$. If $T$ is in the third normal form then

a.   $A$ is not functionally dependent on $\{B, C, D\}$

b.   $B$ is not functionally dependent on $\{A, C, D\}$

c.   $C$ is not functionally dependent on $\{A, D\}$

d.   $C$ is not functionally dependent on $\{B, D\}$

e.   $D$ is not functionally dependent on $\{A, C\}$

f.   $D$ is not functionally dependent on $\{B, C\}$

If any of these conditions is violated there would be a clear redundancy. For example, if $D$ *is* functionally dependent on $\{B, C\}$ then observe the redundancy in the following instantaneous table. We can deduce from the constraint that the '?' in the second row should read '45'

4.   The normalization process can continue further until the arsenal of normal form definitions is exhausted.

After the design is completed, all the schemas but the last one are discarded. Programs, queries, and the like      are designed directly in terms of the final schema.  A diagram of the flow of design by normalization follows.

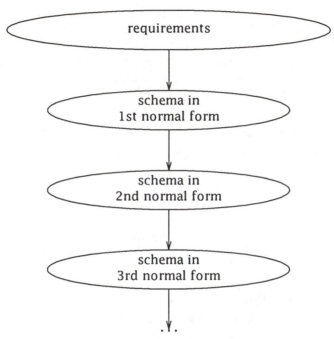

**Figure 4-2.**  Alternative relational database design: Normalization.

## 4.3.  A Comparison of Methodologies

1.   The normalization methodology captures only a few of the aspects of the data base semantic quality, while the methodology suggested in this text attempts to capture all the aspects.

| A | B | C | D |
|---|---|---|---|
| 37 | 15 | 5 | 45 |
| 12 | 15 | 5 | ? |

2.  The normalization methodology is too difficult to be used by most systems analysts and software engineers.

3.  The normalization methodology is "bottom-up": a "bad" data base is designed, and then it is refined by normalization. This is analogous to writing a bad program and then improving its structure.

    This book's methodology is "top-down": good semantic schemas are designed first, and then they are downgraded to meet implementational restrictions, while the original semantic schemas remain to serve as documentation. This is analogous to writing an algorithm first, and then translating it into a structured program, while the algorithm remains as documentation.

Figure 4-4 (page 208) is a "schema" of the world of relational database schemas and two database design processes: the binary-relational conversion according to the methodology of this book and the schema normalization according to the alternative methodology. This "methodology schema" shows:

- Every relational schema is a binary schema.

- Some of the binary schemas, which are not relational schemas, are high-quality schemas according to all the criteria of schema quality.

- Some of the relational schemas satisfy to a certain degree *some* of the non-redundancy criteria. These limited criteria are primarily concerned with the possible redundancy of a table which could be split into two tables. The relational schemas which satisfy these limited criteria to a certain minimal degree (at least) are called the second-normal-form schemas. Some of the second-normal-form schemas satisfy the limited criteria to a higher degree and correspondingly belong to the *THIRD-NORMAL-FORM, FOURTH-NORMAL-FORM, etc.*, subcategories of the second-normal-form schemas.

- Every high-quality relational schema should be in the maximal known normal form, but the opposite is not true: some maximal-normal-form schemas are not of high quality, since they do not address all the quality criteria.

- The process of normalization begins with a very poor relational schema and converts it into a second normal form schema, then into a third normal form schema, and so on.

- The methodology of this book begins with a quality binary schema and downgrades it to a quality relational schema.

Figure 4-3 outlines the "instantaneous database" under the "methodology schema". The individual schemas are points there in a coordinate system of schema quality.

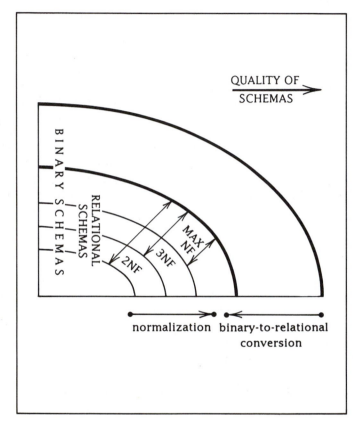

**Figure 4-3.** A comparison between database design methodologies: the "instantaneous database" for the "schema" of conversion methodologies.

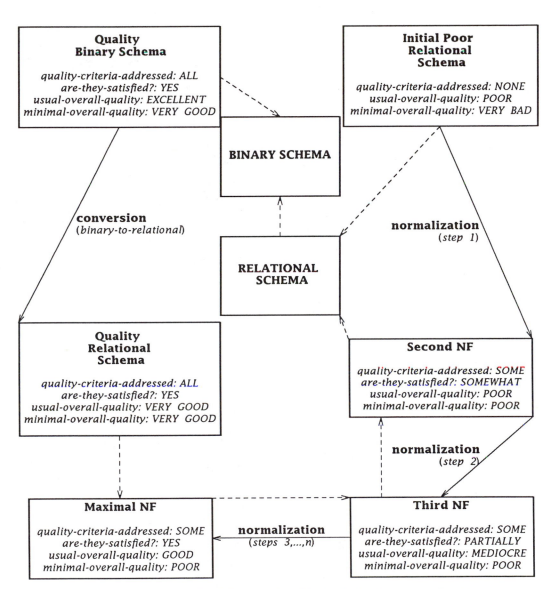

**Figure 4-4.** A "Schema" of Conversion Methodologies: normalization *vs* binary-to-relational conversion. The arrows with dashes show the subcategories among the the categories of schemas.

# 5

# THE NETWORK MODEL

This chapter introduces the Network Data Model. Since the 1970s, this model has been very popular in the industry. An alternative name of the model is **CODASYL/DBTG**, after the name of the committee that produced a standard for the Network Model (CODASYL Data Base Task Group).

## 5.1. Definitions

**Order-less network schema** — a binary schema satisfying the following:

a.  all the abstract categories are pairwise *disjoint*

b.  every relation is either an *attribute* (an m:1 relation to a concrete category), or a 1:*m* relation between *different* abstract categories.

---

*Example 5-1.*

The following could be an order-less network schema for a university, provided there are no persons but students and instructors, and the categories *INSTRUCTOR* and *STUDENT* are disjoint.

---

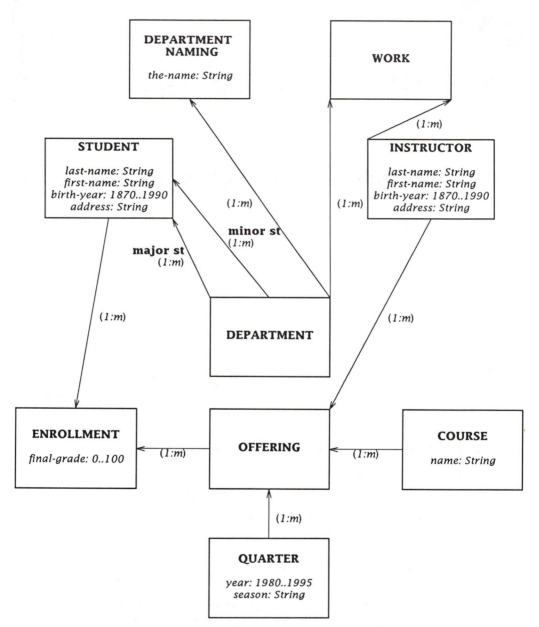

**Figure 5-1.** An order-less network schema for the university application.

*Default names of relations*

It is customary in the network model to name relations as

*domain* **hyphen** *range*

Of course, this convention may be used only when there is no other relation between the same domain and range.

In the graphic representation of network schemas we may omit some of the names of the relations. The omitted names by default conform to the above convention.

---

*Example 5-2.*

- Relation **instructor-work** from *INSTRUCTOR* to *WORK* (*1:m*)

---

**Onto relation** — a relation whose inverse is total.

This means that a relation $R$ from $C_1$ to $C_2$ is onto if for every object $y$ of $C_2$ there is an object $x$ of $C_1$ such that $xRy$.

---

*Example 5-3.*

- Relation    from *STUDENT* to *ENROLLMENT*  (*1:m,onto*)

(it is *onto* because every enrollment has a student related to it).

- Relation    from *INSTRUCTOR* to *WORK*  (*1:m,onto*)

(it is *onto* because every event of work is related to an instructor).

---

The phrase 'relation $R$ is **onto** category $C$' means:

$R$ is an *onto* relation, and its range is $C$.

The phrase 'category $C_2$ **depends on** category $C_1$' means:

there is a *relation* from $C_1$ onto $C_2$

(that is, there is a relation which relates every object of $C_2$ to an object of $C_1$).

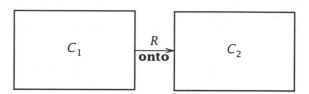

**Figure 5-2.** $C_2$ depends on $C_1$.

---

*Example 5-4.*

- *OFFERING* depends on *COURSE*
- *OFFERING* depends on *QUARTER*
- *OFFERING* depends on *INSTRUCTOR*
- *ENROLLMENT* depends on *OFFERING*
- *ENROLLMENT* depends on *STUDENT*
- *DEPARTMENT-NAMING* depends on *DEPARTMENT*
- *WORK* depends on *DEPARTMENT*
- *WORK* depends on *INSTRUCTOR*

---

The phrase 'category $C_1$ **indirectly depends on** category $C_2$' means (recursively):

> $C_1$ depends on $C_2$, or there exists $C_3$ such that $C_1$ depends on $C_3$ and $C_3$ indirectly depends on $C_2$.

---

*Example 5-5.*

- *ENROLLMENT* indirectly depends on *OFFERING*
  (since *ENROLLMENT* depends on *OFFERING*).
- *ENROLLMENT* indirectly depends on *COURSE*

---

**Independent category** — an abstract category which depends on no category.

*Example 5-6.*

Independent categories:

*STUDENT, INSTRUCTOR, DEPARTMENT, COURSE, QUARTER.*

**Ordered network schema** — a binary system consisting of

a.  an order-less network schema

b.  a category, called *SYSTEM*, in which at all times there is only one and the same object SYSTEM

c.  relations from *SYSTEM onto* some of the abstract categories of the order-less schema, such that every abstract category of the order-less schema would be indirectly dependent on *SYSTEM*

*Example 5-7.*

- Relation   from *SYSTEM* to *STUDENT*   (*1:m,onto*)
- Relation   from *SYSTEM* to *INSTRUCTOR*   (*1:m,onto*)
- Relation   from *SYSTEM* to *DEPARTMENT*   (*1:m,onto*)
- Relation   from *SYSTEM* to *COURSE*   (*1:m,onto*)
- Relation   from *SYSTEM* to *QUARTER*   (*1:m,onto*)

d.  for every relation $R$ between different abstract categories $C_1$ and $C_2$ there is a relation $NEXT_R$ such that

- the domain of $NEXT_R$ is $C_2$,
- the range of $NEXT_R$ is $C_2$,
- for every object $x$ in $C_1$, $NEXT_R$ constitutes a linear order of $C_2$'s objects connected by $R$ to $x$.

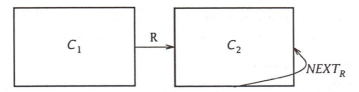

*Example 5-8.*

- Relation **next-system-department** from *DEPARTMENT* to *DEPARTMENT* (*1:1*)

This is a chain connecting all of the departments:

$$d_1 \rightarrow d_2 \rightarrow d_3 \rightarrow d_4$$

*Example 5-9.*

- Relation **next-system-student** from *STUDENT* to *STUDENT* (*1:1*)

This is a chain connecting all of the students:

$$s_1 \rightarrow s_2 \rightarrow s_3 \rightarrow \cdots \rightarrow s_{500}$$

*Example 5-10.*

- Relation **next-major-st** from *STUDENT* to *STUDENT* (*1:1*)

This is a set of chains, one chain per department, connecting all the majoring students of the department.

For department $d_1$:     $s_{11} \rightarrow s_{25} \rightarrow s_3 \rightarrow s_{15}$

For department $d_2$: trivial chain because the department has only 1 majoring student.

For department $d_3$: empty chain because the department has no majoring students.

For department $d_4$:     $s_1 \rightarrow s_{220} \rightarrow s_{31}$

(The remaining 492 students have not declared their majors.)

*Network schema terminology*

The following terms are frequently used in network database management systems. Most of them have synonyms in the binary terminology.

**Record-type** — abstract category.

> *Example 5-11.*
>
> *DEPARTMENT* is a record-type.

**Field** — attribute.

> *Example 5-12.*
>
> *LAST-NAME* is a field.

**Set-type** — a non-attribute relation between different categories.

> *Example 5-13.*
>
> - Relation **major-st** from *DEPARTMENT* to *STUDENT*  (*1:m*)
>
> - Relation **instructor-work** from *INSTRUCTOR* to *WORK* (*1:m*)

**Record occurrence** — a part of an instantaneous database, consisting of exactly one abstract object and all its attributes.

> *Example 5-14.*
>
> A record occurrence of record-type *STUDENT*:
>
> > **ONE student**
> >
> > *last-name:* Jackson
> > *first-name:* Mary
> > *birth-year:* 1970
> > *address:* 123  Dorms

**Set occurrence** of a set-type $R$ for an object $x$ — a part of an instantaneous database consisting only of $x$, all the objects related to $x$ by $R$, and the relation $NEXT_R$ on these objects.

*Example 5-15.*

Let $s_1$, $s_2$, $s_3$, $s_4$ be the only majoring students of department $d$. Then the following may be a set occurrence:

$$d, s_1 \; NEXT_{\text{major-st}} \; s_2 \; NEXT_{\text{major-st}} \; s_3 \; NEXT_{\text{major-st}} \; s_4$$

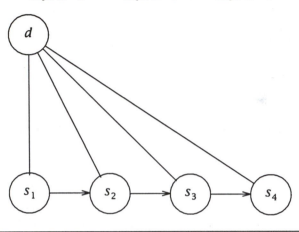

Each set-type whose domain is *SYSTEM* has exactly one set-occurrence, since there is only one object of the record-type *SYSTEM*.

*Example 5-16.*

The following is the set-occurrence of *SYSTEM-STUDENT* in an instantaneous database.

$$SYSTEM \xrightarrow{\;first\;} student_1 \xrightarrow{\;next\;} student_2 \xrightarrow{\;next\;} student_3$$

*Example 5-17.*

The following figure shows a part of a network instantaneous database. This part contains all the record-occurrences of *STUDENT*, *DEPARTMENT*, and *DEPARTMENT-NAMING* and all the set-occurrences of *SYSTEM-STUDENT*, *SYSTEM-DEPARTMENT*, *DEPARTMENT—DEPARTMENT-NAMING*, *MAJOR-ST*, and *MINOR-ST*.

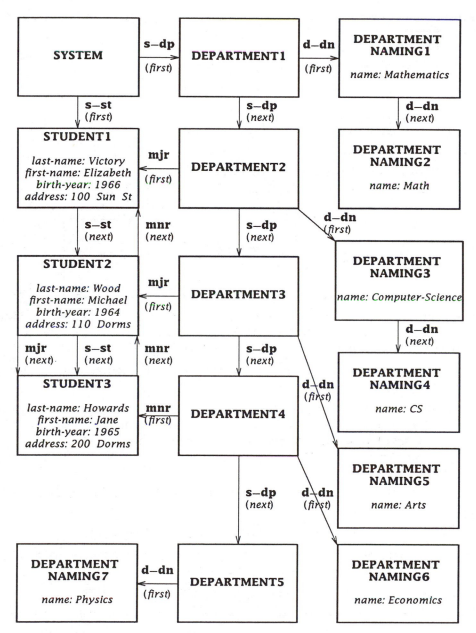

**Figure 5-3.** A part of a network instantaneous database.

**Owner** of a set-type $R$ — its domain.

> *Example 5-18.*
>
> *DEPARTMENT* is the owner of *MAJOR-ST.*

**Member** of a set-type $R$ — its range.

> *Example 5-19.*
>
> *STUDENT* is the member of *MAJOR-ST.*

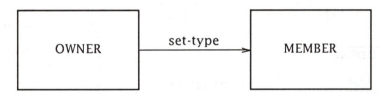

**Order-type** of a set type $R$ — the integrity constraints, the implementational restrictions, or the inference rules regarding the ordering of a set-occurrence (as determined by the relation $NEXT_R$).

Many network database management systems recognize the following order types:

**'order is last'** — the member object last related (in time) to a given owner object becomes the last in the order among all the member objects related by the relation to the owner object.

> *Example 5-20.*
>
> Let the following be the set occurrence of *MAJOR-ST* for department $d$:
>
> $$d, s_1 \; NEXT_{\text{major-st}} \; s_2 \; NEXT_{\text{major-st}} \; s_3 \; NEXT_{\text{major-st}} \; s_4$$
>
> Now assume that another student $s$ becomes a majoring student of $d$. Then the new set occurrence would be
>
> $$d, \quad s_1 \; NEXT_{\text{major-st}} \; s_2 \; NEXT_{\text{major-st}} \; s_3 \; NEXT_{\text{major-st}} \; s_4 \; NEXT_{\text{major-st}} \; s$$

**'order is first'** — the member object last (in time) related to a given owner object becomes the first in the order among all the member objects related by the relation to the owner object.

---

*Example 5-21.*

Let the following be the set occurrence of *MAJOR-ST* for department *d*:

$$d, s_1 \; NEXT_{\text{major-st}} \; s_2 \; NEXT_{\text{major-st}} \; s_3 \; NEXT_{\text{major-st}} \; s_4$$

Now assume that another student *s* becomes a majoring student of *d*. Then the new set occurrence would be

$$d,$$
$$s \; NEXT_{\text{major-st}} \; s_1 \; NEXT_{\text{major-st}} \; s_2 \; NEXT_{\text{major-st}} \; s_3 \; NEXT_{\text{major-st}} \; s_4$$

---

**'order is ascending by field** $f$**'** — the member object last related to a given owner object is put in a position within the order according to the following criterion for every two member objects $y_1$ and $y_2$:

$$\textbf{if } y_1 \; NEXT_R \; y_2 \textbf{ then } y_1.f \leq y_2.f$$

This order type is often also called **"order by key"**. This "key" has nothing to do with the concept of *key* as defined for the relational model. To avoid confusion, the "order by key" terminology is not used in this text.

**'order is descending by field** $f$**'** — the member object last related to a given owner object is put in a position within the order according to the following criterion for every two member objects $y_1$ and $y_2$:

$$\textbf{if } y_1 \; NEXT_R \; y_2 \textbf{ then } y_1.f \geq y_2.f$$

**'order is** $o_1, o_2, ..., o_k$**'**, where each $o_i$ is of the form

**'ascending by field** $f_i$**'** or **'descending by field** $f_i$**'**

— a lexicographic combination of ordering conditions on several fields.

**'order is current'** — no constraints, restrictions, or program-independent rules for the order. Pragmatically, the position of a new object is determined by the application program: the position will be right next to the last object accessed by the program within the same set-occurrence.

## 5.2. Database Design

**Conversion algorithm** of an adequate binary schema into a network schema whose quality is among the highest possible for the latter:

1. **Convert all abstract categories into disjoint ones** as in the conversion for the Relational Model.

   *Note*:

   - In the Network Model, the categories need not have keys. Thus, when the solution *Events* is chosen, its redundancy cannot be controlled in terms of the key. If the supercategory has a 1:1 attribute, then we can specify an integrity constraint controlling the *Events* redundancy in terms of that attribute.

   ---

   *Example 5-22.*

   Suppose we had

   - Relation *ssn* from *PERSON* to the category of values *Integer* *(1:1)*

   After the conversion into *Events* we would have

   - Relation *ssn* from *STUDENT* to the category of values *Integer* *(1:1)*
   - Relation *ssn* from *INSTRUCTOR* to the category of values *Integer* *(1:1)*

   In this case, we can specify a constraint for every relation whose domain or range was the category *PERSON*. For the relation *ADDRESS* such a constraint is:

   **for every** s **in** *STUDENT*:

   **for every** i **in** *INSTRUCTOR*:

       **if** s.*SSN*=i.*SSN*

         **then**

             s.*ADDRESS*=i.*ADDRESS* **or**

           (s *ADDRESS* **null and** i *ADDRESS* **null**)

   ---

   - The available network database management systems usually do not support sophisticated userviews, they support only subschemas, which are trivial userviews. This means that normally the solution

*Union+Events* should not be chosen in the design of a network schema.

2. **Convert every proper 1:m or m:m relation whose range is a concrete category** into a new abstract category and its two functional relations through a relation-split.

3. **Convert every proper many-to-many** relation into a category and two functional relations through a relation-split.

4. **Convert every m:1 non-attribute relation into a 1:m relation** by changing its direction and its name.

---

*Example 5-23.*

Instead of

- Relation **the-student** from *ENROLLMENT* to *STUDENT* (*m:1*)

we have

- Relation **student-enrollment** from *STUDENT* to *ENROLLMENT* (*1:m*)

---

5. **Convert every 1:m relation whose domain and range are the same category** into a new category, a 1:1 onto relation, and a 1:m onto relation, through a relation-split.

---

*Example 5-24.*

If we had

- Relation **subdepartment** from *DEPARTMENT* to *DEPARTMENT* (*1:m*)

then we would convert it into

- Category *event-of-SUBDEPARTMENT*
- Relation **the-event-of-the-same-department** from *DEPARTMENT* to *event-of-SUBDEPARTMENT* (*1:1,onto*)
- Relation **department-subdepartment** from *DEPARTMENT* to *event-of-SUBDEPARTMENT* (*1:m,onto*)

---

> *Example 5-25.*
>
> The binary schema of the university has been converted so far into the order-less network schema of Figure 5-1 on page 212.

6. **Add the category** *SYSTEM*, which always has just one object — the enterprise or the world for which the database is being designed.

7. **Relate every independent category** *C* to *SYSTEM*:

   - Relation **system-***C* from *SYSTEM* to *C*  (*1:m,onto*)

   > *Example 5-26.*
   >
   > - Relation **system-department** from *SYSTEM* to *DEPARTMENT*  (*1:m,onto*)

8. If there are still abstract categories *C* that do not indirectly depend on *SYSTEM* (a very rare case), then relate them to *SYSTEM*:

   - Relation **system-***C* from *SYSTEM* to *C*  (*1:m,onto*)

> *Example 5-27.*
>
> There is no such problem in our schema. Let's spoil our schema a bit to have such a problem. If the relation *MAJOR-ST* were onto:
>
> - Relation **major-st** from *DEPARTMENT* to *STUDENT* (*1:m,onto*)
>
> and in addition we had a relation assigning one student council liaison to several departments:
>
> - Relation **student-council-liaison-for-department** from *SUDENT* to *DEPARTMENT*  (*1:m,onto*)
>
> then the categories *STUDENT* and *DEPARTMENT* would depend on each other. None of the categories would be independent. We have to link at least one of them to *SYSTEM*, so that they would indirectly depend on SYSTEM:
>
> - Relation **system-department** from *SYSTEM* to *DEPARTMENT*  (*1:m,onto*)

9.   Define **order-type** of every non-attribute relation *R* as follows:

If the domain of the relation is *SYSTEM*

(i)   *then* ("order is by ascendance/descendance by fields"):

 (a)  Let *C* be the range of this relation. Pick an attribute of *C*, or a list of attributes, so that the application programs are most likely to access the objects of *C* in the order which can be defined by these attributes.

 (b)  Specify the order-type to preserve the ascendance-descendance of the above attributes.

 (A *list* of attributes establishes precedence between them: the objects are ordered primarily according to the first attribute in the list. Two objects that have the same value of the first attribute in the list are ordered according to the second attribute, and so on.)

 This need not be a *deterministic* (unambiguous) specification of the order — two distinct objects may have equal values in each of the attributes in the list. (In many DBMS's, such two objects are called **duplicates**.)

 The list of attributes may be empty, as it is, for example, when *C* has no attributes at all.

---

*Example 5-28.*

- The order of *SYSTEM-COURSE* is ascending by *NAME*.

- The order of *SYSTEM-QUARTER* is ascending by *YEAR*, descending by *SEASON*. (Fortunately, the alphabetic order of seasons, 'Winter' > 'Spring' > 'Fall', coincides with their natural order.)

- The order of *SYSTEM-INSTRUCTOR* is ascending by *LAST-NAME*, ascending by *FIRST-NAME*.

- The order of *SYSTEM-STUDENT* is ascending by *LAST-NAME*, ascending by *FIRST-NAME*.

- The order of *SYSTEM-DEPARTMENT* has no constraint.

---

(ii)  *else* ("order is last"):

Let the order be the order of insertion/connection, that is, there is a dynamic constraint (restriction) that when an object $x$ becomes connected by $R$ to an object $y$, this $x$ becomes the last by $NEXT_R$ among the objects connected by $R$ to $y$.

10. **Translate the integrity constraints** into the terms of the new schema:

   a.   The constraints of the original schema.

   b.   The additional constraints accumulated during the conversion process.

*Problem 5-1.*

Use the university/network reference schema at the end of this book. Specify in calculus all the integrity constraints which are not covered by this network schema but are covered by the binary schema, that is, the constraints generated during the conversion from the binary schema.

*Problem 5-2.*

Use the university/binary reference schema at the end of this book. Convert this schema into a network schema, assuming

- 50% of the instructors are students and 40% of students are instructors

- an instructor can give the same course several times during one quarter

- the DBMS does not support userviews

Specify the integrity constraints which are not covered by your network schema, but are covered by the binary schema.

*Problem 5-3.*

Use the studio/binary schema (Figure 8-2 on page 281). Design a network schema for the studio application.

Solution on page 348.

*Problem 5-4.*

Use the medical/binary schema (Figure 8-6 on page 287).

1. Design a network schema for the medical application. Your data base shall be equivalent in the information content to the binary data base described by the above binary schema.

2. Specify in calculus all the integrity constraints that have to be added to the schema during conversion.

3. Whenever the conversion algorithm allows a selection between alternatives, discuss the alternatives and justify your selection.

4.    Specify one subschema of your schema.

5.    According to your subschema draw the part of an instantaneous data base.

**In the following problems**, design a network schema equivalent to the appropriate binary schema. Specify the integrity constraints incident to the conversion from the binary schema to the network schema.

*Problem 5-5.*

Use the clan/binary schema (Figure 8-3 on page 282).

Solution on page 349.

*Problem 5-6.*

Use the circuit/binary schema (Figure 8-5 on page 283).

Solution on page 350.

*Problem 5-7.*

Use the sales/binary schema (Figure 8-4 on page 283).

Solution on page 351.

*Problem 5-8.*

Use the cable/binary schema (Figure 8-10 on page 290).

Solution on page 352.

*Problem 5-9.*

Use the busstop/binary schema (Figure 8-11 on page 291).

Solution on page 353.

*Problem 5-10.*

Use the carsale/binary schema (Figure 8-12 on page 292).

*Problem 5-11.*

Use the clinic/binary schema (Figure 8-13 on page 293).

Solution on page 354.

*Problem 5-12.*

Use the newspaper/binary schema (Figure 8-27 on page 310).

Solution on page 356.

*Problem 5-13.*

Use the library/binary schema (Figure 8-7 on page 288).

Solution on page 357.

## 5.3. Network Languages

## 5.3.1. A structured extension of Pascal

Syntactically, this language is the same as the binary extension of Pascal, but used for network schemas. Pragmatically, there is one difference:

- In the Binary and Relational models, there is no order between the objects. Thus, the **for** loops are performed in an arbitrary order, transparent to the application programmer. The DBMS would usually attempt to find the most efficient order dependent on the circumstances of the program run and the physical structure of the database.

- In the Network Model, the loops are performed in the order specified by the *NEXT* ordering relations. This reduces the flexibility of the application program by making it depend on information which is not strictly relevant for the program's goals. Also, this does not allow for optimization of the program by the DBMS.

---

*Example 5-29.*

The university has decided to expel all the students whose average grade is below 60 (out of 100). To prevent this wrong-doing to computer science students, the department offered a fictitious course, Computer-Pass, by Prof. Good, in which all computer science students are to receive a sufficient grade so as to not to be expelled, if possible.

The following program fabricates Prof. Good and the Computer-Pass course, enrolls students in this course, grades them accordingly, and prints the names of those computer science students whom this measure cannot help.

---

**program** Pass (Input, Output, UNIVERSITY-DB, UNIVERSITY-MASTER-VIEW);
**var**       Computer-Pass-Course, Prof-Good, Good-Offer, comp-science,
            work, this-quarter, cs-student, her-enrollment, fictitious-enrollment:
            *ABSTRACT*;
**var**       the-grade, desired-grade, number-of-grades,
            total-of-grades, current-year: *INTEGER*;

**begin**
(* Get the current year from the standard input file.  *)
  read (current-year);
(* Fabricate the course, Prof. Good, and the offering.  *)
    **transaction begin**

        **create new** Computer-Pass-Course **in** *COURSE*;

        Computer-Pass-Course.*NAME* **:=** 'Computer Pass';

        **create new** Prof-Good **in** *INSTRUCTOR*;

        Prof-Good.*LAST-NAME* **:=** 'Good';

        **create new** Good-Offer **in** *OFFERING*;

        **relate**: Computer-Pass-Course *COURSE-OFFERING* Good-Offer;

        **relate**: Prof-Good *INSTRUCTOR-OFFERING* Good-Offer;

        **for** this-quarter **in** *QUARTER*

            **where** (this-quarter.*YEAR* = current-year **and** this-quarter.-
            *SEASON* = 'Winter') **do**

            **relate**: this-quarter *QUARTER-OFFERING* Good-Offer;

    **end**;

(* The following two nested loops will be performed only once.  Inside the
    body of the second loop, the variable *comp-science* will refer to the
    Computer Science Department.  *)

**for** computer-science-name **in** *DEPARTMENT-NAMING*

    **where** (computer-science-name.*NAME*= 'COMPUTER SCIENCE') **do**

        **for** comp-science **in** *DEPARTMENT*

            **where** (computer-science *DEPARTMENT–DEPARTMENT-NAMING*
            comp-science-name) **do**

**begin**

**transaction begin**

    **create new** work in *WORK*;

    **relate**: Prof-Good *INSTRUCTOR-WORK* work;

    **relate**: comp-science *DEPARTMENT-WORK* work

    **end**;

```
for cs-student in STUDENT
    where (comp-science MAJOR-ST cs-student) do
        begin
        (* calculate this student's current statistics: number-of-grades and
            total-of-grades *)
        number-of-grades := 0;
        total-of-grades := 0;
        for her-enrollment in ENROLLMENT
            where (cs-student STUDENT-ENROLLMENT her-enrollment
                and not her-enrollment FINAL-GRADE null) do
            begin
            the-grade :=
            cs-student.FINAL-GRADE;
            number-of-grades := number-of-grades + 1;
            total-of-grades := total-of-grades + the-grade
            end;
        (* calculate the minimal desired grade in the computer-pass course,
            solving the equation
```

$$(total+x)/(number+1)=60 \quad *)$$

```
        desired-grade := 60 * (number-of-grades + 1) − total-of-grades;
        if desired-grade > 100
            then
                (* the student cannot be helped. Print a message *)
                    writeln (' The student ', cs-student.LAST-NAME, '
                        cannot be helped. Sorry!')
        else
            if desired-grade > 60 then
                transaction begin
                    create new fictitious-enrollment in
                    ENROLLMENT;
                    relate: cs-student STUDENT-ENROLLMENT
                    fictitious-enrollment;
```

**relate**: Good-Offer *OFFERING-ENROLLMENT* fictitious-enrollment;

fictitious-enrollment.*FINAL-GRADE* := desired-grade

**end**

**end**

**end**

**end**.

## 5.3.2. Calculus

Since every network schema is a binary schema, we can use the same language of Predicate Calculus as was defined for the Binary Model.

---

*Example 5-30.*

Has every student taken at least one course in 1987?

**for every** st **in** *STUDENT*:

**exists** enrl **in** *ENROLLMENT*:

((st *STUDENT-ENROLLMENT* enrl) **and**

**exists** offer **in** *OFFERING*:

**exists** quarter **in** *QUARTER*:

quarter *QUARTER-OFFERING* offer **and**

offer *OFFERING-ENROLLMENT* enrl **and**

quarter.*YEAR*=1987)

---

*Example 5-31.*

Who took Prof. Smith's courses?

**get** student.*LAST-NAME* **where**

exists enrl **in** *ENROLLMENT*:

**exists** prof **in** *INSTRUCTOR*:

**exists** offer **in** *OFFERING*:

prof.*LAST-NAME*='Smith' **and**

> prof *INSTRUCTOR-OFFERING* offer **and**
>
> offer *OFFERING-ENROLLMENT* enrl **and**
>
> student *STUDENT-ENROLLMENT* enrl

**In the following problems,** translate the request into the Predicate Calculus using the network reference schema for the university application (at the end of this book).

*Problem 5-14.*

Find the names of the students born in 1967.

Solution on page 358.

*Problem 5-15.*

For every student, list the instructors of the student's major department.

Solution on page 358.

*Problem 5-16.*

What instructors work in every department?

Solution on page 358.

*Problem 5-17.*

What instructors taught all the students?

Solution on page 358.

*Problem 5-18.*

Has every student taken at least one course in 1995?

Solution on page 359.

*Problem 5-19.*

Print a table with two columns, which associates students to their teachers.  Only last names are printed.

Solution on page 359.

*Problem 5-20.*

Print the average of grades for every Computer Science student.

Solution on page 359.

*Problem 5-21.*

Print the average of the grades given by Prof. Smith.

Solution on page 360.

*Problem 5-22.*

How many students are there in the university?

Solution on page 360.

*Problem 5-23.*

What students have their average grade below 60?

Solution on page 360.

*Problem 5-24.*

An integrity constraint: No student may be enrolled twice in the very same offering of a course.

Solution on page 361.

*Problem 5-25.*

Define an inferred category of students whose minor is Management.

Solution on page 361.

*Problem 5-26.*

Give the grade 100 to all Computer Science students enrolled in the Databases course given by Prof. Smith in Fall 1995.

Solution on page 361.

*Problem 5-27.*

Let 'CS' be no longer an [alternative] name of a department.

Solution on page 362.

*Problem 5-28.*

Give the grade 100 to the Computer Science student Jack Johnson enrolled in the Databases course given by Prof. Smith. If a grade has been previously given, replace it by the new grade.

Solution on page 362.

*Problem 5-29.*

Increase by 10% the grades of all students ever enrolled in the Databases course given by Prof. Smith.

Solution on page 363.

### 5.3.3. *Navigational extension of Pascal

The language presented here is a lower-level extension of Pascal for network data manipulation. Unlike the structured extension of Pascal, here the user herself is responsible for the organization of loops and for navigating in the labyrinth of the database.

The model language presented in this section is an adaptation to Pascal of the logical features of the network data manipulation language proposed by the standard committee CODASYL/DBTG and used with minor variations in many commercial network database management systems.

1.  *Program heading* — same as in the structured extension.

> *Example 5-32.*
>
> **program** MY (input, output, University-data-base, University-
>     principal-subschema)

2.  There are *automatically-generated Pascal record types* for every record-type of the subschema.

> *Example 5-33.*
>
> **type** DEPARTMENT-NAMING =
>     **record**
>         the-name : String        **end**;
> **type** STUDENT =
>     **record**
>         last-name, first-name : String;
>         birth-year : 1870..1990;
>         address : String        **end**;
> **type** INSTRUCTOR =
>     **record**
>         last-name, first-name : String;

```
                    birth-year : 1870..1990;
                    address : String        end;
    type QUARTER =

        record
                year : 1980..1995;
                season : String        end;

    type COURSE =

        record
                name : String        end;

    type ENROLLMENT =

        record
                final-grade : 0..100        end;

    type NULL-RECORD =

        record

        end;*

    type WORK = NULL-RECORD;

    type DEPARTMENT = NULL-RECORD;

    type OFFERING = NULL-RECORD
```

3. *Automatically generated Pascal record variables* for every record-type in the subschema.

   These variables bear the same names as the corresponding types.

   These variables are called **template variables**. The template variable for a database record-type is used as a buffer to store the attributes of record-occurrences when they are moved between the database and the program.

---

* Standard *Pascal* does not allow records without fields. So, a dummy field may have to be introduced:

```
type DEPARTMENT =
    record
            dummy : 0..0        end;
```

---

*Example 5-34.*

**var** student : STUDENT;

**var** enrollment : ENROLLMENT;

*etc.*

---

4.    Pascal data type *ABSTRACT*.

The variables of type *ABSTRACT* reference database objects.

In many network database management systems this type is called *DBKEY*.

5.    System variables (read-only).

There are several automatically generated system variables. The user may not perform explicit assignments to these variables. These variables are updated by the system as a side-effect of performing user commands.

**var Error-status** : (ok, end-of-set, error)

After the execution of any database command, this variable is automatically assigned one of the following values:

- **end-of-set** — if the user attempted to locate the next record occurrence in a particular set-occurrence, and no next record-occurrence existed;

- **error** — if another logical or physical error occurred;

- **ok** — otherwise.

**var current-of-run-unit** : ABSTRACT

This variable references the last accessed object. Initially, it is the object SYSTEM.

**var current-of-record-type-***record-type* : ABSTRACT

For every record-type in the subschema, there is a variable referencing the last accessed object of that record-type.

---

*Example 5-35.*

**var** current-of-record-type-DEPARTMENT, current-of-record-type-STUDENT, current-of-record-type-INSTRUCTOR, current-of-record-type-QUARTER, current-of-record-type-COURSE, current-of-record-type-OFFERING,  current-of-record-type-ENROLLMENT,  current-of-record-type-WORK,  current-of-record-type-DEPARTMENT-NAMING  :  ABSTRACT

**var current-of-set-type-***set-type* : ABSTRACT

> For every set-type in the subschema, there is a variable referencing the last accessed object of a record-type which is the owner or the member of this set-type. For the set-types whose owner is *SYSTEM*, these variables initially contain the object *SYSTEM*. Otherwise the variables are uninitialized.

---

*Example 5-36.*

**var** current-of-set-type-SYSTEM-INSTRUCTOR, current-of-set-type-SYSTEM-STUDENT, current-of-set-type-SYSTEM-DEPARTMENT, current-of-set-type-SYSTEM-COURSE, current-of-set-type-SYSTEM-QUARTER, current-of-set-type-INSTRUCTOR-WORK, current-of-set-type-DEPARTMENT-WORK, current-of-set-type-DEPARTMENT-DEPARTMENT-NAMING, current-of-set-type-MAJOR-ST, current-of-set-type-MINOR-ST, current-of-set-type-INSTRUCTOR-OFFERING, current-of-set-type-COURSE-OFFERING, current-of-set-type-QUARTER-OFFERING, current-of-set-type-OFFERING-ENROLLMENT, current-of-set-type-STUDENT-ENROLLMENT : ABSTRACT

---

6.  Expressions — there is *no* extension to the syntax of Pascal expressions.

Particularly, there are no operations on the objects of type ABSTRACT. For example, if $x$ is a variable of type ABSTRACT, and $A$ is an attribute, then $x.A$ would be an expression in the structured extension of Pascal, but not in the navigational extension.

However, if $x$ is not an abstract variable, but a variable of a Pascal type **record**, for example

> **var** x: **record**
>
> > A: Integer,
> >
> > B: Integer
>
> **end**

then $x.A$ would be a usual Pascal expression, and thus can be used in the navigational language.

**Statements**

7. **find first within** *set-name*

   The first member object is located in the current set-occurrence of this set-type, the set occurrence to which the object **current-of-set-type-***set-type* belongs.

   If there are no member-objects in the set-occurrence, the system variable Error-status is set to **end-of-set**. (Otherwise, if the instruction is successfully performed, the variable Error-status is set to **ok**.)

   If an object is found, the currency variables are updated: the found object becomes

   - the current of run-unit,

   - the current of this set-type,

   - the current of this object's record-type, and

   - the current of every set-type whose owner or member is the category of this object.

   > *Example 5-37.*
   >
   > Are there any students in the database?
   >
   > > **find first within** SYSTEM-STUDENT;
   > >
   > > **if** Error-status = **end-of-set**
   > >
   > > > **then** writeln (' no');
   > >
   > > **if** Error-status = **ok**
   > >
   > > > **then** writeln (' yes');
   > >
   > > **if** Error-status = **error**
   > >
   > > > **then** writeln (' I do not know. I have system problems.');

8. **get**

   This instruction assigns the attributes' values of the current object of run unit to the template variable corresponding to the category of the object.

   > *Example 5-38.*
   >
   > Print the address of one student.
   >
   > > (* locate one student, the one which happens to be the first in

the order of *SYSTEM-STUDENT* *)

**find first within** *SYSTEM-STUDENT*;

(* assign the attribute values of the student to the variable
*student* *)

**get**;

(* print *)

writeln (' The address of a student is:', student.ADDRESS)

9.   **find next within** *set-name*

The next member object is located in the order of the set-type after the
current object of the set-type.

If there are no next member-objects in the set-occurrence, the system
variable Error-status is set to **end-of-set**.

If an object is found, the currency variables are updated: the found object
becomes the current of run-unit, the current of this set-type, the current
of this object's record-type, and the current of every set-type whose
owner or member is the category of this object.

---

*Example 5-39.*

Print names and addresses of all the students.

**find first within** *SYSTEM-STUDENT*;

**while** (Error-status ≠ end-of-set) **do**

**begin**

(* assign the attribute values of the current student to the
variable *student* *)

**get**;

(* print *)

writeln (' The address of Student', student.*LAST-NAME*,
' is: ', student.ADDRESS)

**find next within** *SYSTEM-STUDENT*

**end**;

10. **find owner within** *set-name*

The owner object of the set occurrence of the current object of the set-type is located.

The currency variables are updated: the found object becomes the current of run-unit, the current of this set-type, the current of this object's record-type, and the current of every set-type whose owner or member is the category of this object.

---

*Example 5-40.*

Print names and major departments of all the students.

 **find first within** *SYSTEM-STUDENT*;

 **while** (Error-status ≠ end-of-set) **do**

  **begin**

  (* assign the attribute values of the current student to the variable *student* *)

   **get**;

  (* find the major department of the student *)

   **find owner within** *MAJOR-ST*;

  (* find the name of the department; if the department has more than one name, the first found will do. *)

   **find first within** *DEPARTMENT–DEPARTMENT-NAMING* ;

  (* assign the attribute value of the current department-naming to the variable *department-naming* *)

   **get**

  (* print *)

   writeln (' The major department of Student', student.*LAST-NAME*, ' is: ', department-naming.-*NAME*);

  **find next within** *SYSTEM-STUDENT*

  **end**;

---

11. **find db-key is** *variable-of-type-ABSTRACT*

(This statement is used to find and restore the currency of an object which was previously accessed by the program and whose reference was saved in a variable.)

The object referred to by the variable is located. The currency variables are updated: the found object becomes the current of run-unit and the current of every set-type whose owner or member is the category of this object.

---

*Example 5-41.*

For every student, print the names of the students of the same major.

> **var** student-to-remember: ABSTRACT;
>
> **begin**
>
> **find first within** *SYSTEM-STUDENT*;
>
> **while** (Error-status $\neq$ end-of-set) **do begin**
>
> > (* assign the attribute values of the current student to the variable *student* *)
> >
> > > **get**;
> >
> > (* find the major department of the student *)
> >
> > > **find owner within** *MAJOR-ST*;
> >
> > (* print a heading for the current student's list of co-majors. *)
> >
> > > writeln (' Student', student.*LAST-NAME*, ' has the same major as the following students: ');
> >
> > (* remember the current student, so that we can return to her after we have finished processing the co-majors. *)
> >
> > > student-to-remember := current-of-set-type-SYSTEM-STUDENT;
> >
> > (* process the students connected in the set-type MAJOR-ST to the current department *)
> >
> > > **find first within** *MAJOR-ST*;
> > >
> > > **while** (Error-status $\neq$ end-of-set) **do**
> > >
> > > > **begin**

---

**get**;

write (student.*LAST-NAME*);

**find next within** *MAJOR-ST*

**end**;

---

Example 5-41 continued.

(* restore the currency of the student of the principal
      loop. *)

    **find db-key is** student-to-remember;

**find next within** *SYSTEM-STUDENT*

**end**;

**end**.

---

12. **find within** *set-name* **using** *attribute*

Among the member objects in the set occurrence of the current object of
the set-type, find the first object whose value of the *attribute* is the same
as in the template variable of the member record-type.

The currency variables are updated: the found object becomes the current
of run-unit, the current of this set-type, the current of this object's
record-type, and the current of every set-type whose owner or member is
the category of this object.

This is roughly equivalent to the following program, where $S$ is the set-
type and *rec* is the member record-type:

attribute-to-compare := *rec.attribute*;

**find first within** $S$;

found := false;

**while** (Error-status $\neq$ end-of-set) **and** (**not** found) **do**

    **begin**

    **get**;

    found **:=** (*rec.attribute* = attribute-to-compare);

        **if not** found

             *then*   **find next within** *S*

        **end**;

---

*Example 5-42.*

How many times was the *Databases* course offered?

    (* find the *Databases* course  *)

        *course.NAME* := 'Databases';

        **find within** *SYSTEM-COURSE* **using** *NAME*;

    (* count the offerings  *)

        number := 0;

        **find first within** *COURSE-OFFERING*;

        **while** Error-status $\neq$ end-of-set **do**

            **begin**

            number := number+1;

            **find next within** *COURSE-OFFERING*;

            **end**

        writeln (' Databases was offered ', number, ' times.')

---

13. **modify** *record-type*

The attributes' values of the current object of this record-type are updated according to the values in the template variable of this record-type.

---

*Example 5-43.*

Change the name of every Fall quarter to *Autumn*.

        **find first within** *SYSTEM-QUARTER*;

        **while** (Error-status $\neq$ end-of-set) **do**

            **begin**

            **if** Error-status = error **then begin**

                writeln (' SYSTEM ERROR'); stop   **end**;

            **get**;

> **if** quarter.*SEASON* = 'Fall' **then**
>
>     **begin**
>
>     quarter.*SEASON* := 'Autumn';
>
>     **modify** *QUARTER*;
>
>     **end**;
>
> **find next within** *SYSTEM-QUARTER*
>
> **end**;

14. **erase** *record-type*

The current object of the *record-type* is deleted from the database.

If the object is the owner of a set-occurrence of a set-type *onto* the member, then all the member objects of that set occurrence are automatically erased. This process is recursive: the deletion of some objects may trigger deletion of more objects.

> *Example 5-44.*
>
> Cancel everything that happened in any summer.
>
>     **find first within** *SYSTEM-QUARTER*;
>
>     **while** (Error-status ≠ end-of-set) **do**
>
>         **begin**
>
>         **if** Error-status = error **then begin**
>
>             writeln (' SYSTEM ERROR'); stop      **end**;
>
>         **get**;
>
>         **if** quarter.*SEASON* = 'Summer' **then**
>
>             **erase** *QUARTER*;
>
>         **find next within** *SYSTEM-QUARTER*
>
>         **end**;

15. **connect** *record-type* **to** *set-type*

The current object of the *record-type* is inserted as a member into the current set-occurrence of the set-type — the set-occurrence in which the current object of the set-type is the owner or a member.

*Example 5-45.*

Let every student have the same minor as his major, assuming that every student had (until now) a major and no minor department.

>    **find first within** *SYSTEM-STUDENT*;
>
>    **while** (Error-status ≠ end-of-set) **do**
>
>>        **begin**
>>
>>        **if** Error-status = error **then begin**
>>
>>>            writeln (' SYSTEM ERROR'); stop      **end**;
>>
>>        **get**;
>>
>>        **find owner within** *MAJOR-ST*;
>>
>>        **if** Error-status = error **then**
>>
>>>            writeln (' Oh-oh. Wrong assumption about having a
>>>            major department for ', student.*LAST-NAME*);
>>
>>        **connect** *STUDENT* **to** *MINOR-ST*;
>>
>>        **if** Error-status = error **then**
>>
>>>            writeln (' Oh-oh. Wrong assumption about not having a
>>>            minor department for ', student.*LAST-NAME*);
>>
>>        **find next within** *SYSTEM-STUDENT*
>>
>>        **end**;

16. **disconnect** *record-type* **from** *set-type*

The current object of the *record-type* will no longer be a member in the current set-occurrence of the set-type (the set-occurrence in which the current object of the set-type is the owner or a member).

*Example 5-46.*

Let every student have the same minor as his major, by canceling the present minors. Assume that every student had a major department.

>    **find first within** *SYSTEM-STUDENT*;
>
>    **while** (Error-status ≠ end-of-set) **do**
>
>>        **begin**

```
      if Error-status = error then begin
          writeln (' SYSTEM ERROR'); stop      end;
      get;
      disconnect STUDENT from MINOR-ST;
      find owner within MAJOR-ST;
      if Error-status = error then
          writeln (' Oh-oh. Wrong assumption about having a
              major department for ', student.LAST-NAME);
      connect STUDENT to MINOR-ST;
      find next within SYSTEM-STUDENT
      end;
```

17. **reconnect** *record-type* **to** *set-type*

The current object of the *record-type* will no longer be a member in its former set-occurrence of the set-type.

Instead, the current object of the *record-type* is inserted as a member into the current set-occurrence of the set-type (the set-occurrence in which the current object of the set-type is the owner or a member).

---

*Example 5-47.*

Let every student have the same minor as his major, canceling the present minor, assuming that every student had a major department.

```
      find first within SYSTEM-STUDENT;
      while (Error-status ≠ end-of-set) do
          begin
          if Error-status = error then begin
              writeln (' SYSTEM ERROR'); stop      end;
          get;
          find owner within MAJOR-ST;
          if Error-status = error then
              writeln (' Oh-oh. Wrong assumption about having a
```

> major department for ', student.*LAST-NAME*);
>
> **reconnect** *STUDENT* **to** *MINOR-ST*;
>
> **find next within** *SYSTEM-STUDENT*
>
> **end**;

18. **store** *record-type*

    A new object of the *record-type* is created.

    The object automatically gets the values of its attributes from the template variable of this record-type.

    This object becomes the current of the *record-type*.

19. **transaction** *compound-statement*

    — as in the structured extension of Pascal.

---

*Example 5-48.*

Let Prof. Asteroid (a unique name for this instructor, so no confusion with other instructors is possible) offer the course *Databases* every quarter.

```
instructor.LAST-NAME = 'Asteroid';
course.NAME := 'Databases';
find within INSTRUCTOR using LAST-NAME;
find within COURSE using NAME;
find first within SYSTEM-QUARTER;
while (Error-status ≠ end-of-set) do
    begin
    if Error-status = error then begin
        writeln (' SYSTEM ERROR'); stop    end;
    get;
    transaction begin
        store OFFERING;
        connect OFFERING to QUARTER-OFFERING;
        connect OFFERING to COURSE-OFFERING;
```

> **connect** *OFFERING* **to** *INSTRUCTOR-OFFERING*
>
> **end**
>
> **find next within** *SYSTEM-QUARTER*
>
> **end**;

---

*Example 5-49.*

A navigational program for the expulsion prevention problem which has been previously solved in the structured extension of Pascal.

---

**program** Pass (Input, Output, UNIVERSITY-DB, UNIVERSITY-PRINCIPAL-SUBSCHEMA);

> (* The comments in the boxes are the corresponding program fragments in the structured extension of Pascal. It is recommended, that when a program needs to be written in the navigational language, it should first be written in the higher level-language. Then, when the higher-level program is translated into the lower-level navigational language, the commands of the original program should become algorithmic comments within the navigational program. *)

**var** Good-Offer: *ABSTRACT*;

**var** the-grade, desired-grade, number-of-grades, total-of-grades, current-year: *INTEGER*;

**const** null-year = 1870 (* to represent missing birth-year, assuming nobody was born in 1870*);

**const** null-name = '' (* to represent missing names *);

**const** null-address = '' (* to represent missing addresses *);

**const** null-grade = 0 (* to represent missing grades, assuming that 0 is never given as a real grade† *);

---

† If the type of the variable *enrollment.Final-grade* technically allows for negative values, then a better representation of the missing grade is '-1'.

**begin** (* Get the current year from the standard input file.  *)

    read (current-year);

**transaction begin**

> (*
>
> **create new** Computer-Pass-Course **in** *COURSE*;
>
> Computer-Pass-Course.*NAME* **:=** 'Computer Pass';  *)

course.*NAME* **:=** 'Computer Pass';

**store** *COURSE*;

**connect** *COURSE* **to** *SYSTEM-COURSE*;

> (*
>
> **create new** instructor **in** *INSTRUCTOR*;
>
> instructor.*LAST-NAME* **:=** 'Good';  *)

instructor.*LAST-NAME* **:=** 'Good';

instructor.*FIRST-NAME* **:=** null-name;

instructor.*BIRTH-YEAR* **:=** null-year;

instructor.*ADDRESS* **:=** null-address;

**store** *INSTRUCTOR*;

**connect** *INSTRUCTOR* **to** *SYSTEM-INSTRUCTOR*;

> (*
>
> **create new** Good-Offer **in** *OFFERING*;
>
> **relate**: Computer-Pass-Course *COURSE-OFFERING* Good-Offer;
>
> **relate**: Prod-Good *INSTRUCTOR-OFFERING* Good-Offer;  *)

**store** *OFFERING*;

**connect** *OFFERING* **to** *INSTRUCTOR-OFFERING*;

**connect** *OFFERING* **to** *COURSE-OFFERING*;

*Good-Offer* **:=** current-of-record-type-OFFERING;

```
    (*
for quarter in QUARTER
        where (quarter.YEAR = current-year and quarter.SEASON
            = 'Winter') do
        relate: quarter QUARTER-OFFERING Good-Offer;
         *)
```

found := **false**;

**find first within** *SYSTEM-QUARTER*;

**while** (Error-status ≠ end-of-set **and not** found) **do**

    **begin**;

    **if** Error-status = error **then begin**

        writeln (' SYSTEM ERROR'); stop    **end**;

    **get**;

    found := (quarter.YEAR = 1987 **and** quarter.SEASON = 'Winter');

    **if not** found **then**

    **find next within** *SYSTEM-QUARTER*

    **end**;

**connect** *OFFERING* **to** *QUARTER-OFFERING*;

**end** (* transaction*);

```
(* Prepare-Department:
for department-naming in DEPARTMENT-NAMING
        where (department-naming.NAME= 'COMPUTER SCIENCE') do
            for department in DEPARTMENT
                where (department DEPARTMENT–DEPARTMENT-
                    NAMING department-naming) do
         *)
```

found := **false**;

**find first within** *SYSTEM-DEPARTMENT*;

**while** (Error-status ≠ end-of-set **and not** found) **do**

    **begin**;

```
if Error-status = error then begin
    writeln (' SYSTEM ERROR'); stop    end;
get;
found := false;
find first within DEPARTMENT–DEPARTMENT-NAMING;
while (Error-status ≠ end-of-set and not found) do
    begin;
    if Error-status = error then begin
        writeln (' SYSTEM ERROR'); stop    end;
    get;
    found := (department-naming.NAME = 'Computer Science');
    if not found then
    find next within DEPARTMENT–DEPARTMENT-NAMING
    end;
if not found then
find next within SYSTEM-DEPARTMENT
end;
(**end Prepare-department**)
transaction begin
```

```
    (*
    create new work in WORK;
    relate: instructor INSTRUCTOR-WORK work;
    relate: department DEPARTMENT-WORK work    *)
```

```
store WORK;
connect WORK to INSTRUCTOR-WORK;
connect WORK to DEPARTMENT-WORK;
end (* transaction *);
```

```
(* Student-loop:

for student in STUDENT
        where (department MAJOR-ST student) do   *)
```

**find first within** *MAJOR-ST*;

**while** (Error-status ≠ end-of-set) **do**

   **begin**

   **if** Error-status = error **then begin**

      writeln (' SYSTEM ERROR'); stop    **end**;

  **get**;

     (**end of the opening of Student-loop **)

(* calculate this student's current statistics: number-of-grades and total-of-grades  *)

    number-of-grades **:=**  0;

    total-of-grades **:=**  0;

```
(* Enrollment-loop:

for enrollment in ENROLLMENT
        where (student STUDENT-ENROLLMENT enrollment and
              not enrollment FINAL-GRADE null) do   *)
```

   **find first within** *STUDENT-ENROLLMENT*;

   **while** (Error-status ≠ end-of-set) **do**

     **begin**

     **if** Error-status = error **then begin**

        writeln (' SYSTEM ERROR'); stop    **end**;

    **get**;

     **if** student.*FINAL-GRADE* ≠ null-grade **then**

       **begin**

         (**end of the opening of Enrollment-loop **)

       the-grade **:=** student.*FINAL-GRADE*;

       number-of-grades **:=** number-of-grades + 1;

       total-of-grades **:=** total-of-grades + the-grade

(**closing Enrollment-loop **)

> **end**;

**find next within** *STUDENT-ENROLLMENT*

**end**;

(**end Enrollment-loop **)

(* calculate the minimal desired grade in the computer-pass course, solving the equation $(total+x)/(number+1)=60$  *)

desired-grade **:=**  60 * (number-of-grades + 1) − total-of-grades;

**if** desired-grade > 100

> **then**
>
>> (* the student cannot be helped. Print a message  *)
>>
>>> writeln (' The student ', student.*LAST-NAME*, ' cannot be helped. Sorry!')

> **else**
>
>> **if** desired-grade > 60 **then**
>>
>>> **transaction begin**

> > > > ```
> > > > (*
> > > > create new fictitious-enrollment in EN-
> > > >     ROLLMENT;
> > > > relate: student STUDENT-ENROLLMENT
> > > >     fictitious-enrollment;
> > > > relate: Good-Offer OFFERING-
> > > >     ENROLLMENT fictitious-enrollment;
> > > > fictitious-enrollment.FINAL-GRADE :=
> > > >     desired-grade   *)
> > > > ```

> > enrollment.*FINAL-GRADE* **:=** desired-grade;
>
> > **store** *ENROLLMENT*;
>
> > **connect** *ENROLLMENT* **to** *STUDENT-ENROLLMENT*;
>
> > **find db-key is** Good-Offer; (* We have to restore the currency of the fabricated offering remembered in the variable Good-Offer, because the currency may have changed in the meantime.  *)

                **connect** *ENROLLMENT* **to** *OFFERING-ENROLLMENT*;

                **end**

        (\*\*closing Student-loop\*\*)

    **find next within** *MAJOR-ST*

    **end**;

    (\*\*end Student-loop \*\*)

**end.**

*Problem 5-30.*

Use the university/binary reference schema at the end of this book. Write a navigational program to find the average teaching load of *full-time* computer science instructors this quarter. ('Full time' means working for no other department.)

# 6
# THE HIERARCHICAL MODEL

The Hierarchical Model requires the schema and the instantaneous database to be trees.

The Hierarchical Model is the oldest (albeit, not the best) major database model. However, it is still widely used in the industry.

This chapter presents a "modern view" of the hierarchical model. Some technicalities, particularly the clearly obsolete ones, are ignored.

## 6.1. Definitions

**Hierarchical schema** — a network schema such that for every category, excluding *SYSTEM*, there is exactly one relation coming into it from another category.

> *Example 6-1.*
>
> A hierarchical schema for the university application follows. Only the order-less part is shown in the figure.

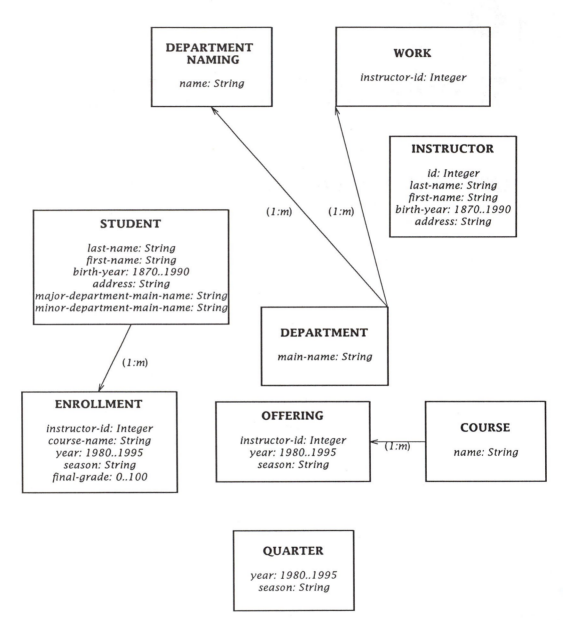

**Figure 6-1.** An order-less hierarchical schema for the university application.

*Note:*  We can prove the truth of the following statements from the definition of the hierarchical schemas:

a.   The relations between the abstract categories of any order-less hierarchical schema form a set of directed trees.  (This is the reason for the name *'hierarchical'.*)

b.   The root of every tree is an independent category.

c.   All the relations between distinct abstract categories are *onto.*

d.   Since every category *C* has only one entering relation $R_C$ from another category, every category has only one order $NEXT_{R_C}$. Thus, we can speak about *the* order of the objects of a category.

---

*Example 6-2.*

The following figures represent an instantaneous database for the schema of Figure 6-1.  This instantaneous database represents the same state of the application's real world as the binary instantaneous database of Figure 1-1 on page 22.

---

**INSTRUCTOR**

| id | last-name | first-name | birth-year | address |
|-------|-----------|------------|------------|-----------------|
| 11332 | Brown     | George     | 1956       | 112 Lucky Dr.   |
| 14352 | Whatson   | Mary       | 1953       | 231 Fortune Dr. |
| 24453 | Blue      | John       | 1950       | 536 Orange Dr.  |

**Figure 6-2.** An instantaneous database for the hierarchical schema of the university application. Part I. The flat tree of *INSTRUCTOR.*

**STUDENT**

| last-name | first-name | birth-year | address | major-dept-main-name | minor-dept-main-name |
|-----------|------------|------------|---------|----------------------|----------------------|
| Victory | Elizabeth | 1966 | 100 Sun St. | Computer Science | Economics |

    **COURSE ENROLLMENT**

| instructor-id | course-name | year | season | final-grade |
|---------------|-------------|------|--------|-------------|
| 11332 | Gastronomy | 1987 | Fall | 100 |

**STUDENT**

| last-name | first-name | birth-year | address | major-dept-main-name | minor-dept-main-name |
|-----------|------------|------------|---------|----------------------|----------------------|
| Howards | Jane | 1965 | 200 Dorms | Arts | Economics |

    **COURSE ENROLLMENT**

| instructor-id | course-name | year | season | final-grade |
|---------------|-------------|------|--------|-------------|
| 11332 | Gastronomy | 1987 | Fall | 70 |
| 11332 | Databases | 1987 | Fall | 80 |

**STUDENT**

| last-name | first-name | birth-year | address | major-dept-main-name | minor-dept-main-name |
|-----------|------------|------------|---------|----------------------|----------------------|
| Wood | Michael | 1964 | 110 Dorms | Arts | Economics |

**Figure 6-3.** An instantaneous database for the hierarchical schema of the university application. Part II. The tree of *STUDENT*.

**DEPARTMENT**

| main-name |
|---|
| Computer Science |

**DEPARTMENT NAMING**

| name |
|---|
| CS |

**WORK**

| instructor-id |
|---|
| 11332 |

**DEPARTMENT**

| main-name |
|---|
| Mathematics |

**DEPARTMENT NAMING**

| name |
|---|
| Math |

**WORK**

| instructor-id |
|---|
| 11332 |
| 24453 |

**DEPARTMENT**

| main-name |
|---|
| Physics |

**WORK**

| instructor-id |
|---|
| 14352 |

**DEPARTMENT**

| main-name |
|---|
| Arts |
| Economics |

**Figure 6-4.** An instantaneous database for the hierarchical schema of the university application. Part III. The tree of *DEPARTMENT*.

**COURSE**

| name |
|------|
| Databases |

**COURSE OFFERING**

| instructor-id | year | season |
|---------------|------|--------|
| 11332 | 1987 | Fall |

**COURSE**

| name |
|------|
| Football |

**COURSE OFFERING**

| instructor-id | year | season |
|---------------|------|--------|
| 11332 | 1987 | Fall |

**COURSE**

| name |
|------|
| Gastronomy |

**COURSE OFFERING**

| instructor-id | year | season |
|---------------|------|--------|
| 11332 | 1987 | Fall |

**Figure 6-5.** An instantaneous database for the hierarchical schema of the university application. Part V. The tree of *COURSE*.

**QUARTER**

| year | season |
|------|--------|
| 1987 | Fall |
| 1987 | Winter |
| 1987 | Spring |

**Figure 6-6.** An instantaneous database for the hierarchical schema of the university application. Part V. The flat tree of *QUARTER*.

*Hierarchical schema terminology*

**Segment type** — record type.

> *Example 6-3.*
>
> *DEPARTMENT.*

**Segment occurrence** — record occurrence.

> *Example 6-4.*
>
> One course and its name.

> *Example 6-5.*
>
> One student and his/her last name, first name, address, and the main names of his/her major and minor departments.

If there is a relation from a segment-type $C_1$ to another $C_2$, then $C_1$ is the **parent** of $C_2$ and $C_2$ is a **child** of $C_1$.

> *Example 6-6.*
>
> *DEPARTMENT* is the parent of *DEPARTMENT-NAMING*.
>
> *DEPARTMENT-NAMING* is a child of *DEPARTMENT*.

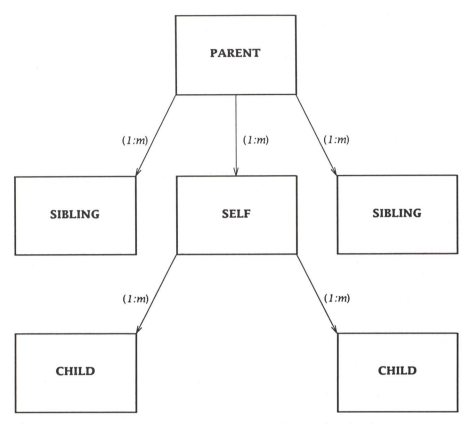

**Figure 6-7.** Family relations in a hierarchical schema.

**Root segment type** — a segment type whose *parent* is *SYSTEM*.

> *Example 6-7.*
>
> *DEPARTMENT, INSTRUCTOR, STUDENT, COURSE, QUARTER.*

The hierarchical model is not the most natural model to describe the real world of an application. One should notice that what is sometimes called "a hierarchical real world" usually implies a hierarchical *relation* between objects in the real world, not a hierarchical *schema*.

---

*Example 6-8.*

Consider an oversimplified military world, where every soldier has at most one commander. A binary schema for this world is:

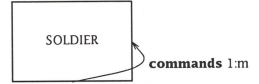

This is not a hierarchical schema, since it contains a cycle. No hierarchical schema can represent this world in a *natural* way.

---

## 6.2.  Database Design

**Conversion algorithm** of an adequate binary schema into a **hierarchical** schema whose quality is among the highest possible for the latter.

1.    Convert the binary schema into a **network schema.**

2.    For every abstract category, excluding *SYSTEM*, choose its **parent-relation** *R* so that

> When all the relations, except the parent relations, are removed from the schema, every abstract category would still indirectly depend on *SYSTEM*.

*Note*:   The parent relation for category *C* must be *onto C.*

---

*Example 6-9.*

The parent relation of *OFFERING* may be *COURSE-OFFERING* or *INSTRUCTOR-OFFERING* or *QUARTER-OFFERING.*

The parent relation for *ENROLLMENT* may be *OFFERING-ENROLLMENT* or *STUDENT-ENROLLMENT.*

The parent relation for *WORK* may be *DEPARTMENT-WORK* or *INSTRUCTOR-WORK.*

The parent relation for DEPARTMENT-NAMING is *DEPARTMENT–DEPARTMENT-NAMING.*

---

*Note*: The parent relations of independent categories are from *SYSTEM*.

---

*Example 6-10.*

The parent relation of *STUDENT* is *SYSTEM-STUDENT*.

The parent relation of *INSTRUCTOR* is *SYSTEM-INSTRUCTOR*.

The parent relation of *DEPARTMENT* is *SYSTEM-DEPARTMENT*.

The parent relation of *COURSE* is *SYSTEM-COURSE*.

The parent relation of *QUARTER* is *SYSTEM-QUARTER*.

---

3. Convert the schema into a **tree**: for every abstract category $C$ that has more than one entering relation, do the following.

Let $R$ be its parent relation and $R_1, \ldots, R_n$ the other entering relations, whose domains are $C_1, \ldots, C_n$.

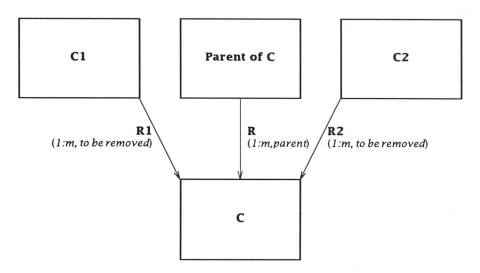

For each of the relations $R_i$ perform the following:

a. Find a key for the category $C_i$. ($C_i$ is the domain of the relation $R_i$ which we intend to eliminate.) Add the key to the schema (if this key has not been added yet.)

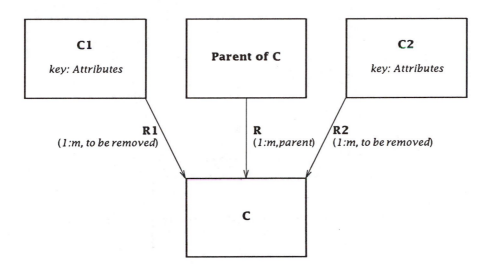

b.   Add to *C* a new attribute, or a group of attributes, that is the composition of the inverse of $R_i$ on the key of $C_i$.

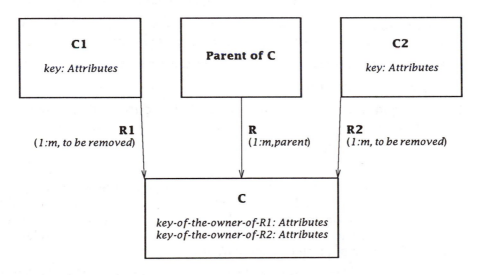

c.   Remove the relation $R_i$ (and its order.)

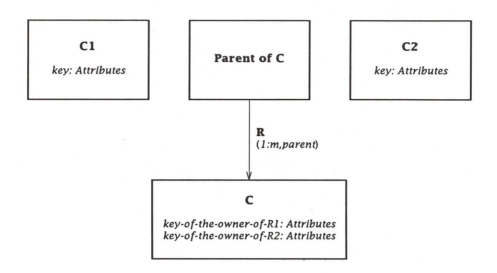

d.  Add the referential integrity constraints that the values of the new attributes of *C* must refer to the values of the keys of the categories $C_i$. (This is similar to what is done in the relational model.)

4.  **Remove** from every category attributes which can be **inferred** from other attributes of that category, its *parent*, or its *ancestors*.

5.  **Translate the integrity constraints** into the terms of the new schema:

    a.  The constraints of the original schema.

    b.  The additional constraints accumulated during the conversion process.


*Remark*

•   In the first step, it is not strictly necessary to go all the way through in the conversion from the binary schema to the network schema. We can omit the substep where the 1:m relations from a category to itself are eliminated. Later, in Step 3 of the hierarchical conversion, these relations will be taken care of as all the non-parent relations.

    If we do this in Step 3 rather than in Step 1 we get a slightly better hierarchical schema. If we were to follow the network conversion in Step 1 fully, we could get one extra category for the relation-split of each 1:m relation from a category to itself.

**In the following problems**, design a hierarchical schema equivalent to the appropriate binary schema. Specify the integrity constraints incident to the conversion from the binary schema to the hierarchical schema.

*Problem 6-1.*

Use the clan/binary schema (Figure 8-3 on page 282).

Solution on page 364.

*Problem 6-2.*

Use the wholesaler/binary schema (Figure 8-1 on page 280).

Solution on page 365.

*Problem 6-3.*

Use the busstop/binary schema (Figure 8-11 on page 291).

Solution on page 367.

*Problem 6-4.*

Use the cable/binary schema (Figure 8-10 on page 290).

Solution on page 368.

*Problem 6-5.*

Use the circuit/binary schema (Figure 8-5 on page 283).

Solution on page 369.

*Problem 6-6.*

Use the clinic/binary schema (Figure 8-13 on page 293).

Solution on page 370.

*Problem 6-7.*

Use the library/binary schema (Figure 8-7 on page 288).

Solution on page 372.

*Problem 6-8.*

Use the sales/binary schema (Figure 8-4 on page 283).

Solution on page 373.

*Problem 6-9.*

Use the studio/binary schema (Figure 8-2 on page 281).

Solution on page 374.

## 6.3. Hierarchical Languages

## 6.3.1. A structured extension of Pascal

Syntactically, this language is the same as the binary extension of Pascal, but is used for the hierarchical schema (every hierarchic schema is a binary schema.) Pragmatically, there is one difference: the **for** loops are performed in the order corresponding to the ordering of objects in the database. (In the Binary Model, the order in which a **for** loop is performed is transparent to the application programmer.)

---

*Example 6-11.*

The university has decided to expel all the students whose average grade is below 60 (out of 100). To prevent this wrong-doing to computer science students, the department offered a fictitious course, Computer-Pass, by Prof. Good, in which all computer science students are to receive a sufficient grade so as to not to be expelled, if possible.

The following program fabricates Prof. Good and the Computer-Pass course, enrolls students in this course, grades them accordingly, and prints the names of those computer science students whom this measure cannot help.

---

**program** Pass (Input, Output, UNIVERSITY-DB, UNIVERSITY-MASTER-VIEW);

**var** Computer-Pass-Course, Prof-Good, Good-Offer, comp-science, comp-science-name, Good-employment, cs-student, her-enrollment, fictitious-enrollment: *ABSTRACT*;

**var** the-grade, desired-grade, number-of-grades, total-of-grades, current-year: *INTEGER*;

**begin** (* Get the current year from the standard input file. *)

    read (current-year);

**transaction begin**

    **create new** Computer-Pass-Course **in** *COURSE*;

    Computer-Pass-Course.*NAME* **:=** 'Computer Pass';

    **create new** Prof-Good **in** *INSTRUCTOR*;

    Prof-Good.*LAST-NAME* **:=** 'Good';

Prof-Good.*ID* **:=** 1234;

**create new** Good-Offer **in** *OFFERING*;

**relate**: Computer-Pass-Course *OFFERING* Good-Offer;

Good-Offer.*INSTRUCTOR-ID* **:=** 1234;

Good-Offer.*YEAR* **:=** current-year;

Good-Offer.*SEASON* **:=** 'Winter';

**end**

**for**          comp-science-name **in** *DEPARTMENT-NAMING*

          **where** (comp-science-name.*NAME*= 'COMPUTER SCIENCE') **do**

     **for**          comp-science **in** *DEPARTMENT*

               **where** (comp-science *DEPARTMENT–DEPARTMENT-NAME*
               comp-science-name) **do begin**

          **transaction begin**

               **create new** Good-employment in *WORK*;

               **relate**: comp-science *DEPARTMENT-WORK* Good-employment;

               Good-employment.*ID* **:=** 1234

               **end**;

          **for** cs-student **in** *STUDENT*

                    **where** (cs-student.*MAJOR-DEPARTMENT-MAIN-NAME* =
                    comp-science.*MAIN-NAME*) **do begin**

               (* calculate this student's current statistics: number-of-grades
                    and total-of-grades  *)

               number-of-grades **:=**  0;

               total-of-grades **:=**  0;

               **for** her-enrollment **in** *ENROLLMENT*

                         **where** (cs-student *ENROLLMENT* her-enrollment
                              **and not** her-enrollment *FINAL-GRADE* **null**) **do**
                              **begin**

                    the-grade **:=**

                    her-enrollment.*FINAL-GRADE*;

```
                number-of-grades :=
                number-of-grades + 1;
                total-of-grades := total-of-grades + the-grade
            end;
        (* calculate the minimal desired grade in the computer-pass
            course, solving the equation (total+x)/(number+1)=60  *)
        desired-grade :=  60 * (number-of-grades + 1) — total-of-
            grades;
    if desired-grade > 100
        then
                (* the student cannot be helped. Print a message  *)
                    writeln (' The student ', cs-student.LAST-NAME, '
                        cannot be helped. Sorry!')
        else if desired-grade > 60 then
        transaction begin
                create new fictitious-enrollment in ENROLLMENT;
                relate: cs-student ENROLLMENT fictitious-
                    enrollment;
                fictitious-enrollment.FINAL-GRADE := desired-
                    grade;
                fictitious-enrollment.YEAR := current-year;
                fictitious-enrollment.SEASON := 'Winter';
                fictitious-enrollment.INSTRUCTOR-ID := 1234;
                fictitious-enrollment.COURSE-NAME := 'Computer
                    Pass'
            end
        end
    end
end.
```

## 6.3.2.  Calculus

Since every hierarchical schema is a binary schema, we can use the same language of Predicate Calculus as was defined for the binary model.

---

*Example 6-12.*

Has every student taken at least one course in 1987?

> **for every** st **in** *STUDENT:*
>
> > **exists** enrl **in** *ENROLLMENT:*
> >
> > > ((st *STUDENT-ENROLLMENT* enrl ) **and**
> > >
> > > (enrl.*YEAR*=1987))

---

*Example 6-13.*

Who took Prof. Smith's courses?

> **get** student.*LAST-NAME* **where**
>
> > **exists** enrl **in** *ENROLLMENT:*
> >
> > > (student *STUDENT-ENROLLMENT* enrl **and**
> > >
> > > exists inst **in** *INSTRUCTOR:*
> > >
> > > > (inst.*LAST-NAME* = 'Smith' **and**
> > > >
> > > > enrl.*INSTRUCTOR-ID* = inst.*ID*))

---

*Example 6-14.*

What students have their average grade below 60?

> **get** std.*LAST-NAME*
>
> **where** 60 >
>
> > **average** enrl.*FINAL-GRADE*
> >
> > > **where**
> > >
> > > > std *STUDENT-ENROLLMENT* enrl

---

*Example 6-15.*

Print the average of grades for every computer science student.

> **get** student.*LAST-NAME*,
>
>> (**average** enrollment.*FINAL-GRADE*
>>
>>> **where**
>>>
>>>> student *STUDENT-ENROLLMENT*
>>> enrollment)
>
> **where** student **is a** *STUDENT* and
>
>> (student.*MAJOR-DEPARTMENT-MAIN-NAME* = 'Computer Science')

---

*Example 6-16.*

How many students are there in the university?

> **get** (**count** std **where** std **is a** *STUDENT*)

---

*Problem 6-10.*

Solve the programming problems of Chapter 3 in the languages of the Hierarchical Model.

# 7
# COMPARATIVE REVIEW OF THE FOUR MODELS

Four database models were introduced in this text. Each of the models provides a certain degree of **data independence** — the isolation of the application programmer from representational or implementational details. The following table illustrates five levels of data independence.

| Level | What is transparent to the user? | Database model |
|-------|----------------------------------|----------------|
| V | The representation of *information* by *data* | **Semantic Binary** |
| IV | The organization of access to data | **Relational** |
| III | The physical implementation of the logical data-access structure | **Network** |
| II | The physical implementation of the special data structure *Hierarchy* | **Hierarchical** |
| I | The physical implementation of logical files by bytes on disks | File management Systems |

**Figure 7-1.** Levels of data independence.

The Relational, Network, and Hierarchical models were derived from the Binary Model as its subsets. A schema in any one of those models is a binary schema satisfying certain criteria. Those criteria are related to the implementational restrictions of the model. The following diagram shows the subsets of the Binary Model.

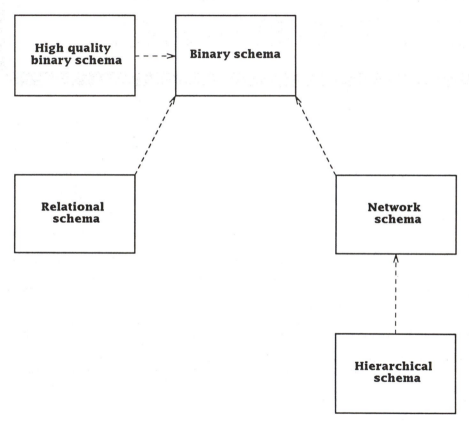

**Figure 7-2.** The generalization of data models. For example, the relational schemas form a subcategory of the binary schemas.

The following figure depicts the schema design methodologies presented in this text. The goal of the methodologies is to produce high-quality databases in the Relational, Network, and Hierarchical models.

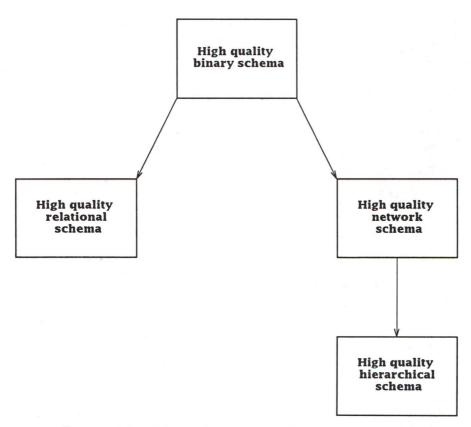

**Figure 7-3.** The schema-conversion methodologies studied in this text.

To review and compare some of the structural characteristics of the four database models studied in this text, the following series of examples solves the same query in the predicate calculus language, using, in turn, each of the four database models.

The examples use the four reference schemas of the university application at the end of this book. The query prints the pairs of the names of students and instructors, where the instructor works in the student's major department.

*Example 7-1.*

*Binary*:

    **get** s.*LAST-NAME*, i.*LAST-NAME*

    **where** i *WORKS-IN* s.*MAJOR-DEPARTMENT*

---

*Example 7-2.*

*Relational*:

    **get** s.*LAST-NAME*, i.*LAST-NAME*

    **where**

        i **is an** *INSTRUCTOR* **and**

        s **is a** *STUDENT* **and**

    **exists** w **in** *WORK*:

        (w.*INSTRUCTOR-ID-in-key* = i.*ID-key* **and**

        s.*MAJOR-DEPARTMENT-MAIN-NAME* =
            w.*DEPARTMENT-MAIN-NAME-in-key*)

---

*Example 7-3.*

*Network*:

    **get** s.*LAST-NAME*, i.*LAST-NAME*

    **where**

        i **is an** *INSTRUCTOR* **and**

        s **is a** *STUDENT* **and**

    **exists** w **in** *WORK*:

        (i *INSTRUCTOR-WORK* w **and**

        **exists** d **in** *DEPARTMENT*:

            (d *DEPARTMENT-WORK* w **and**

            d *MAJOR-ST* s))

*Example 7-4.*

*Hierarchical*:

    **get** s.*LAST-NAME*, i.*LAST-NAME*

    **where**

        i **is an** *INSTRUCTOR* **and**

        s **is a** *STUDENT* **and**

        **exists** w **in** *WORK*:

            (i.*ID* = w.*INSTRUCTOR-ID* **and**

            **exists** d **in** *DEPARTMENT*:

                (d *DEPARTMENT-WORK* w **and**

                d.*MAIN-NAME* = s.*MAJOR-DEPARTMENT-MAIN-NAME*))

# 8

# SOLVED CASE STUDY PROBLEMS

This chapter contains solutions for most of the case-study problems. For many problems, only a part of the problem is solved here — the reader is expected to complete the rest.

### Solution for Problem 1-1 on page 12

Works-in m:m, name 1:m (department may have several names, but every name is unique), last-name m:1, first-name m:1, birth-year m:1, address m:1, major m:1, minor m:1, year m:1, season m:1, name of COURSE 1:1.

### Solution for Problem 1-2 on page 13

{ }; {(a1 R a1)}; {(a1 R a2)}; {(a1 R a1), (a1 R a2)}
{(a2 R a1)}; {(a2 R a2)}; {(a2 R a1), (a2 R a2)};
{(a1 R a1), (a2 R a1)}; {(a1 R a1), (a2 R a2)}; {(a1 R a1), (a2 R a1), (a2 R a2)};
{(a1 R a2), (a2 R a1)}; {(a1 R a2), (a2 R a2)}; {(a1 R a2), (a2 R a1), (a2 R a2)};
{(a1 R a1), (a1 R a2), (a2 R a1)}; {(a1 R a1), (a1 R a2), (a2 R a2)}; {(a1 R a1), (a1 R a2), (a2 R a1), (a2 R a2)};

### Solution for Problem 1-3 on page 13

Each object of *A* has four choices to be paired with one of the objects (including itself). Thus, the total number of choices is 4×4×4×4=256. Thus, 256 different sets of pairs are possible.

### Solution for Problem 1-4 on page 13

Each object of *A* has five choices: to be paired with one of the four objects (including itself), or to be paired with no object. Thus, a total number of choices is 5×5×5×5=625. Thus, 625 different sets of pairs are possible.

### Solution for Problem 1-5 on page 24

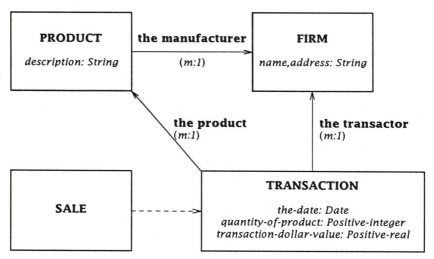

**Figure 8-1.** A binary schema for a wholesaler. The transactions which are not *sales*, are purchases.

**Solution for Problem 1-6 on page 24**

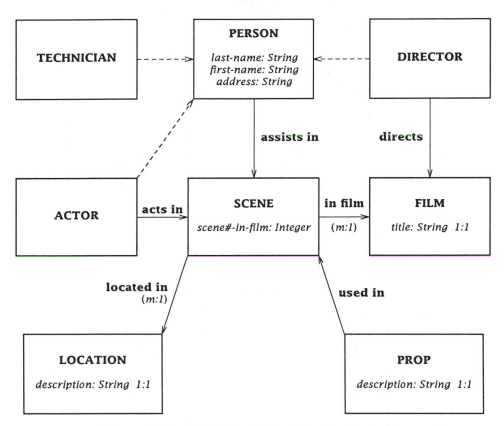

**Figure 8-2.** A binary schema for a movie studio.

**Solution for Problem 1-7 on page 24**

All the members of the clan have the same last name, so it is absent from the schema. *MARRIED* is a many-to-many relation (between current and ex-spouses). If the society described by the database does not allow divorce and a widower may not remarry, then the relation MARRIED would be one-to-one.

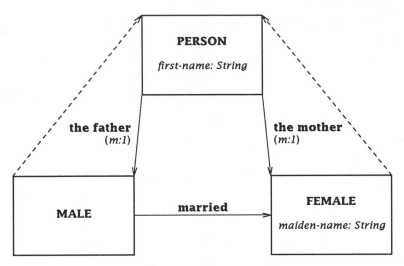

**Figure 8-3.** A binary schema for a clan.

**Solution for Problem 1-8 on page 24**

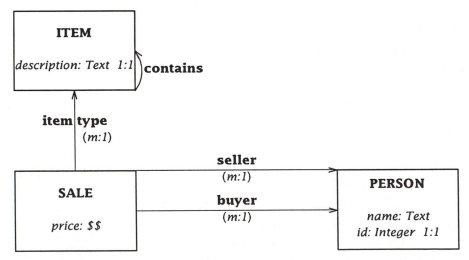

**Figure 8-4.** A binary schema to record sale transactions.

A *sale* is a transaction of a merchandise of the *item-type* for the *price* between the *seller* and the *buyer*. The many-to-many relation *contains* forms a bill of material of item-types.

**Solution for Problem 1-9 on page 24**

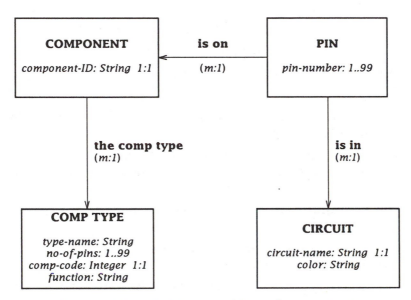

**Figure 8-5.** A binary schema for a circuit board.

Note:   No pin is in two circuits because a circuit is defined as containing a full set of electrically common wires.

**Solution for Problem 1-10 on page 32**

The concepts incorporated in the binary schema are marked with "☞".

1.   A catalogue of names of known diseases.

  ☞   Category *DISEASE*

  ☞   Relation *name* from *DISEASE* to the category of values *String*   (*m:1* )

2.   A catalogue of descriptions of known symptoms: their names and the units in which the magnitude of their intensity/acuteness is measured.

☞ Category *SYMPTOM-TYPE*

☞ Relation *name* from *SYMPTOM-TYPE* to the category of values *String* (*m:1* )

☞ Relation *magnitude-unit* from *SYMPTOM-TYPE* to the category of values *String* (*m:1* )

3. For every disease there is a list of its possible symptoms, in which

> for every possible symptom
>
> for some magnitudes of its acuteness
>
> there is a probability estimation whether
>
> > the symptom should accompany the disease with such magnitude at least.

☞ Category *SYMPTOM'S-POSSIBILITY-FOR-A-DISEASE* (Every object of this category is an event of the possibility of a symptom for a disease.)

☞ Relation **may-have** from *DISEASE* to *SYMPTOM'S-POSSIBILITY-FOR-A-DISEASE* (*1:m*)

☞ Relation **may-indicate** from *SYMPTOM-TYPE* to *SYMPTOM'S-POSSIBILITY-FOR-A-DISEASE* (*1:m*)

☞ Relation *magnitude* from *SYMPTOM'S-POSSIBILITY-FOR-A-DISEASE* to the category of values *Number* (*m:1* )

☞ Relation *probability* from *SYMPTOM'S-POSSIBILITY-FOR-A-DISEASE* to the category of values *0-100%* (*m:1* )

4. A catalogue of names of known drugs.

☞ Category *DRUG*

☞ Relation *name* from *DRUG* to the category of values *String* (*m:1* )

5. For every disease there are lists of factors which may aggravate, cause or cure the disease: drugs, drug combinations, other diseases.

☞ Category *FACTOR-INFLUENCING-DISEASES* (Every factor is either DRUG or or DRUG-INTERACTION or DISEASE. The three subcategories are disjoint.)

☞ Subcategory *DRUG* of the category *FACTOR-INFLUENCING-DISEASES*

☞ Subcategory *DISEASE* of the category *FACTOR-INFLUENCING-DISEASES*

☞ Subcategory *DRUG-INTERACTION* of the category *FACTOR-INFLUENCING-DISEASES* (Every object of the category DRUG-INTERACTION stands for a combination of drugs which jointly can produce influence.)

☞ Relation **in** from *DRUG* to *DRUG-INTERACTION* (*m:m*) (A drug may participate **in** everal drug-interactions)

☞ Relation **may-cure** from *FACTOR-INFLUENCING-DISEASES* to *DISEASE* (*m:m*)

☞ Relation **may-aggravate** from *FACTOR-INFLUENCING-DISEASES* to *DISEASE* (*m:m*)

☞ Relation **may-cause** from *FACTOR-INFLUENCING-DISEASES* to *DISEASE* (*m:m*)

6. Names, addresses, and dates of birth of patients, names and addresses of physicians. Some physicians are also known as patients. Some persons relevant to the database are neither patients nor physicians. For these persons we have names and addresses.

☞ Category *PERSON*

☞ Relation *name* from *PERSON* to the category of values *String* (*m:1* )

☞ Relation *address* from *PERSON* to the category of values *String* (*m:1* )

☞ Subcategory *PATIENT* of the category *PERSON*

☞ Subcategory *PHYSICIAN* of the category *PERSON*

☞ Relation *born* from *PATIENT* to the category of values *Date* (*m:1* )

7. Physicians' areas of specialization (diseases).

☞ Relation **specializes-in** from *PHYSICIAN* to *DISEASE* (*m:m*)

8. Every patient's medical history, including

● all his/her present and past illnesses

- their duration,

- their diagnosing physicians,

- drugs prescribed for them;

☞ Category *PATIENT'S-SICKNESS* (Every object of this category is an event of a patient having a disease during a period of time.)

☞ Relation **had** from *PATIENT* to *PATIENT'S-SICKNESS* (*1:m*)

☞ Relation **occurred** from *DISEASE* to *PATIENT'S-SICKNESS* (*1:m*)

☞ Relation *from* from *PATIENT'S-SICKNESS* to the category of values *Date* (*m:1*)

☞ Relation *to* from *PATIENT'S-SICKNESS* to the category of values *Date* (*m:1*)

☞ Relation **diagnosed** from *PHYSICIAN* to *PATIENT'S-SICKNESS* (*m:m*)

● all his/her reported symptoms with

  - the duration of the symptom's occurrences,

  - an indication of the magnitude of intensity/acuteness of the symptom's occurrence,

  - a record of the persons (names and addresses) who reported or measured the symptom's occurrence (the occurrence can be reported, for example, by the patient himself, his relatives, medical personnel), and

  - the physicians who confirmed the symptom's occurrence.

☞ Category *SYMPTOM'S-INSTANCE-FOR-A-PATIENT* (Every object of this category is an event of a a patient having a certain symptom with a certain magnitude during a certain period of time.)

☞ Relation **had** from *PATIENT* to *SYMPTOM'S-INSTANCE-FOR-A-PATIENT* (*1:m*)

☞ Relation **appeared** from *SYMPTOM-TYPE* to *SYMPTOM'S-INSTANCE-FOR-A-PATIENT* (*1:m*)

☞ Relation *from* from *SYMPTOM'S-INSTANCE-FOR-A-PATIENT* to the category of values *Date* (*m:1*)

☞ Relation *to* from *SYMPTOM'S-INSTANCE-FOR-A-PATIENT* to the category of values *Date* (*m:1*)

☞ Relation *magnitude* from *SYMPTOM'S-INSTANCE-FOR-A-PATIENT* to the category of values *Number* (*m:1*)

☞ Relation **reported** from *PERSON* to *SYMPTOM'S-INSTANCE-FOR-A-PATIENT* (*m:m*)

☞ Relation **confirmed** from *PHYSICIAN* to *SYMPTOM'S-INSTANCE-FOR-A-PATIENT* (*m:m*)

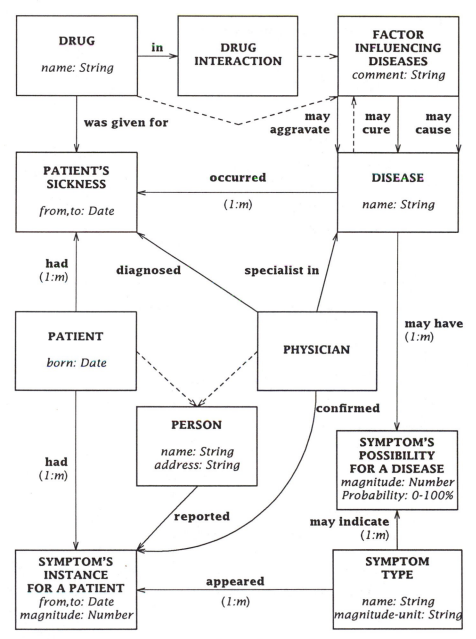

**Figure 8-6.** A binary schema for a medical application.

**Solution for Problem 1-12 on page 42**

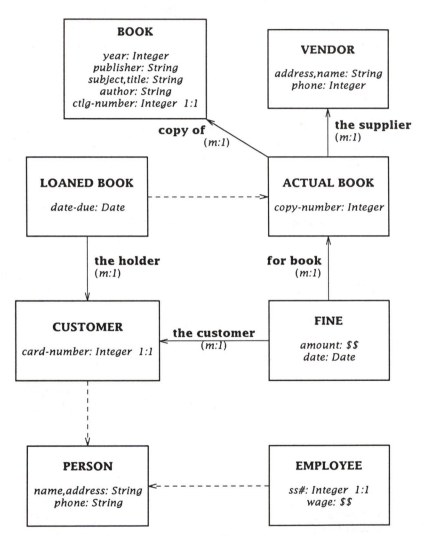

**Figure 8-7.** A binary schema for a library.

```
                        FINE

              violator's-name: String
              violator's-address: String
              violator's-phone: String
violator's-card-number: Integer (m:1, unlike in the schema)
                  amount: $$
                   date: Date
       ctlg-number: Integer (m:1, unlike in the schema)
            book-copy-number: Integer
```

**Figure 8-8.** A userview of the library schema for billing of customers.

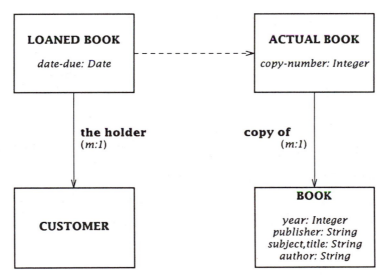

**Figure 8-9.** A subschema of the library schema for statistical analysis of reading habits. All the information that can help identify a particular person is concealed from this subschema.

**Solution for Problem 1-13 on page 50**

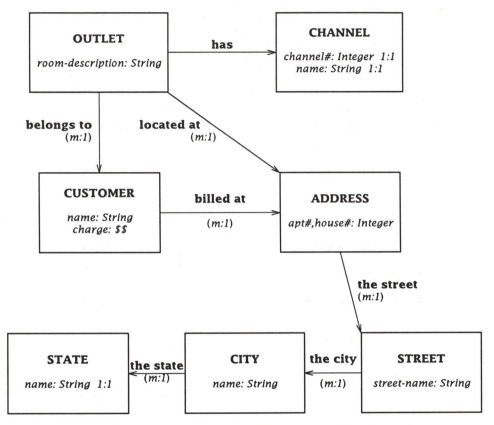

**Figure 8-10.** A binary schema for a cable distribution network.

**Solution for Problem 1-14 on page 51**

The schema appears on the following page.

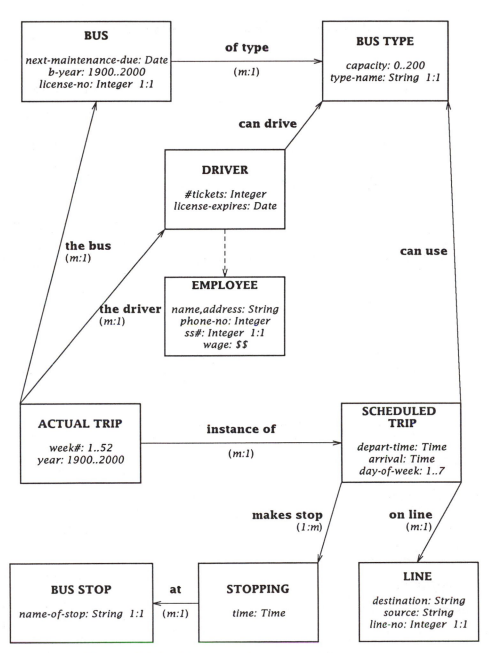

**Figure 8-11.** A binary schema for a bus company.

**Solution for Problem 1-15 on page 52**

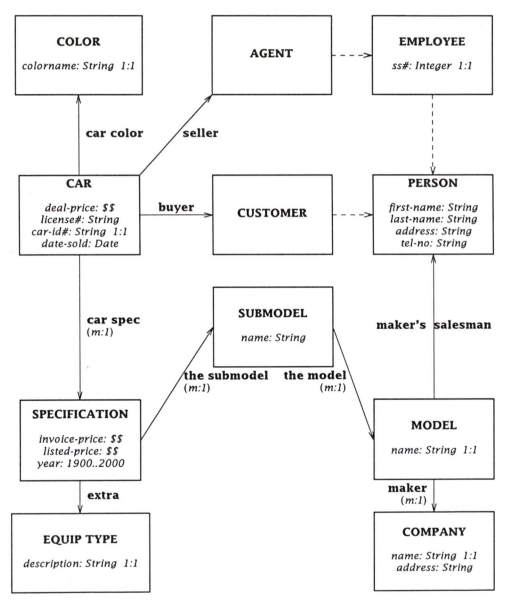

**Figure 8-12.** A binary schema for a car dealer.

**Solution for Problem 1-16 on page 52**

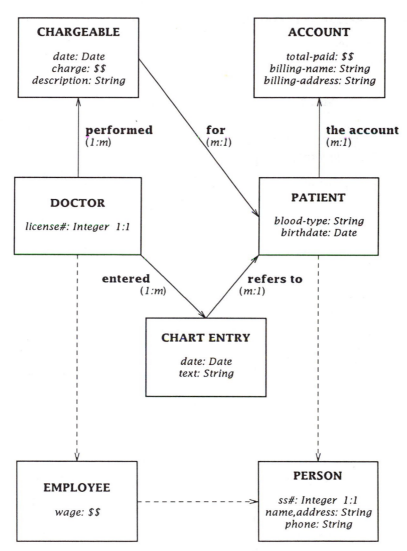

**Figure 8-13.** A binary schema for a medical clinic.

Explanation follows.

- Several patients, such as a family, can use a joint account with the clinic. No patient has two accounts — otherwise we would not know where to bill him.

- A chart entry is a doctor's memo written during a patient's visit.

- A chargeable is any activity which is performed by a doctor and is billable to a patient.

**Solution for Problem 1-17 on page 52**

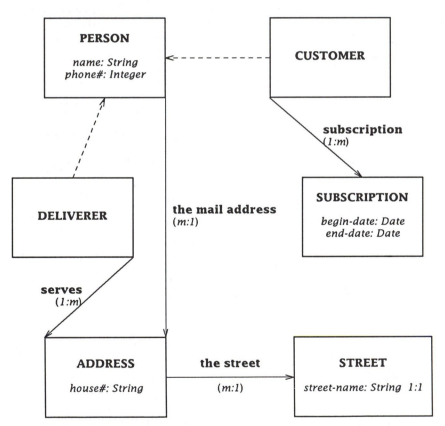

**Figure 8-14.** A binary schema for a newspaper distribution department.

Assumptions follow.

- All the subscriptions of one person are delivered to that person's mailing address. Otherwise, we would have a separate relation from *SUBSCRIPTION* to *ADDRESS*.

- For any address, there is only one deliverer who serves it.

- It is a local newspaper. All its customers and deliverers reside within one city. Thus, the name of the city does not appear in the address. All the addresses in the city are composed of a street name and house number.

- For the distribution department, the addresses are more than just character strings: they are topographical locations which are grouped into sets according to the streets of the city. Thus, there is a separate abstract category *ADDRESS*.

### Solution for Problem 2-4 on page 72

(* Normalization formula:

$$\text{new grade} := \text{old grade} + \text{factor}*(100 - \text{old grade})$$

where

$$75 = \text{AVERAGE (new grade)} =$$
$$\text{AVERAGE (old grade)} + \text{factor}*(100 - \text{AVERAGE(old grade))}$$

Thus:

$$\text{factor} = (75 - \text{average})/ (100 - \text{average})$$

(For simplification, the effect of a grade going below 0 is neglected.)     *)

**Program** Normalize (output, UNIVERSITY-DB, UNIVERSITY-MASTER-VIEW) ;

**var**

co,ce : ABSTRACT ;

iscsmajor : Boolean ;

number-of-grades, total, average: Integer ;

factor: Real;

**begin**

**for** co **in** *COURSE-OFFERING* **where** true **do begin**

total := 0;

number-of-grades :=0;

```
for ce in COURSE-ENROLLMENT where (ce.THE-OFFER = co) do begin
    iscsmajor := false ;
    for d in DEPARTMENT where (d NAME 'Computer Science' and
        ce.THE-STUDENT MAJOR d) do

        iscsmajor := true ;

    if (not iscsmajor) and not (ce FINAL-GRADE null) then begin
        total := total + ce.FINAL-GRADE ;

        number-of-grades := number-of-grades + 1 ;

        end

    end (* enrollment loop  *)

if number-of-grades>0 then begin
    average := total/number-of-grades ;

    factor := (75. − average)/ (100 − average)

    transaction begin
        for ce in COURSE-ENROLLMENT where (ce.THE-OFFER = co) do
            begin
            iscsmajor := false ;

            for d in DEPARTMENT where (d NAME 'Computer Science'
                and ce.THE-STUDENT MAJOR d) do

                iscsmajor := true ;

            if (not iscsmajor) and not (ce FINAL-GRADE null) then

                ce.FINAL-GRADE := ce.FINAL-GRADE + factor * (100 −
                    ce.FINAL-GRADE );

            end (* enrollment loop  *)

        end (* transaction  *)

    end

end (* course offering loop  *)
end. (* program  *)
```

### Solution for Problem 2-7 on page 102

A.  A simplified solution. We assume that *TO-DATE* is a total relation on the category *SICKNESS*.

**get** sickness.*THE-PATIENT.NAME*, sickness.*THE-DISEASE.NAME*

**where**

    sickness **is a** *SICKNESS* **and**

    **exists** possibility **in** *SYMTOM'S-POSSIBILITY*:

          possibility.*THE-DISEASE*=sickness.*THE-DISEASE* **and**

          possibility.*PROBABILITY* $\geq$ 0.9 **and**

          **not exists** instance **in** *SYMTOM'S-INSTANCE*:

               instance.*THE-PATIENT*=sickness.*THE-PATIENT* **and**

               instance.*THE-SYMPTOM*=possibility.*THE-SYMPTOM* **and**

               instance.*FROM-DATE*$\leq$sickness.*FROM-DATE* **and**

               instance.*TO-DATE*$\geq$sickness.*FROM-DATE*

B.  A full solution. It is possible that a sickness has no *TO-DATE*, which means that the sickness has not ended yet.

**get** sickness.*THE-PATIENT.NAME*, *sickness.THE-DISEASE.NAME*

**where**

    sickness **is a** *SICKNESS* **and**

    **exists** possibility **in** *SYMTOM'S-POSSIBILITY*:

          possibility.*THE-DISEASE*=sickness.*THE-DISEASE* **and**

          possibility.*PROBABILITY* $\geq$ 0.9 **and**

          **not exists** instance **in** *SYMTOM'S-INSTANCE*:

               instance.*THE-PATIENT*=sickness.*THE-PATIENT* **and**

               instance.*THE-SYMPTOM*=possibility.*THE-SYMPTOM* **and**

               instance.*FROM-DATE*$\leq$sickness.*FROM-DATE***and**

               (instance.*TO-DATE*$\geq$sickness.*FROM-DATE* **or**

               **not exists** d **in** *DATE*: instance *TO-DATE* d)

**Solution for Problem 3-1 on page 116**

EMPLOYEE[id-key: Integer, name: Text, boss-id: Integer]

PROJECT [proj-name-key: Text]

WORK [empl-id-in-key: Integer, proj-name-in-key: Text]

SUBPROJECT [subproj-name-in-key: Text, proj-name-in-key: Text]

**Figure 8-15.** A relational schema for project information.

**Solution for Problem 3-6 on page 151**

| MALE |
| --- |
| *first-name: String*<br>*the-mother--person-id: Integer*<br>*the-father--person-id: Integer*<br>*person-id-key: Integer* |

| FEMALE |
| --- |
| *first-name: String*<br>*the-mother--person-id: Integer*<br>*the-father--person-id: Integer*<br>*person-id-key: Integer*<br>*maiden-name: String* |

| MARRIAGE |
| --- |
| *husband--person-id-in-key: Integer*<br>*wife--person-id-in-key: Integer* |

**Figure 8-16.** A relational schema for a clan.

*Some of the Integrity Constraints Generated During Schema Conversion*
(**for every** x **in** *MARRIAGE*:

   **exists** y **in** *MALE*:

      x.*husband--person-id-in-key* = y.*person-id-key*)
**and**

(**for every** x **in** *FEMALE*:

   x *the-mother-person-id* **null  or**

   **exists** y **in** *FEMALE*:

      x.*the-mother--person-id* = y.*person-id-key*)
   **and**

(**for every** x **in** *FEMALE*:

   x *the-father-person-id* **null  or**

   **exists** y **in** *MALE*:

      x.*the-father--person-id* = y.*person-id-key*)

### Solution for Problem 3-7 on page 152

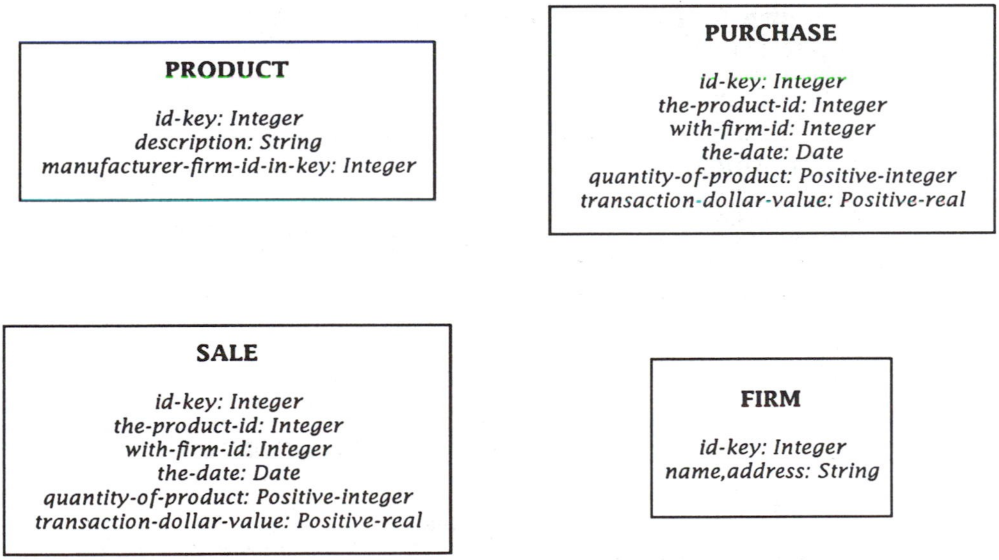

PRODUCT

id-key: Integer
description: String
manufacturer-firm-id-in-key: Integer

PURCHASE

id-key: Integer
the-product-id: Integer
with-firm-id: Integer
the-date: Date
quantity-of-product: Positive-integer
transaction-dollar-value: Positive-real

SALE

id-key: Integer
the-product-id: Integer
with-firm-id: Integer
the-date: Date
quantity-of-product: Positive-integer
transaction-dollar-value: Positive-real

FIRM

id-key: Integer
name,address: String

**Figure 8-17.** A relational schema for a wholesaler. Alternative I.

```
┌─────────────────────────────────────┐      ┌──────────────────────────────┐
│              PRODUCT                 │      │            FIRM              │
│                                      │      │                              │
│           id-key: Integer           │      │        id-key: Integer       │
│         description: String         │      │    name,address: String      │
│  manufacturer-firm-id-in-key: Integer│      │                              │
└─────────────────────────────────────┘      └──────────────────────────────┘
```

```
┌─────────────────────────────────────┐
│            TRANSACTION               │
│                                      │
│           id-key: Integer            │
│        the-product-id: Integer       │
│         with-firm-id: Integer        │
│            the-date: Date            │
│   quantity-of-product: Positive-integer│
│  transaction-dollar-value: Positive-real│
│           is-a-sale: Boolean         │
└─────────────────────────────────────┘
```

**Figure 8-18.** A relational schema for a wholesaler. Alternative II.

```
┌──────────────────────────────────┐      ┌─────────────────────────────┐
│             PRODUCT              │      │            FIRM             │
│                                  │      │                             │
│      product-id-key: Integer     │      │      firm-id-key: Integer   │
│        description: String       │      │     address,name: String    │
│  the-manufacturer--firm-id: Integer│      │                             │
└──────────────────────────────────┘      └─────────────────────────────┘
```

```
┌──────────────────────────┐      ┌──────────────────────────────────────────┐
│           SALE           │      │               TRANSACTION                  │
│                          │      │                                            │
│ transaction-id-key: Integer│      │        transaction-id-key: Integer        │
│                          │      │     quantity-of-product: Positive-integer  │
└──────────────────────────┘      │   transaction-dollar-value: Positive-real  │
                                   │             the-date: Date                 │
                                   │     the-product--product-id: Integer       │
                                   │     the-transactor--firm-id: Integer       │
                                   └────────────────────────────────────────────┘
```

**Figure 8-19.** A relational schema for a wholesaler. Alternative III.

## Solution for Problem 3-8 on page 152

| ASSISTANCE | PERSON | DIRECTION |
|---|---|---|
| person-id-in-key: Integer<br>film-title-in-key: String<br>scene-#-in-key: Integer | person-id-key: Integer  1:1<br>last-name: String<br>first-name: String<br>address: String<br>is-a-DIRECTOR: Boolean<br>is-an-ACTOR: Boolean<br>is-a-TECHNICIAN: Boolean | director-id-in-key: Integer<br>film-title-in-key: String |

| ACTING | SCENE | FILM |
|---|---|---|
| actor-id-in-key: Integer<br>film-title-in-key: String<br>scene-#-in-key: Integer | film-title-in-key: String<br>scene#-in-film-in-key: Integer<br>location-description: String | title-key: String  1:1 |

| LOCATION | PROP USE | PROP |
|---|---|---|
| description-key: String  1:1 | prop-description-in-key: String<br>film-title-in-key: String<br>scene-#-in-key: String | description-key: String  1:1 |

**Figure 8-20.** A relational schema for a movie studio.

*Integrity Constraints*

1.  Every *ACTOR-ID-in-key* of an *ACTING* corresponds to the *PERSON-ID-key* of a *PERSON* whose attribute *IS-AN-ACTOR* is *true.*

2.  Every *DIRECTOR-ID-in-key* of a *DIRECTION* corresponds to the *PERSON-ID-key* of a *PERSON* whose attribute *IS-A-DIRECTOR* is *true.*

3.  Every *PERSON-ID-in-key* of a *ASSISTANCE* corresponds to the *PERSON-ID-key* of a *PERSON.*

4. Every *FILM-TITLE-in-key* of a *DIRECTION* corresponds to the *FILM-TITLE-key* of a *FILM*.

5. Every *PROP-DESCRIPTION-in-key* of a *PROP-USE* corresponds to the *PROP-DESCRIPTION-key* of a *PROP*.

6. Every *LOCATION-DESCRIPTION-in-key* of a *SCENE* corresponds to the *LOCATION-DESCRIPTION-key* of a *LOCATION*.

7. For every *ACTING*, its *FILM-TITLE-in-key* and *SCENE-#-in-key* correspond to the *FILM-TITLE-in-key* and *SCENE-#-in-key* of one *SCENE*.

8. For every *PROP-USE*, its *FILM-TITLE-in-key* and *SCENE-#-in-key* correspond to the *FILM-TITLE-in-key* and *SCENE-#-in-key* of one *SCENE*.

**Solution for Problem 3-9 on page 152**

```
┌─────────────────────────────┐         ┌──────────────────────────────────────┐
│                             │         │                 PIN                    │
│         COMPONENT           │         │   is-on--component-ID-in-key: String   │
│                             │         │      pin-number-in-key: 1..99          │
│    component-ID-key: String │         │     is-in--circuit-name: String        │
│  the-comp-type--comp-code: Integer │  └──────────────────────────────────────┘
└─────────────────────────────┘


    ┌──────────────────────────┐         ┌──────────────────────────────┐
    │       COMP TYPE          │         │          CIRCUIT             │
    │  comp-code-key: Integer  │         │   circuit-name-key: String   │
    │     no-of-pins: 1..99    │         │        color: String         │
    │    type-name: String     │         └──────────────────────────────┘
    │    function: String      │
    └──────────────────────────┘
```

**Figure 8-21.** A relational schema for a circuit board.

*Some of the Integrity Constraints Generated During Schema Conversion*
(**for every** x **in** *PIN*:

    x *is-in--circuit-name* **null  or**

    **exists** y **in** *CIRCUIT*:  x.*is-in--circuit-name* = y.*circuit-name-key*) **and**
(**for every** x **in** *COMPONENT*:

    **exists** y **in** *COMP-TYPE*:   x.*the-comp-type--comp-code* = y.*comp-code-key*)

        *A Constraint Translated From an Original Constraint*

**for every** p **in** *PIN*:

    **exists** cmp **in** *COMPONENT*:

        p.*is-on-component-ID-in-key* = cmp.*component-ID-key* **and**

        **exists** ct **in** *COMP-TYPE*:

            x.*the-comp-type--comp-code* = ct.*comp-code-key* **and**

            p.*pin-number-in-key* $\leq$ ct.*no-of-pins*

### Solution for Problem 3-10 on page 152

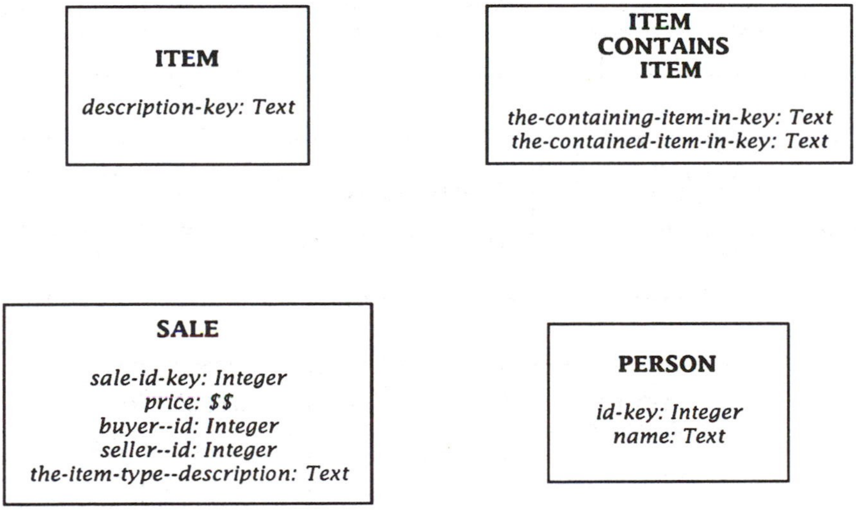

**Figure 8-22.** A relational schema of sale transactions.

*Some of the Integrity Constraints Generated During Schema Conversion*

(**for every** x **in** *SALE*:

    **exists** y **in** *PERSON*:   x.*seller--id* = y.*id-key*) **and**

(**for every** x **in** *SALE*:

    **exists** y **in** *ITEM*:   x.*the-item-type--description* = y.*description-key*)

**Solution for Problem 3-11 on page 152**

| SYMPTOM'S INSTANCE |
|---|
| *symptom's-instance-id-key: Integer*<br>*to,from: Date*<br>*magnitude: Number*<br>*the-patient-had--person-id: Integer*<br>*the-symptom-appeared--name: String* |

| SYMPTOM'S POSSIBILITY |
|---|
| *symptom's-possibility-id-key: Integer*<br>*probability: 0-100%*<br>*magnitude: Number*<br>*the-disease-may-have--factor-id: Integer*<br>*the-symptom-may-indicate--name: String* |

| FACTOR |
|---|
| *factor-id-key: Integer*<br>*comment: Text* |

| DRUG |
|---|
| *factor-id-key: Integer*<br>*name: String* |

| DISEASE |
|---|
| *factor-id-key: Integer*<br>*name: String* |

| PERSON |
|---|
| *person-id-key: Integer*<br>*address,name: String* |

| PHYSICIAN |
|---|
| *person-id-key: Integer* |

| PATIENT |
|---|
| *person-id-key: Integer*<br>*born: Date* |

| DRUG INTERACTION |
|---|
| *factor-id-key: Integer* |

| SYMPTOM |
|---|
| *name-key: String*<br>*magnitude-unit: String* |

| SICKNESS |
|---|
| *sickness-id-key: Integer*<br>*to,from: Date*<br>*the-patient-had--person-id: Integer*<br>*the-disease-occurred--factor-id: Integer* |

**Figure 8-23.** A relational schema for a medical application. Part I: tables representing the categories.

```
┌──────────────────────────────────────────────────┐
│                     DRUG                           │
│                  PARTICIPATES                      │
│                     DRUG                           │
│                  INTERACTION                       │
│                                                    │
│         the-drug--factor-id-in-key: Integer        │
│   the-drug-interaction--factor-id-in-key: Integer  │
└──────────────────────────────────────────────────┘
```

```
┌──────────────────────────────────────────┐
│                  FACTOR                    │
│                 MAY-CURE                   │
│                 DISEASE                    │
│                                            │
│      the-factor--factor-id-in-key: Integer │
│     the-disease--factor-id-in-key: Integer │
└──────────────────────────────────────────┘
```

```
┌──────────────────────────────────────────┐
│                  FACTOR                    │
│              MAY-AGGRAVATE                 │
│                 DISEASE                    │
│                                            │
│      the-factor--factor-id-in-key: Integer │
│     the-disease--factor-id-in-key: Integer │
└──────────────────────────────────────────┘
```

```
┌──────────────────────────────────────────┐
│                  FACTOR                    │
│                MAY-CAUSE                   │
│                 DISEASE                    │
│                                            │
│      the-factor--factor-id-in-key: Integer │
│     the-disease--factor-id-in-key: Integer │
└──────────────────────────────────────────┘
```

```
┌──────────────────────────────────────────┐
│                 PHYSICIAN                  │
│                 DIAGNOSED                  │
│                 SICKNESS                   │
│                                            │
│   the-physician--person-id-in-key: Integer │
│       the-sickness-id-in-key: Integer      │
└──────────────────────────────────────────┘
```

```
+-------------------------------------------------+
|                    PERSON                       |
|                  REPORTED                       |
|                  SYMPTOM'S                      |
|                  INSTANCE                        |
|                                                 |
|         the-person-id-in-key: Integer           |
|    the-symptom's-instance-id-in-key: Integer    |
+-------------------------------------------------+
```

```
+-------------------------------------------------+
|                  PHYSICIAN                      |
|                  CONFIRMED                       |
|                  SYMPTOM'S                      |
|                  INSTANCE                        |
|                                                 |
|    the-physician--person-id-in-key: Integer     |
|    the-symptom's-instance-id-in-key: Integer    |
+-------------------------------------------------+
```

```
+-------------------------------------------+
|                   DRUG                    |
|             WAS-GIVEN-FOR                  |
|               SICKNESS                     |
|                                           |
|    the-drug--factor-id-in-key: Integer    |
|     the-sickness-id-in-key: Integer       |
+-------------------------------------------+
```

```
+-------------------------------------------+
|                PHYSICIAN                  |
|             SPECIALIZES-IN                 |
|                 DISEASE                    |
|                                           |
|  the-physician--person-id-in-key: Integer |
|  the-disease--factor-id-in-key: Integer   |
+-------------------------------------------+
```

**Figure 8-24.** A relational schema for a medical application. Part II: tables representing the m:m relationships.

## Solution for Problem 3-12 on page 152

### BUS

*license-no-key: Integer*
*b-year: 1900..2000*
*next-maintenance-due: Date*
*type-name: String*

### BUS TYPE

*type-name-key: String*
*capacity: 0..200*

### DRIVER

*ss#-key: Integer*
*#tickets: Integer*
*license-expires: Date*

### DRIVER CAN-DRIVE BUS TYPE

*ss#-in-key: Integer*
*type-name-in-key: String*

### EMPLOYEE

*ss#-key: Integer*
*address,name: String*
*phone-no: Integer*
*wage: $$*

### SCHEDULED TRIP CAN-USE BUS TYPE

*scheduled-trip-id-in-key: Integer*
*type-name-in-key: String*

### ACTUAL TRIP

*actual-trip-id-key: Integer*
*year: 1900..2000*
*week#: 1..52*
*the-driver--ss#: Integer*
*the-bus--license-no: Integer*
*instance-of--scheduled-trip-id: Integer*

### SCHEDULED TRIP

*scheduled-trip-id-key: Integer*
*arrival: Time*
*day-of-week: 1..7*
*depart-time: Time*
*on-line--line-no: Integer*

### BUS STOP

*name-of-stop-key: String*

### STOPPING

*stopping-id-key: Integer*
*time: Time*
*scheduled-trip-id: Integer*
*at--name-of-stop: String*

### LINE

*line-no-key: Integer*
*source: String*
*destination: String*

**Solution for Problem 3-13 on page 152**

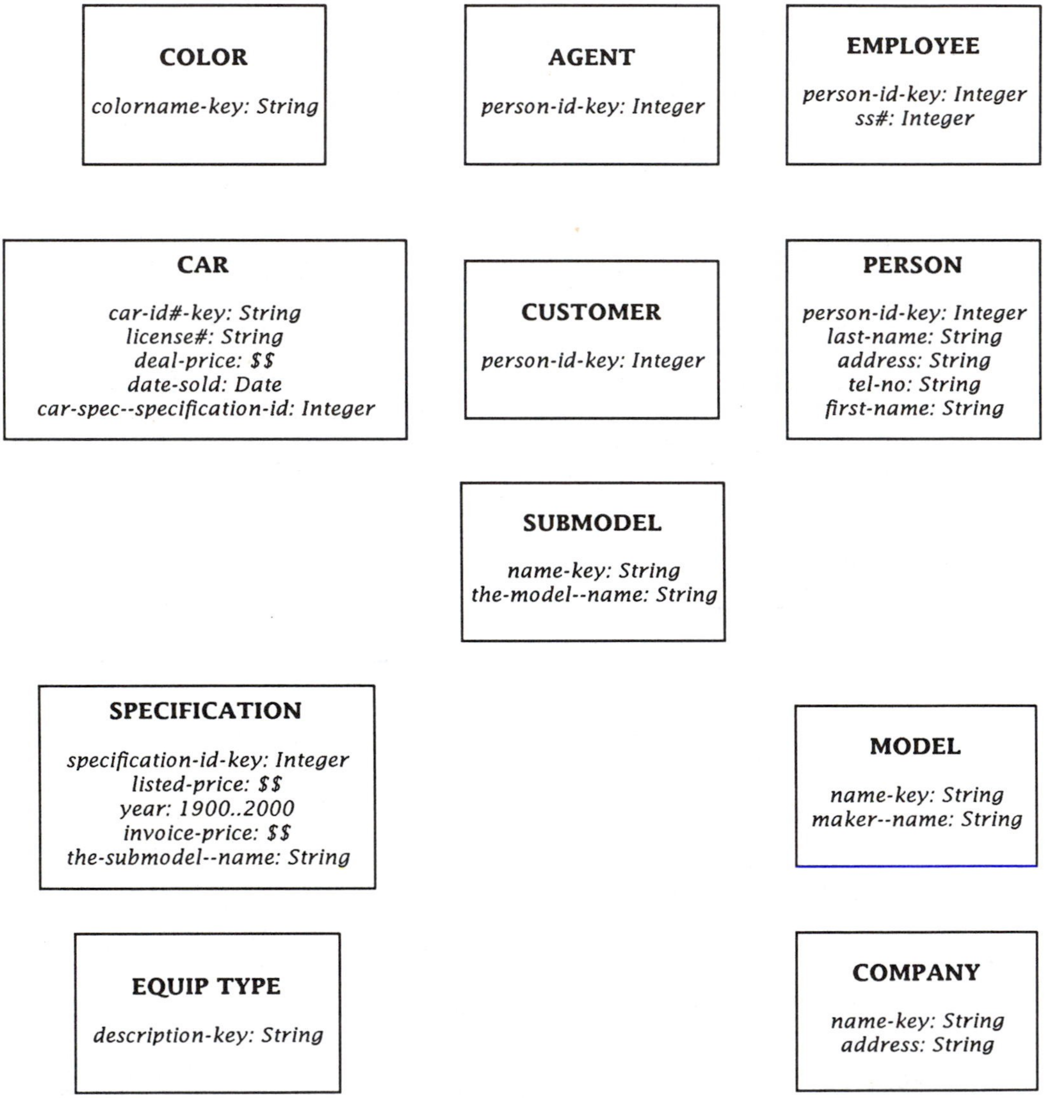

**COLOR**

*colorname-key: String*

**AGENT**

*person-id-key: Integer*

**EMPLOYEE**

*person-id-key: Integer*
*ss#: Integer*

**CAR**

*car-id#-key: String*
*license#: String*
*deal-price: $$*
*date-sold: Date*
*car-spec--specification-id: Integer*

**CUSTOMER**

*person-id-key: Integer*

**PERSON**

*person-id-key: Integer*
*last-name: String*
*address: String*
*tel-no: String*
*first-name: String*

**SUBMODEL**

*name-key: String*
*the-model--name: String*

**SPECIFICATION**

*specification-id-key: Integer*
*listed-price: $$*
*year: 1900..2000*
*invoice-price: $$*
*the-submodel--name: String*

**MODEL**

*name-key: String*
*maker--name: String*

**EQUIP TYPE**

*description-key: String*

**COMPANY**

*name-key: String*
*address: String*

**Figure 8-25.** A relational schema for a car dealer. Part I: tables representing the categories.

| PURCHASE |
|---|
| *the-car-id#-in-key: String*<br>*the-customer--person-id-in-key: Integer* |

| SALE |
|---|
| *the-car-id#-in-key: String*<br>*the-agent--person-id-in-key: Integer* |

| CAR COLOR |
|---|
| *the-car-id#-in-key: String*<br>*the-color--colorname-in-key: String* |

| SPECIFICATION<br>EXTRA EQUIP<br>TYPE |
|---|
| *the-specification--id-in-key: Integer*<br>*the-equip-type--description-in-key: String* |

| MODEL<br>MAKER'S-SALESMAN<br>PERSON |
|---|
| *the-model--name-in-key: String*<br>*the-person-id-in-key: Integer* |

**Figure 8-26.** A relational schema for a car dealer. Part II: tables representing the m:m relationships.

*Some of the Integrity Constraints Generated During Schema Conversion*

(**for every** x **in** *CUSTOMER*:

    **exists** y **in** *PERSON*:   x.*person-id-key* = y.*person-id-key*) **and**

(**for every** x **in** *EMPLOYEE*:

    **exists** y **in** *PERSON*:   x.*person-id-key* = y.*person-id-key*) **and**

(**for every** x **in** *AGENT*:

    **exists** y **in** *PERSON*:   x.*person-id-key* = y.*person-id-key*) **and**

(**for every** x **in** *PURCHASE*:

    **exists** y **in** *CAR*:   x.*the-car-id#-in-key* = y.*car-id#-key*)

### Solution for Problem 3-14 on page 153

```
┌─────────────────────────────────────────────┐
│                   PERSON                      │
│                                               │
│            person-id-key: Integer             │
│               phone#: Integer                 │
│                 name: String                  │
│  the-mail-address--the-street--street-name: String │
│       the-mail-address--house#: String        │
└─────────────────────────────────────────────┘

┌──────────────────────────────┐
│           CUSTOMER            │
│                               │
│     person-id-key: Integer    │
└──────────────────────────────┘
```

```
┌──────────────────────────┐   ┌───────────────────────────────────────────────┐
│        DELIVERER          │   │                  SUBSCRIPTION                   │
│                           │   │                                                 │
│   person-id-key: Integer  │   │          subscription-id-key: Integer           │
│                           │   │                  end-date: Date                 │
│                           │   │                 begin-date: Date                │
│                           │   │  the-customer-subscription--person-id: Integer  │
└──────────────────────────┘   └───────────────────────────────────────────────┘
```

```
┌────────────────────────────────────────────┐   ┌────────────────────────────┐
│                  ADDRESS                     │   │            STREET           │
│                                              │   │                             │
│   the-street--street-name-in-key: String     │   │    street-name-key: String  │
│           house#-in-key: String              │   │                             │
│   the-deliverer-serves--person-id: Integer    │   │                             │
└────────────────────────────────────────────┘   └────────────────────────────┘
```

**Figure 8-27.** A relational schema for a newspaper distribution department.

*Some of the Integrity Constraints Generated During Schema Conversion*

(**for every** x **in** DELIVERER:

    **exists** y **in** PERSON:

        x.person-id-key = y.person-id-key)

## Solution for Problem 3-15 on page 153

**CHARGEABLE**

*chargeable-id-key: Integer*
*charge: $$*
*description: String*
*date: Date*
*the-doctor-performed--id: Integer*
*for--id: Integer*

**ACCOUNT**

*account-id-key: Integer*
*billing-name: String*
*billing-address: String*
*total-paid: $$*

**DOCTOR**

*id-key: Integer*
*license#: Integer*

**PATIENT**

*id-key: Integer*
*blood-type: String*
*birthdate: Date*
*the-account-id: Integer*

**CHART ENTRY**

*chart-entry-id-key: Integer*
*text: String*
*date: Date*
*refers-to--id: Integer*
*the-doctor-entered--id: Integer*

**EMPLOYEE**

*id-key: Integer*
*wage: $$*

**PERSON**

*id-key,ss#: Integer*
*name,address: String*
*phone: String*

**Figure 8-28.** A relational schema for a medical clinic.

**Solution for Problem 3-16 on page 153**

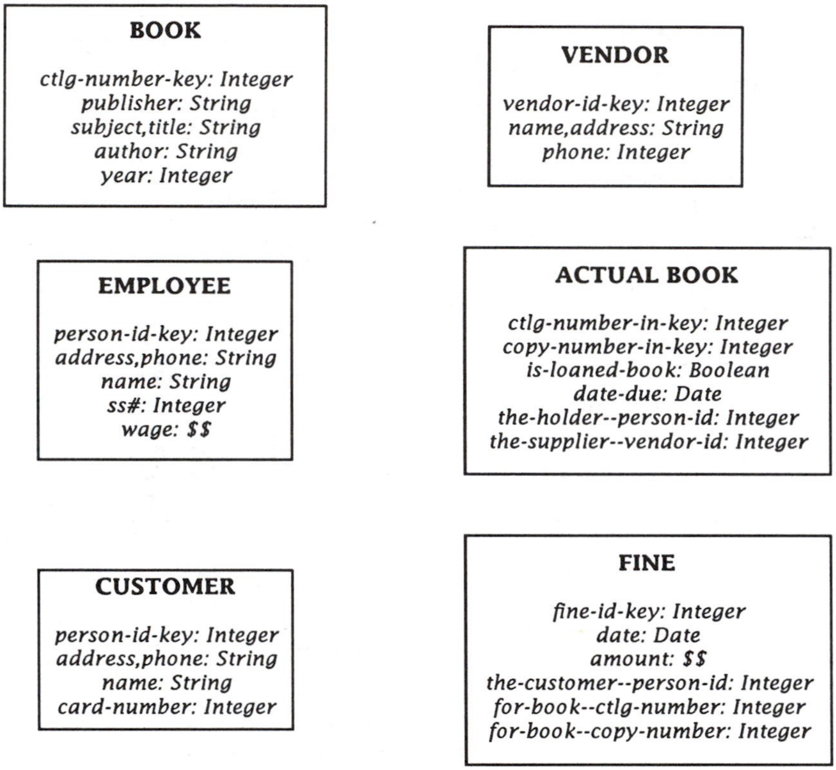

**BOOK**

ctlg-number-key: Integer
publisher: String
subject,title: String
author: String
year: Integer

**VENDOR**

vendor-id-key: Integer
name,address: String
phone: Integer

**EMPLOYEE**

person-id-key: Integer
address,phone: String
name: String
ss#: Integer
wage: $$

**ACTUAL BOOK**

ctlg-number-in-key: Integer
copy-number-in-key: Integer
is-loaned-book: Boolean
date-due: Date
the-holder--person-id: Integer
the-supplier--vendor-id: Integer

**CUSTOMER**

person-id-key: Integer
address,phone: String
name: String
card-number: Integer

**FINE**

fine-id-key: Integer
date: Date
amount: $$
the-customer--person-id: Integer
for-book--ctlg-number: Integer
for-book--copy-number: Integer

**Figure 8-29.** A relational schema for a library. Alternative I.

*Some of the Integrity Constraints Generated During Schema Conversion*

(**for every** x **in** *ACTUAL-BOOK*:   **if not** x *date-due* **null**   **then** x.*is-loaned-book*) **and**

(**for every** x **in** *ACTUAL-BOOK*:   **if not** x *the-holder--person-id* **null**   **then** x.*is-loaned-book*) **and**

(**for every** x **in** *EMPLOYEE*:

   **for every** y **in** *CUSTOMER*:

(* if x and y have equal keys, then all their other attributes are
   respectively equal or null  *)

    **if**

        (x.*address* $\neq$ y.*address* **or**

        x.*phone* $\neq$ y.*phone* **or**

        x.*name* $\neq$ y.*name*)

    **then**

        x.*person-id-key* $\neq$ y.*person-id-key*)

**and**

(**for every** x **in** *FINE*:

    **exists** y **in** *CUSTOMER*:

        x.*the-customer--person-id* = y.*person-id-key*)

    **and**

(**for every** x **in** *ACTUAL-BOOK*:

    x *the-holder--person-id* **null or**

    **exists** y **in** *CUSTOMER*:

        x.*the-holder--person-id* = y.*person-id-key*)

    **and**

(**for every** x **in** *FINE*:

    **exists** y **in** *ACTUAL-BOOK*:

        (x.*for-book--ctlg-number* = y.*ctlg-number-in-key* **and**

        x.*for-book--copy-number* = y.*copy-number-in-key*))

    **and**

(**for every** x **in** *ACTUAL-BOOK*:

    **exists** y **in** *VENDOR*:

        x.*the-supplier--vendor-id* = y.*vendor-id-key*)

    **and**

(**for every** x **in** *ACTUAL-BOOK*:

    **exists** y **in** *BOOK*:

        x.*ctlg-number-in-key* = y.*ctlg-number-key*)

```
┌─────────────────────────────────┐        ┌───────────────────────────────┐
│             BOOK                │        │           VENDOR              │
│                                 │        │                               │
│ ctlg-number-key: Number         │        │   vendor-id-key: Integer      │
│    publisher: String            │        │   name,address: String        │
│   subject,title: String         │        │      phone: Integer           │
│      author: String             │        │                               │
│       year: Integer             │        │                               │
└─────────────────────────────────┘        └───────────────────────────────┘
```

```
┌─────────────────────────────────────┐    ┌─────────────────────────────────────┐
│           LOANED BOOK               │    │           ACTUAL BOOK               │
│                                     │    │                                     │
│ copy-of--ctlg-number-in-key: Number │    │ copy-of--ctlg-number-in-key: Number │
│   copy-number-in-key: Integer       │    │   copy-number-in-key: Integer       │
│       date-due: Date                │    │  the-supplier--vendor-id: Integer   │
│  the-holder--person-id: Integer     │    │                                     │
└─────────────────────────────────────┘    └─────────────────────────────────────┘
```

```
                                        ┌─────────────────────────────────────────┐
                                        │                 FINE                    │
                                        │                                         │
┌───────────────────────────────┐       │        fine-id-key: Integer             │
│          CUSTOMER             │       │             date: Date                  │
│                               │       │           amount: $$                    │
│  person-id-key: Integer       │       │   the-customer--person-id: Integer      │
│  card-number: Integer         │       │ for-book--copy-of--ctlg-number: Number  │
│                               │       │   for-book--copy-number: Integer        │
└───────────────────────────────┘       └─────────────────────────────────────────┘
```

```
┌───────────────────────────────┐        ┌───────────────────────────────┐
│            PERSON             │        │          EMPLOYEE             │
│                               │        │                               │
│  person-id-key: Integer       │        │   person-id-key: Integer      │
│  address,phone: String        │        │      ss#: Integer             │
│      name: String             │        │      wage: $$                 │
└───────────────────────────────┘        └───────────────────────────────┘
```

**Figure 8-30.** A relational schema for a library.    Alternative II.

*Some of the Integrity Constraints Generated During Schema Conversion*
(**for every** x **in** *EMPLOYEE*:

  **exists** y **in** *PERSON*:

          x.*person-id-key* = y.*person-id-key*)
    **and**
(**for every** x **in** *CUSTOMER*:
    **exists** y **in** *PERSON*:
          x.*person-id-key* = y.*person-id-key*)
    **and**
(**for every** x **in** *LOANED-BOOK*:
    **exists** y **in** *ACTUAL-BOOK*:
          x.*copy-of--ctlg-number-in-key* = y.*copy-of--ctlg-number-in-key* and
          x.*copy-number-in-key* = y.*copy-number-in-key*)
    **and**
(**for every** x **in** *FINE*:
    **exists** y **in** *CUSTOMER*:
          x.*the-customer--person-id* = y.*person-id-key*)
    **and**
(**for every** x **in** *LOANED-BOOK*:
    **exists** y **in** *CUSTOMER*:
          x.*the-holder--person-id* = y.*person-id-key*)
    **and**
(**for every** x **in** *FINE*:
    **exists** y **in** *ACTUAL-BOOK*:
          x.*for-book--copy-of--ctlg-number* = y.*copy-of--ctlg-number-in-key* and
          x.*for-book--copy-number* = y.*copy-number-in-key*)
    **and**
(**for every** x **in** *ACTUAL-BOOK*:
    **exists** y **in** *VENDOR*:
          x.*the-supplier--vendor-id* = y.*vendor-id-key*)

### Solution for Problem 3-17 on page 161

**program** Jane (STUDIO-DB, STUDIO-FULL-SCHEMA);
**var** Jane, memories, new-scene, old-acting: ABSTRACT;

```
var current-new-scene-#: Integer;
begin
for Jane in PERSON
            where (Jane.LAST-NAME = 'Smith' and Jane.FIRST-NAME = 'Jane' and
                Jane.IS-AN-ACTOR)
        do
        transaction begin
            create new memories in FILM;
            memories.FILM-TITLE-key := 'Memories of Actress Jane Smith';
            current-new-scene-# := 0
            for old-acting in ACTING where (old-acting.ACTOR-ID-in-key =
                Jane.PERSON-ID-key) do
        begin
                create new new-scene in SCENE;
                current-new-scene-# := current-new-scene-# +1;
                new-scene.SCENE-#-in-key := current-new-scene-#;
                new-scene.FILM-TITLE-in-key := 'Memories of Actress Jane
                    Smith';
                new-scene.LOCATION-DESCRIPTION := Jane.ADDRESS
            end
        end
    end.
```

### Solution for Problem 3-18 on page 161

```
for e in EMPLOYEE where (e.BOSS-ID-in-key=555) do
    for w in WORK where (w.EMPL-ID-in-key=e.ID-key) do
        begin
        present:= false
        for w1 in WORK where
            (w1.PROP-NAME-in-key = w.PROP-NAME-in-key and
            w1.EMPL-ID-in-key = 555)
            do present:= true
        if not present then transaction
            begin
```

     **create new** w1 **in** *WORK*;
     w1.*PROJ-NAME-in-key*:= w.*PROJ-NAME-in-key*;
     w1.*EMPL-ID-in-key*:= 555
    **end**
   **end**

### Solution for Problem 3-19 on page 164

**get** p.*NAME*

**where** p **is a** *PERSON* **and**

**exists** act **in** *ACTING*:

  **exists** ast **in** *ASSISTANCE*:

    act.*ACTOR-ID-in-key* = p.*PERSON-ID-key* **and**

    ast.*PERSON-ID-in-key* = p.*PERSON-ID-key* **and**

    ast.*FILM-TITLE-in-key* = act.*FILM-TITLE-key*

  **or exists** dir **in** *DIRECTION*:

    act.*ACTOR-ID-in-key* = p.*PERSON-ID-key* **and**

    dir.*PERSON-ID-in-key* = p.*PERSON-ID-key* **and**

    dir.*FILM-TITLE-in-key* = act.*FILM-TITLE-key*

### Solution for Problem 3-20 on page 164

**get** e.*NAME* **where** e **is an** *EMPLOYEE* **and**

  **exists** s **in** *EMPLOYEE*: s.*BOSS-ID* = e.*ID-key* **and**

  **not exists** w **in** *WORK*: w.*EMPL-ID-in-key* = e.*ID-key*

### Solution for Problem 3-22 on page 164

**for every** x **in** *T*:

**for every** y **in** *T*:

  **if** (x.*A*=y.*A* **and** x.*B*=y.*B*) **then** x.*D*=y.*D*

### Solution for Problem 3-23 on page 173

PERSON

[PERSON-ID = DIRECTOR-ID-in-key]

DIRECTION

□

PROP-USE [PROP-DESCRIPTION-in-key = 'Helicopter']

[LAST-NAME]

### Solution for Problem 3-24 on page 173

(EMPLOYEE[name='Smith']) [EMPLOYEE.id-key=WORK.empl-id-in-key] WORK
[proj-name-in-key > 'Z'] [proj-name-in-key]

### Solution for Problem 3-25 on page 193

**select** *DIRECTION.FILM-TITLE-in-key*

**from** *DIRECTION, PERSON*

**where**

   *PERSON.LAST-NAME* = 'Fellini' **and**

   *PERSON.PERSON-ID-key* =

   *DIRECTION.DIRECTOR-ID-in-key*

### Solution for Problem 3-26 on page 193

**select distinct** *PROJ-NAME-in-key*

**from** *SUBPROJECT*

**where** TRUE

### Solution for Problem 3-27 on page 193

   **select**  *ID-key*

   **from**  *PERSON*

**where** *NAME* = 'Johnson'

### Solution for Problem 3-28 on page 194

**select** *ITEM-TYPE-DESCRIPTION*

**from** *SALE, PERSON*

**where** *SALE.BUYER-ID = PERSON.ID-KEY* **and** *PERSON.NAME* = 'Johnson'

### Solution for Problem 3-29 on page 194

**select** p.*NAME*

**from** *PERSON* p, *SALE* s, *PERSON* r

**where** r.*NAME* = 'Rothschild' **and** s.*SELLER-ID* = r.*ID-key* **and** s.*BUYER-ID* = p.*ID-key*

### Solution for Problem 3-30 on page 194

**select** *PRICE*

**from** *SALE*

**where** *ITEM-TYPE-DESCRIPTION* = 'nail'

### Solution for Problem 3-31 on page 194

**select** *

**from** *SALE*

**where** *PRICE* > 100

### Solution for Problem 3-32 on page 194

**select** *NAME, ID-key*

**from** *PERSON, SALE* s1, *SALE* s2

**where** *PERSON.ID-key* = s1.*SELLER-ID* **and** *PERSON.ID-key* = s2.*BUYER-ID* **and** s1.*PRICE* < s2.*PRICE*

### Solution for Problem 3-33 on page 194

**select** **count** (✳)
**from** *SALE*
**where** *PRICE* = 1

### Solution for Problem 3-34 on page 194

**select** **avg**(*PRICE*)
**from** *SALE*
**where** *ITEM-TYPE-DESCRIPTION* = 'nail'

### Solution for Problem 3-35 on page 195

**select** **distinct** *ITEM-TYPE-DESCRIPTION*
**from** *SALE, PERSON*
**where** *PERSON.NAME* = 'Tsai' **and** *PERSON.ID-key* = *SALE.BUYER-ID*

### Solution for Problem 3-36 on page 195

**select** **count**(**distinct** *ITEM-TYPE-DESCRIPTION*)
**from** *SALE, PERSON*
**where** *PERSON.NAME* = 'Tsai' **and** *PERSON.ID-key* = *SALE.BUYER-ID*

### Solution for Problem 3-37 on page 195

**select** *ITEM-TYPE-DESCRIPTION*, **avg**(*PRICE*)
**from** *SALE*
**group by** *ITEM-TYPE-DESCRIPTION*

### Solution for Problem 3-38 on page 195

**select** *ITEM-TYPE-DESCRIPTION*

**from** *SALE*

**group by** *ITEM-TYPE-DESCRIPTION*

**having avg**(*PRICE*) > 1000

### Solution for Problem 3-39 on page 195

**select** *ITEM-TYPE-DESCRIPTION*

**from** *SALE*

**where** *PRICE* > 10

**group by** *ITEM-TYPE-DESCRIPTION*

**having avg**(*PRICE*) > 1000

### Solution for Problem 3-40 on page 195

**select** *

**from** *PERSON*

**order by** *NAME*

### Solution for Problem 3-41 on page 195

**delete from** *PERSON*

**where** *ID-key = 555*

### Solution for Problem 3-42 on page 195

**delete from** *SALE*

**where** *ITEM-TYPE-DESCRIPTION = 'car'*

### Solution for Problem 3-43 on page 196

**insert into** *PERSON*

ID-key, NAME

**values**

333, 'Vasudha'

### Solution for Problem 3-44 on page 196

**insert into** *SALE*
*SALE-ID-key, BUYER-ID, SELLER-ID, ITEM-TYPE-DESCRIPTION, PRICE*
**select** *SALE-ID-key+100000, BUYER-ID, SELLER-ID, 'Nail', PRICE*.01*
**from** *SALE*
**where** *ITEM-TYPE-DESCRIPTION = 'Hammer'*

### Solution for Problem 3-45 on page 196

**update** *SALE*
   **set** *PRICE = PRICE * .90*
   **where** *PRICE > 90*

### Solution for Problem 3-46 on page 196

**create table** *PERSON*
*ID-key*                Integer
*NAME*                String

### Solution for Problem 3-47 on page 196

**create view** *BOUGHT*
*PERSON, ITEM*
**as**
   **select** *BUYER-ID, ITEM-TYPE-DESCRIPTION*
   **from** *SALE*

### Solution for Problem 3-48 on page 196

**insert into** *ITEM*

*DESCRIPTION-key*
**values** :item

### Solution for Problem 3-49 on page 196

**var** item: String;
**begin**
**while not** eof(Input) **do begin**
    **readln** (item);
    **insert into** *ITEM*
        *DESCRIPTION-key* **values** :item
    **end**
**end**.

### Solution for Problem 3-50 on page 197

**select  count** (✶)
**from** *SALE*
**where** PRICE < 10
**into** :total

### Solution for Problem 3-51 on page 197

**declare** current-sale **cursor for**
        **select** *ITEM-TYPE-DESCRIPTION*
        **from** *SALE*
        **where** *PRICE* = 20;
**open** current-sale;
**repeat**
    **fetch** current-sale **into** :item;
    **if** sqlstatus ≠ not-found **then** writeln(item)
**until** sqlstatus = not-found

### Solution for Problem 3-52 on page 197

```
declare current-sale cursor for
        select  PRICE
        from  SALE;
open current-sale;
repeat
    fetch current-sale into :price;
    price := modify(price);
    if sqlstatus ≠ not-found then
        update SALE
            set PRICE := price
            where current of current-sale
until sqlstatus = not-found
```

### Solution for Problem 3-53 on page 197

```
declare current-item cursor for
        select DESCRIPTION-key
        from  ITEM
open current-item;
repeat
    fetch current-item into :item;
    if sqlstatus ≠ not-found then begin
        writeln (' Would you like to delete ', item, '?');
        readln (answer);
        if answer='yes' then
            delete from ITEM
                where current of current-item
    end
```

**until** sqlstatus = not-found

### Solution for Problem 3-54 on page 197

**select** P.*THE_COMP_ID_KEY*, P.*PIN_NUMBER_KEY*, F.*FUNCTION*

**from** *PIN* P, *COMPONENT* C, *COMP_TYPE* F

**where** P.*THE_CKT_NAME* = 'DATABIT01' **and** P.*THE_COMP_ID_KEY* = C.*COMP_ID_KEY* **and** C.*THE_COMP_CODE* = F.*COMP_CODE_KEY*

**order by** *THE_COMP_ID_KEY*, *PIN_NUMBER_KEY*

### Solution for Problem 3-55 on page 197

**select** *THE_CKT_NAME*, *THE_COMP_ID_KEY*, *PIN_NUMBER_KEY*

**from** *PIN*

**order by** *THE_CKT_NAME*, *THE_COMP_ID_KEY*, *PIN_NUMBER_KEY*

### Solution for Problem 3-56 on page 198

**select** *THE_CKT_NAME*

**from** *PIN*

**group by** *THE_CKT_NAME*

**having count**($*$) = 1

### Solution for Problem 3-57 on page 198

**select distinct** CT.*TYPE_NAME*

**from** *COMP_TYPE* CT, *COMPONENT* C, *PIN* P, *CIRCUIT* CI

**where** CI.COLOR = 'RED' **and** CI.*CIRCUIT_NAME_KEY* = P.*THE_CKT_NAME* **and** P.*PIN_NUMBER_KEY* = 14 **and** P.*THE_COMP_ID_KEY* = C.*COMP_ID_KEY* **and** C.*THE_COMP_CODE* = CT.*COMP_CODE_KEY*

### Solution for Problem 3-58 on page 198

**select** *COMP_ID_KEY*, *TYPE_NAME*, *FUNCTION*

**from** *COMPONENT* X, *COMP_TYPE* Y
**where** X.*THE_COMP_CODE* = Y.*COMP_CODE_KEY*
**order by** *COMP_ID_KEY*

### Solution for Problem 3-59 on page 198

**update** *CIRCUIT*
**set** *CIRCUIT_NAME_KEY* = 'databit02'
**where** *CIRCUIT_NAME_KEY* = 'databit01';

**update** *PIN*
**set** *THE_CKT_NAME* = 'databit02'
**where** *THE_CKT_NAME* = 'databit01'

### Solution for Problem 3-60 on page 199

Find the names of the persons born in 1967.

*Calculus for the binary schema*

**get** person.*LAST-NAME*
    **where** (person.*BIRTH-YEAR* = 1967)

*Calculus for the relational schema*

**get** person.*LAST-NAME*
    **where** ((person **is a** *STUDENT*) **and** (person.*BIRTH-YEAR* = 1967)) **or**
    ((person **is an** *INSTRUCTOR*) **and** (person.*BIRTH-YEAR* = 1967))

*Ext. Pascal for the relational schema*

*A. If duplicates may be printed*

**for** s **in** *STUDENT* **where** s.*BIRTH-YEAR* = 1967 **do**
    **writeln**( s.*LAST-NAME* );
**for** i **in** *INSTRUCTOR* **where** i.*BIRTH-YEAR* = 1967 **do**
    **writeln**( i.*LAST-NAME* );

*B. Without duplicates*

**for** s **in** *STUDENT* **where** s.*BIRTH-YEAR* = 1967 **do**

    **writeln**( s.*LAST-NAME* );

**for** i **in** *INSTRUCTOR*

    **where** i.*BIRTH-YEAR* = 1967

    **do begin**

        already-printed := **false**;

        **for** s **in** *STUDENT*

            **where** i.*ID-key* = s.*ID-key*

            **do** already-printed := **true**;

        **if not** already-printed **then writeln**( i.*LAST-NAME* )

        **end**

                                Algebra for the relational schema

(*STUDENT* [*BIRTH-YEAR* = 1967] [*LAST-NAME*]) $\cup$

(*INSTRUCTOR* [*BIRTH-YEAR* = 1967] [*LAST-NAME*])

                                  SQL for the relational schema

(* The following pair of queries will print duplicates; it's too hard to eliminate duplication *)

**select** *LAST-NAME* **from** *STUDENT* **where** *BIRTH-YEAR* = 1967;

**select** *LAST-NAME* **from** *INSTRUCTOR* **where** *BIRTH-YEAR* = 1967

### Solution for Problem 3-61 on page 199

For every student, list the instructors of the student's major department.

                                  Calculus for the binary schema

**get** student.*FIRST-NAME*, student.*LAST-NAME*, instructor.*FIRST-NAME*, instructor.*LAST-NAME*

    **where** (instructor   *WORKS-IN*   student.*MAJOR*)

                                  Calculus for the relational schema

**get** s.*FIRST-NAME*, s.*LAST-NAME*, i.*FIRST-NAME*, i.*LAST-NAME*

    **where**

(s **is an** *STUDENT*) **and** (i **is an** *INSTRUCTOR*) **and**

(**exists** w **in** *WORK*:

> i.*ID-key* = w.*INSTRUCTOR-ID-in-key* **and** s.*MAJOR-DEPT-MAIN-NAME* = w.*DEPT-MAIN-NAME-in-key*)

> > Ext. Pascal for the relational schema

**for** s **in** *STUDENT*

> **where true**

> **do**

> > **for** w **in** *WORK*

> > > **where** (w.*DEPT-MAIN-NAME-in-key* = s.*MAJOR-DEPT-MAIN-NAME*)

> > **do**

> > > **for** i **in** *INSTRUCTOR*

> > > > **where** w.*INSTRUCTOR-ID-in-key* = i.*ID-key*

> > > > **do writeln**( s.*FIRST-NAME*, s.*LAST-NAME*, i.*FIRST-NAME*, i.*LAST-NAME* )

> > > > > Algebra for the relational schema

All-instructors-with-renamed-attributes =
  *INSTRUCTOR* [*ID-key/INSTR-ID-key*] [*FIRST-NAME/INSTR-FIRST-NAME*] [*LAST-NAME/INSTR-LAST-NAME*]

All-instructors-and-their-departments =
  All-instructors-with-renamed-attributes [*INSTR-ID-key* = *INSTRUCTOR-ID-in-key*] *WORK*

Pairs-student-instructor =
  *STUDENT* [*MAJOR-DEPT-MAIN-NAME* = *DEPT-MAIN-NAME-in-key*] All-instructors-and-their-departments

Result =
  Pairs-student-instructor [*FIRST-NAME*, *LAST-NAME*, *INSTR-FIRST-NAME*, *INSTR-LAST-NAME*]

> > > > SQL for the relational schema

**select** s.*FIRST-NAME*, s.*LAST-NAME*, i.*FIRST-NAME*, i.*LAST-NAME*

**from** *STUDENT* s, *INSTRUCTOR* i

**where** <i.*ID-key*, s.*MAJOR-DEPT-MAIN-NAME*> **in**

    **select** *INSTRUCTOR-ID-in-key, DEPT-MAIN-NAME-in-key*

    **from** *WORK*

    **where** TRUE

### Solution for Problem 3-62 on page 199

What instructors work in every department? (Each relevant instructor shares her time between all the departments.)

Calculus for the binary schema

**get** instructor.*LAST-NAME* **where**

    (**for every** d **in** *DEPARTMENT*:

       instructor *WORKS-IN* d)

Calculus for the relational schema

**get** instructor.*LAST-NAME*

    **where** (instructor **is an** *INSTRUCTOR*) **and**

       **for every** d **in** *DEPARTMENT*:

          (**exists** w **in** *WORK*:

             instructor.*ID-key* = w.*INSTRUCTOR-ID-in-key* **and** d.*MAIN-NAME-key* = w.*DEPT-MAIN-NAME-in-key*)

Ext. Pascal for the relational schema

**for** i **in** *INSTRUCTOR*

    **where true**

    **do begin**

       instructor-OK := **true**;

       **for** d **in** *DEPARTMENT*

          **where** instructor-OK

          **do begin**

             works-in := **false**;

    **for** w **in** *WORK*

        **where** (w.*INSTRUCTOR-ID-in-key* = i.*ID-key*) **and**
            (w.*DEPT-MAIN-NAME-in-key* = d.*MAIN-NAME-key*)
        **and** (**not** works-in)

        **do** works-in := **true**;

    **if not** works-in **then** instructor-OK := **false**

    **end**;

  **if** instructor-OK **then writeln**(i.*LAST-NAME*)

  **end**

Algebra for the relational schema

(* {all instructors} − {instructors who do not work in every department}  *)

Pairs-inst-dpt-where-the-instructor-does-not-work-in-the-department =
    (*INSTRUCTOR* [*ID-key*] × *DEPARTMENT*) −
    (*WORK* [*INSTRUCTOR-ID-in-key/ID-key*] [*DEPARTMENT-MAIN-NAME-in-key/MAIN-NAME-key*])

Instructors-who-do-not-work-every-department =
    Pairs-inst-dpt-where-the-instructor-does-not-work-in-the-department
    [*INSTRUCTOR-ID-in-key*]

Instructors-who-work-in-every-department =
    *INSTRUCTOR* [*ID-key*] − Instructors-who-do-not-work-every-department

Names-of-instructors-who-work-in-every-department =
    (Instructors-who-work-in-every-department □ *INSTRUCTOR*) [*LAST-NAME*]

SQL for the relational schema

**select** i.*LAST-NAME*

**from** *INSTRUCTOR* i

**where**

    **select** w.*DEPT-MAIN-NAME-in-key*

    **from** *WORK* w

    **where** w.*INSTRUCTOR-ID-in-key* = i.*ID-key*

  **contains**

    **select** d.*MAIN-NAME-key*

  **from** *DEPARTMENT* d

  **where true**

### Solution for Problem 3-63 on page 199

What instructors taught every student?

        Calculus for the binary schema

**get** instructor.*LAST-NAME* **where**

  **for every** s **in** *STUDENT*:

    **exists** enrl **in** *COURSE-ENROLLMENT*:

     (enrl *THE-STUDENT* s **and**

     enrl.*THE-OFFERING.THE-INSTRUCTOR* = instructor)

        Calculus for the relational schema

**get** instructor.*LAST-NAME*

  **where** (instructor **is an** *INSTRUCTOR*) **and**

   (**for every** s **in** *STUDENT*:

    **exists** enrl **in** *COURSE-ENROLLMENT*:

     enrl.*STUDENT-ID-in-key* = s.*ID-key* **and** enrl.*INSTRUCTOR-ID-in-key* = instructor.*ID-key*)

        Ext. Pascal for the relational schema

**for** i **in** *INSTRUCTOR*

  **where true**

  **do begin**

   instructor-OK := **true**;

   **for** s **in** *STUDENT*

    **where** instructor-OK

    **do begin**

     has-taught-the-student := **false**;

     **for** enrl **in** *COURSE-ENROLLMENT*

      **where** (enrl.*INSTRUCTOR-ID-in-key* = i.*ID-key*) **and**
       (enrl.*STUDENT-ID-in-key* = s.*ID-key*) **and** (**not** has-

taught-the-student)

        **do** has-taught-the-student := **true**;

     **if not** has-taught-the-student **then** instructor-OK := **false**

     **end**;

   **if** instructor-OK **then writeln**(i.*LAST-NAME*)

   **end**

Algebra for the relational schema

All-pairs-instructor-teaching-student =
   *COURSE-ENROLLMENT* [*INSTRUCTOR-ID-in-key*, *STUDENT-ID-in-key*]

All-pairs-instructor-student =
   (*INSTRUCTOR* [*ID-key*][*ID-key/INSTRUCTOR-ID-in*-key]) × (*STUDENT* [*ID-key*] [*ID-key/STUDENT-ID-in-key*])

All-pairs-instructor-not-teaching-student =
   All-pairs-instructor-student − All-pairs-instructor-teaching-student

The-instructors-not-teaching-all-students =
   All-pairs-instructor-not-teaching-student [*INSTRUCTOR-ID-in-key*]

The-instructors-teaching-all-students =
   *INSTRUCTOR* [*ID-key*] − The-instructors-not-teaching-all-students

The-names-of-the-instructors-teaching-all-students =
   (The-instructors-teaching-all-students □ *INSTRUCTOR*) [*LAST-NAME*]

SQL for the relational schema

**select** i.*LAST-NAME*

**from** *INSTRUCTOR* i

**where**

    **select** enrl.*STUDENT-ID-in-key*

    **from** COURSE-ENROLLMENT enrl

    **where** enrl.*INSTRUCTOR-ID-in-key* = i.*ID-key*

  **contains**

    **select** s.*ID-key*

    **from** *STUDENT* s

    **where true**

### Solution for Problem 3-64 on page 199

Who took Prof. Smith's courses?

*Calculus for the binary schema*

**get** student.*LAST-NAME* **where**

   **exists** enrl **in** *COURSE-ENROLLMENT*:

     (enrl.*THE-STUDENT*=student **and** enrl.*THE-OFFERING. THE-INSTRUCTOR. LAST-NAME*='Smith')

*Calculus for the relational schema*

**get** s.*LAST-NAME*

   **where** s **is a** *STUDENT* **and**

     **exists** enrl **in** *COURSE-ENROLLMENT*:

       enrl.*STUDENT-ID-in-key* = s.*ID-key* **and**

         (**exists** i **in** *INSTRUCTOR*:

           enrl.*INSTRUCTOR-ID-in-key* = i.*ID-key* **and** i.*LAST-NAME* = 'Smith')

*Ext. Pascal for the relational schema*

(* This program is allowed to print a student's name twice *)

**for** i **in** *INSTRUCTOR*

   **where** i.*LAST-NAME* = 'Smith'

   **do begin**

     **for** enrl **in** *COURSE-ENROLLMENT*

       **where** enrl.*INSTRUCTOR-ID-in-key* = i.*ID-key*

       **do begin**

         **for** s **in** *STUDENT*

           **where** enrl.*STUDENT-ID-in-key* = s.*ID-key*

           **do writeln**(s.*LAST-NAME*)

       **end**

   **end**

Algebra for the relational schema

The-enrollments-of-instructor-Smith =
    INSTRUCTOR [LAST-NAME = 'Smith'] [ID-key] [ID-key/INSTRUCTOR-ID-in-key] □ COURSE-ENROLLMENT

The-enrollments-and-students-of-instructor-Smith =
    The-enrollments-of-instructor-Smith [STUDENT-ID-in-key = ID-key] STUDENT)

The-students-of-instructor-Smith =
    The-enrollments-and-students-of-instructor-Smith [LAST-NAME]

SQL for the relational schema

**select** s.LAST-NAME

**from** STUEDNT s

**where** s.ID-key **in**

    **select** enrl.STUDENT-ID-in-key

    **from** COURSE-ENROLLMENT enrl

    **where** enrl.INSTRUCTOR-ID-in-key **in**

        **select** i.ID-key

        **from** INSTRUCTOR i

        **where** i.LAST-NAME = 'Smith'

### Solution for Problem 3-65 on page 199

Display 'TRUE' if every student took at least one course.

Calculus for the binary schema

**get**

    (**for every** s **in** STUDENT:

        **exists** enrl **in** COURSE-ENROLLMENT:

            s=enrl.THE-STUDENT)

Calculus for the relational schema

**get**

    (**for every** s **in** STUDENT:

> **exists** enrl **in** *COURSE-ENROLLMENT*:
>> s.*ID-key* = enrl.*STUDENT-ID-in-key*)

Ext. Pascal for the relational schema

OK := **true**;

**for** s **in** *STUDENT*

   **where** OK

   **do begin**

      student-OK := **false**;

      **for** enrl **in** *COURSE-ENROLLMENT*

         **where not** student-OK

         **do if** enrl.*STUDENT-ID-in-key* = s.*ID-key* **then** student-OK :=
            **true**;

      **if not** student-OK **then** OK := **false**

      **end**;

**if** OK **then writeln**('TRUE')

SQL for the relational schema

**select distinct** 'TRUE' (* This constant is printed if the **where** condition is
   satisfied. Otherwise, nothing is printed.  *)

**from** *DEPARTMENT* (* The table *DEPARTMENT* is irrelevant, but we have to
   specify a table. We are "retrieving" a constant.  *)

**where**

     **select** *STUDENT-ID-in-key*

     **from** *COURSE-ENROLLMENT*

     **where true**

   **contains**

     **select** *ID-key*

     **from** *STUDENT*

     **where true**

### Solution for Problem 3-66 on page 199

Print a table with two columns, which associates students to their teachers. Only last names are printed.

Calculus for the binary schema

**get** Teacher: instructor.*LAST-NAME*, Student-taught: student.*LAST-NAME*
 **where**

   **exists** enrl **in** *COURSE-ENROLLMENT*:

      enrl.*THE-STUDENT* = student **and**

      enrl.*THE-OFFER. THE-INSTRUCTOR* = instructor

Calculus for the relational schema

**get** Teacher: i.*LAST-NAME*, Student-taught: s.*LAST-NAME*

   **where** (s **is a** *STUDENT*) **and** (i **is an** *INSTRUCTOR*) **and**

      (**exists** enrl **in** *COURSE-ENROLLMENT*:

         enrl.*STUDENT-ID-in-key* = s.*ID-key* **and** enrl.*INSTRUCTOR-ID-in-key* = i.*ID-key*)

Ext. Pascal for the relational schema

(* It is a rather inefficient program, but other possibilities are either very hard to program or produce redundant output  *)

**writeln**('Teacher', 'Student-taught');

**for** i **in** *INSTRUCTOR*

   **where true**

   **do**

      **for** s **in** *STUDENT*

         **where true**

         **do begin**

            (* find whether i taught s  *)

            taught := **false**;

            **for** enrl **in** *COURSE-ENROLLMENT*

               **where** (enrl.*INSTRUCTOR-ID-in-key* = i.*ID-key* **and**
               enrl.*STUDENT-ID-in-key* = s.*ID-key*)

**do** taught := **true**;

**if** taught **then writeln**(i.*LAST-NAME*, s.*LAST-NAME*)

**end**

Algebra for the relational schema

(*INSTRUCTOR* [*ID-key, LAST-NAME*] [*ID-key/INSTRUCTOR-ID-in-key*])

□

*COURSE-ENROLLMENT*

□

(*STUDENT* [*ID-key/STUDENT-ID-in-key*] [*LAST-NAME/ST-LAST-NAME*]))
[*LAST-NAME, ST-LAST-NAME*]

SQL for the relational schema

**select** i.*LAST-NAME*, s.*LAST-NAME*

**from** *INSTRUCTOR* i, *STUDENT* s

**where** <i.*ID-key*, s.*ID-key*> **in**

**select** enrl.*INSTRUCTOR-ID-in-key*, enrl.*STUDENT-ID-in-key*,

**from** *COURSE-ENROLLMENT* enrl

**where true**


**Solution for Problem 3-67 on page 200**

Find the average birth year of the students.

Calculus for the relational schema

**get** (**average** s.*BIRTH-YEAR* **where** s **is a** *STUDENT*)

Ext. Pascal for the relational schema

number := 0;

sum-of-birthyear := 0;

**for** s **in** *STUDENT*

**where true**

**do begin**

number := number + 1;

sum-of-birthyear := sum-of-birthyear + s.*BIRTH-YEAR*

**end**;
**writeln**(sum-of-birthyear/number)

SQL for the relational schema

**select avg** (*BIRTH-YEAR*)
**from** *STUDENT*
**where true**

### Solution for Problem 3-68 on page 200

Find the number of pairs (*INSTRUCTOR, DEPARTMENT*) where the instructor works in the department.

Calculus for the relational schema

**get** (**count** w
    **where** w **is a** *WORK*)

Ext. Pascal for the relational schema

pair-count := 0;
**for** w **in** *WORK*
    **where true**
    **do** pair-count := pair-count + 1;
**writeln**(pair-count)

SQL for the relational schema

**select count** (*)
**from** *WORK*
**where true**

### Solution for Problem 3-69 on page 200

Find the average of grades of Student Jane Howard.

Calculus for the relational schema

**get average** enrl.*FINAL-GRADE*

**where** (enrl **is a** *COURSE-ENROLLMENT*) **and**

    (**exists** s **in** *STUDENT*:

        s.*LAST-NAME* = 'Howard' **and** s.*FIRST-NAME* = 'Jane' **and**

        s.*ID-key* = enrl.*STUDENT-ID-in-key*)

                         Ext. Pascal for the relational schema

**for** s **in** *STUDENT*

    **where** (s.*LAST-NAME* = 'Howard') **and** (s.*FIRST-NAME* = 'Jane')

    **do begin**

        sum-grade := 0;

        number-grade := 0;

        **for** enrl **in** *COURSE-ENROLLMENT*

            **where** s.*ID-key* = enrl.*STUDENT-ID-in-key*

            **do begin**

                sum-grade := sum-grade + enrl.*FINAL-GRADE*;

                number-grade := number-grade + 1

            **end**;

        **writeln**(sum-grade/number-grade)

        **end**

                       SQL for the relational schema

**select avg** (enrl.*FINAL-GRADE*)

**from** *COURSE-ENROLLMENT* enrl

**where**

    **exists**

        (**select** *

        **from** *STUDENT* s

        **where**

            s.*LAST-NAME* = 'Howards' **and** s.*FIRST-NAME* = 'Jane' **and**

            s.*ID-key* = enrl.*STUDENT-ID-in-key*)

### Solution for Problem 3-70 on page 200

Print the average of all grades given by Prof. Brown.

*Calculus for the relational schema*

**get** (**average** enrl.*FINAL-GRADE*
    **where** (enrl **is a** *COURSE-ENROLLMENT*) **and**
      (**exists** i **in** *INSTRUCTOR*:
        i.*LAST-NAME* = 'Brown' **and**
        i.*ID-key* = enrl.*INSTRUCTOR-ID-in-key*))

*Ext. Pascal for the relational schema*

**for** i **in** *INSTRUCTOR*
    **where** i.*LAST-NAME* = 'Brown'
    **do begin**
      sum-grade := 0;
      number-grade := 0;
      **for** enrl **in** *COURSE-ENROLLMENT*
        **where** i.*ID-key* = enrl.*INSTRUCTOR-ID-in-key*
        **do begin**
          sum-grade := sum-grade + enrl.*FINAL-GRADE*;
          number-grade := number-grade + 1
        **end**;
      **writeln**(sum-grade/number-grade)
    **end**

*SQL for the relational schema*

**select avg** (enrl.*FINAL-GRADE*)
**from** *COURSE-ENROLLMENT* enrl
**where exists**
    (**select** *
    **from** *INSTRUCTOR* i

**where** i.*LAST-NAME* = 'Brown' **and**

> i.*ID-key* = enrl.*INSTRUCTOR-ID-in-key*)

### Solution for Problem 3-71 on page 200

How many students are there in the university?

> Calculus for the relational schema

**get** (**count** s

> **where** s **is a** *STUDENT*)

> Ext. Pascal for the relational schema

total := 0;

**for** s **in** *STUDENT*

> **where true**
>
> **do** total := total + 1;

**writeln**(total)

> SQL for the relational schema

**select count** (*)
**from** *STUDENT*
**where true**

### Solution for Problem 3-72 on page 200

What students have their average grade above 90?

> Calculus for the relational schema

**get** s.*FIRST-NAME*, s.*LAST-NAME*

> **where** s **is a** *STUDENT* **and** $90 \leq$
>
> > (**average** enrl.*FINAL-GRADE*
> >
> > > **where** enrl **is a** *COURSE-ENROLLMENT* **and** s.*ID-key* = enrl.*STUDENT-ID-in-key*)

Ext. Pascal for the relational schema

```
for s in STUDENT
    where true
    do begin
        total := 0;
        count := 0;
        for enrl in COURSE-ENROLLMENT
            where s.ID-key = enrl.STUDENT-ID-in-key
            do begin
                total := total + enrl.FINAL-GRADE;
                count := count + 1
            end;
        if (90 <= total/count) then writeln(s.FIRST-NAME, s.LAST-NAME)
    end
```

SQL for the relational schema

```
select s.FIRST-NAME, s.LAST-NAME
from STUDENT s
where 90 <=
    (select avg enrl.FINAL-GRADE
    from COURSE-ENROLLMENT enrl
    where s.ID-key = enrl.STUDENT-ID-in-key)
```

### Solution for Problem 3-73 on page 200

What are the last names of all the students?

Calculus for the relational schema

```
get s.LAST-NAME
    where s is a STUDENT
```

Ext. Pascal for the relational schema

**for** s **in** *STUDENT*
　　**where true**
　　**do writeln**(s.*LAST-NAME*)

Algebra for the relational schema

(\* distinct *LAST-NAME*s  \*)
*STUDENT* [*LAST-NAME*]

SQL for the relational schema

**select** *LAST-NAME*
**from** *STUDENT*
**where true**

### Solution for Problem 3-74 on page 200

When was Student Russel born?

Calculus for the relational schema

**get** s.*BIRTH-YEAR*
　　**where** (s **is a** *STUDENT*) **and** (s.*LAST-NAME* = 'Russel')

Ext. Pascal for the relational schema

**for** s **in** *STUDENT*
　　**where** s.*LAST-NAME* = 'Russel'
　　**do writeln**(s.*BIRTH-YEAR*)

Algebra for the relational schema

(*STUDENT* [*LAST-NAME* = 'Russel']) [*BIRTH-YEAR*]

### Solution for Problem 3-75 on page 200

What courses has Prof. Graham taught?

Calculus for the relational schema

**get** enrl.*COURSE-NAME-in-key*

    **where** (enrl **is a** *COURSE-ENROLLMENT*) **and**

      (**exists** i **in** *INSTRUCTOR*:

        i.*ID-key* = enrl.*INSTRUCTOR-ID-in-key* **and** i.*LAST-NAME* =
        'Graham')

Ext. Pascal for the relational schema

(* a very inefficient program in order to eliminate duplicates  *)

**for** c **in** *COURSE*

    **where true**

    **do begin**

      OK := false;

      **for** i **in** *INSTRUCTOR*

        **where** i.*LAST-NAME* = 'Graham'

        **do**

          **for** enrl **in** *COURSE-ENROLLMENT*

            **where** (enrl.*INSTRUCTOR-ID-in-key* = i.*ID-key*) **and**
              (c.*NAME-key* = enrl.COURSE-NAME-in-key)

            **do** OK := true;

      **if** OK **then writeln**(c.*NAME-key*)

    **end**

Algebra for the relational schema

((*INSTRUCTOR* [*LAST-NAME* = 'Graham']) [*ID-key* = *INSTRUCTOR-ID-in-key*]
    *COURSE-OFFERING*) [*COURSE-NAME-in-key*]


### Solution for Problem 3-76 on page 201

Print the names of the pairs of students who live together.

Calculus for the relational schema

**get** s1.*LAST-NAME*, s2.*LAST-NAME*

**where** (s1 **is a** *STUDENT*) **and** (s2 **is a** *STUDENT*) **and** (s1.*ADDRESS* = s2.*ADDRESS*) **and not**(s1.*ID-key* = s2.*ID-key*)

Ext. Pascal for the relational schema

(* Both (s1, s2) and (s2, s1) are printed  *)

**for** s1 **in** *STUDENT*

**where true**

**do**

    **for** s2 **in** *STUDENT*

    **where** s1.*ADDRESS* = s2.*ADDRESS* **and** s1.*ID-key* <> s2.*ID-key*

    **do writeln**(s1.*LAST-NAME*, s2.*LAST-NAME*)

Algebra for the relational schema

*STUDENT* [*ID-key/ID-key1*] [*LAST-NAME/LAST-NAME1*]
(* rename columns to prepare for join with another copy of table STUDENT *)
[*ID-key1, ADDRESS, LAST-NAME1*]
(* the attribute ADDRESS is for natural join, the others are to produce the results *)
□
*STUDENT*
(* natural join: two students are paired if their addresses are equal *)
[*ID-key* ≠ *ID-key1*]
(* remove the trivial pairs of a student with himself *)
[*LAST-NAME1, LAST-NAME*]
(* produce the names of the pairs of students *)

### Solution for Problem 3-77 on page 201

Print the names and the addresses of all computer science students.

Calculus for the relational schema

**get** s.*LAST-NAME*, s.*ADDRESS*

    **where** (s **is a** *STUDENT*) **and** (s.*MAJOR-DEPT-MAIN-NAME* = 'Computer Science')

Ext. Pascal for the relational schema

**for** s **in** *STUDENT*

    **where** s.*MAJOR-DEPT-MAIN-NAME* = 'Computer Science'

**do writeln**(s.*LAST-NAME*, s.*ADDRESS*)

Algebra for the relational schema

(*STUDENT* [MAJOR-DEPT-MAIN-NAME = 'Computer Science']) [*LAST-NAME*, *ADDRESS*]

### Solution for Problem 3-78 on page 201

How many computer science students are there in the database?

Calculus for the relational schema

**get** (**count** s

  **where** (s **is a** *STUDENT*) **and** (s.*MAJOR-DEPT-MAIN-NAME* = 'Computer Science'))

Ext. Pascal for the relational schema

sum := 0;

**for** s **in** *STUDENT*

  **where** s.*MAJOR-DEPT-MAIN-NAME* = 'Computer Science'

  **do** sum := sum + 1;

**writeln**(sum)

### Solution for Problem 3-79 on page 201

What is the average grade in the *Databases* course?

Calculus for the relational schema

**get** (**average** enrl.*FINAL-GRADE*

  **where** (enrl **is a** *COURSE-ENROLLMENT*) **and** (enrl.*COURSE-NAME-in-key* = 'DATABASES'))

Ext. Pascal for the relational schema

sum := 0;

grades := 0;

**for** enrl **in** *COURSE-ENROLLMENT*

  **where** enrl.*COURSE-NAME-in-key* = 'DATABASES'

**do begin**
> sum := sum + 1;
> grades := grades + enrl.*FINAL-GRADE*
> **end**;

**writeln**(grades/sum)

### Solution for Problem 3-80 on page 201

List the distinct addresses of the students.

Calculus for the relational schema

**get** n **where** (**exists** s **in** *STUDENT*:   n = s.*ADDRESS*)

Algebra for the relational schema

*STUDENT* [*ADDRESS*]

### Solution for Problem 3-81 on page 201

Find the names of the students who never took a course.

Calculus for the relational schema

**get** s.*LAST-NAME*
> **where** (s **is a** *STUDENT*) **and**
> > (**not exists** enrl **in** *COURSE-ENROLLMENT*:
> > > enrl.*STUDENT-ID-in-key* = s.*ID-key*)

Ext. Pascal for the relational schema

**for** s **in** *STUDENT* **do begin**
> OK := **true**;
> **for** enrl **in** *COURSE-ENROLLMENT*
> > **where** enrl.*STUDENT-ID-in-key* = s.*ID-key*
> > **do** OK := **false**;
> **if** OK **then writeln**(s.*LAST-NAME*)
> **end**

**Solution for Problem 5-3 on page 226**

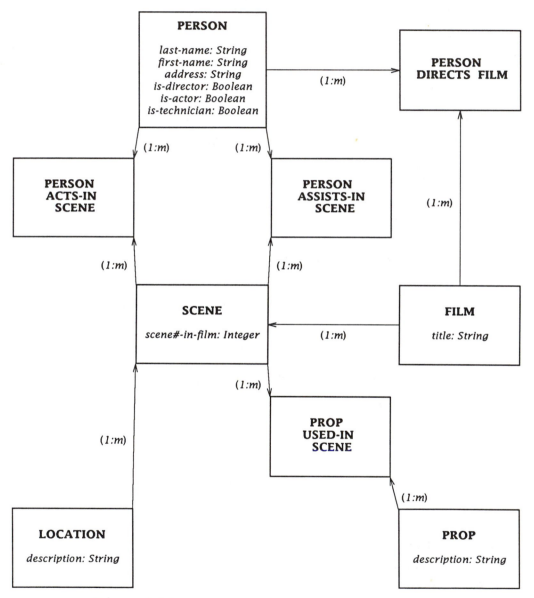

**Figure 8-31.** A network schema for a movie studio.

**Solution for Problem 5-5 on page 227**

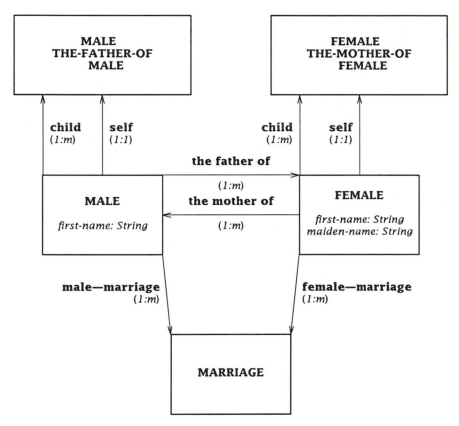

**Figure 8-32.**  A network schema for a clan.

*A constraint*

(**for every** x **in** *MALE*:
    **for every** z **in** *FEMALE*:
       **for every** y1 **in** *MARRIAGE*:
         **for every** y2 **in** *MARRIAGE*:
            **if** (x *male—marriage* y1 **and** z *female—marriage* y1) **and**
               (x *male—marriage* y2 **and** z *female—marriage* y2)
            **then** y1=y2)

**Solution for Problem 5-6 on page 227**

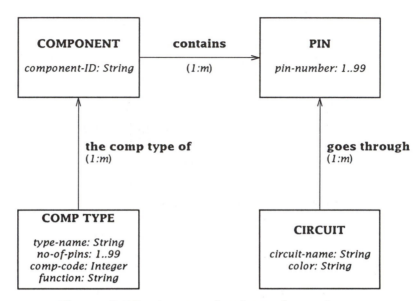

**Figure 8-33.** A network schema for a circuit board.

*Some of the Integrity Constraints Generated During Schema Conversion*

(**for every** x1 **in** *COMPONENT*:

   **for every** x2 **in** *COMPONENT*:

      **if** x1.*component-ID*=x2.*component-ID* **then** x1=x2)
   **and**

(**for every** x1 **in** *CIRCUIT*:

   **for every** x2 **in** *CIRCUIT*:

      **if** x1.*circuit-name*=x2.*circuit-name* **then** x1=x2)
   **and**

(**for every** x1 **in** *COMP-TYPE*:

   **for every** x2 **in** *COMP-TYPE*:

      **if** x1.*comp-code*=x2.*comp-code* **then** x1=x2)

**Solution for Problem 5-7 on page 227**

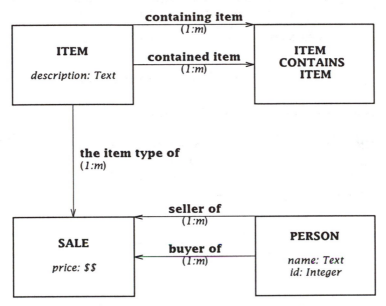

**Figure 8-34.** A network schema of sale transactions.

*Some of the Integrity Constraints Generated During Schema Conversion*

(**for every** x1 **in** *PERSON*:

    **for every** x2 **in** *PERSON*:

        **if** x1.*id*=x2.*id* **then** x1=x2)

    **and**

(**for every** x1 **in** *ITEM*:

    **for every** x2 **in** *ITEM*:

        **if** x1.*description*=x2.*description* **then** x1=x2)

    **and**

(**for every** x **in** *ITEM*:

    **for every** z **in** *ITEM*:

        **for every** y1 **in** *ITEM--CONTAINS--ITEM*:

**for every** y2 **in** *ITEM--CONTAINS--ITEM*:

    **if** (x *containing-item* y1 **and** z *contained-item* y1) **and**
        (x *containing-item* y2 **and** z *contained-item* y2)

    **then** y1=y2)

### Solution for Problem 5-8 on page 227

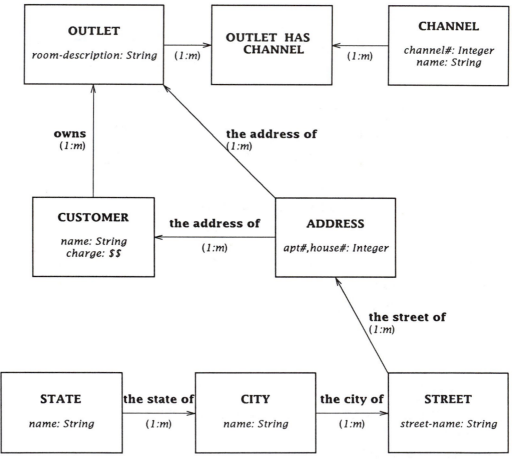

**Figure 8-35.** A network schema for a cable distribution network.

**Solution for Problem 5-9 on page 227**

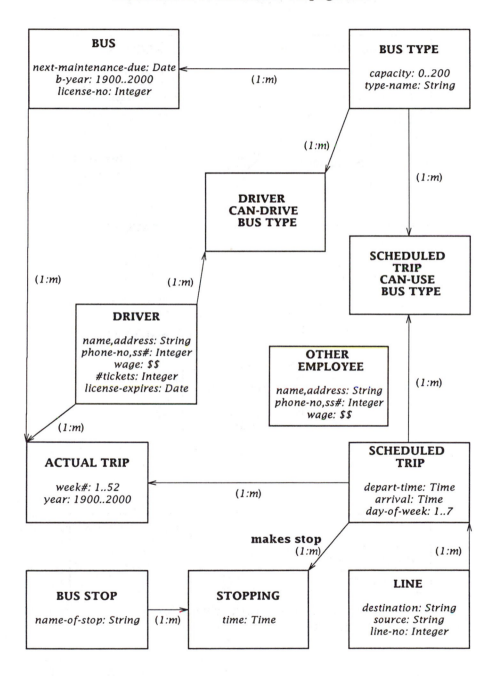

**Solution for Problem 5-11 on page 227**

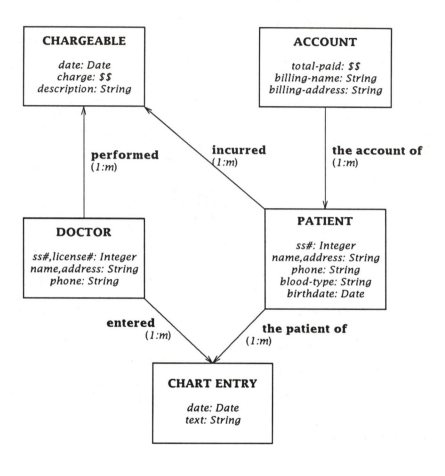

**Figure 8-36.** A network schema for a medical clinic. Alternative I.

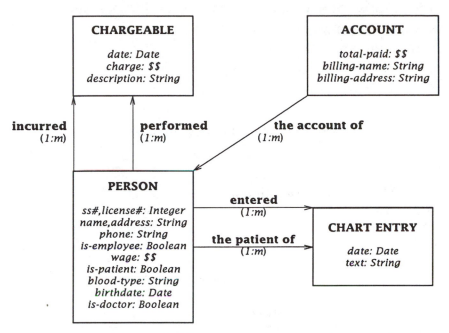

**Figure 8-37.** A network schema for a medical clinic. Alternative II.

*Some of the Integrity Constraints Generated During Schema Conversion*

(**for every** x **in** *PERSON*:   **if** x.*is-doctor* **then** x.*is-employee*) **and**

(**for every** x **in** *PERSON*:   **if not** x *wage* **null**   **then** x.*is-employee*) **and**

(**for every** x **in** *PERSON*:   **if not** x *blood-type* **null**   **then** x.*is-patient*) **and**

(**for every** x **in** *PERSON*:   **if not** x *birthdate* **null**   **then** x.*is-patient*) **and**

(**for every** x **in** *PERSON*:   **for every** y **in** *CHART-ENTRY*:
    **if** x *the-patient-of* y **then** x.*is-patient*) **and**

(**for every** x **in** *PERSON*:

    **for every** y **in** *ACCOUNT*:

        **if** y *the-account-of* x **then** x.*is-patient*)
    **and**

(**for every** x **in** *PERSON*:   **for every** y **in** *CHARGEABLE*:
    **if** x *incurred* y **then** x.*is-patient*) **and**

(**for every** x **in** *PERSON*:   **if not** x *license#* **null**   **then** x.*is-doctor*) **and**

(**for every** x **in** *PERSON*:   **for every** y **in** *CHART-ENTRY*:
   **if** x *entered* y **then** x.*is-doctor*) **and**

(**for every** x **in** *PERSON*:   **for every** y **in** *CHARGEABLE*:
   **if** x *performed* y **then** x.*is-doctor*)

### Solution for Problem 5-12 on page 227

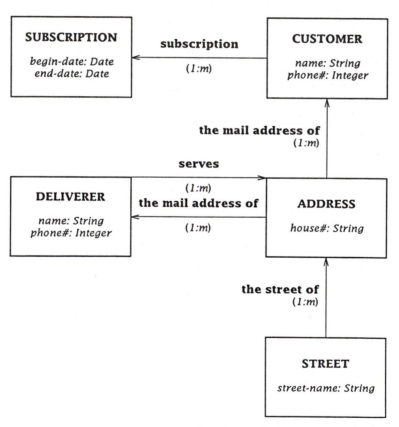

**Figure 8-38.** A network schema for a newspaper distribution department.

**Solution for Problem 5-13 on page 228**

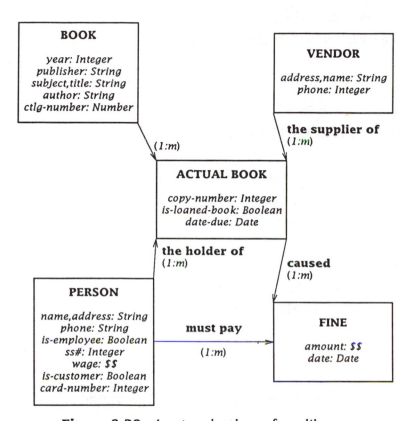

**Figure 8-39.** A network schema for a library.

*Some of the Integrity Constraints Generated During Schema Conversion*

(**for every** x **in** *PERSON*:  **if not** x *ss#* **null**   **then** x.*is-employee*) **and**

(**for every** x **in** *PERSON*:  **if not** x *wage* **null**   **then** x.*is-employee*) **and**

(**for every** x **in** *PERSON*:  **if not** x *card-number* **null**   **then** x.*is-customer*) **and**

(**for every** x **in** *PERSON*:  **for every** y **in** *FINE*:
   **if** x *must-pay* y **then** x.*is-customer*) **and**

(**for every** x **in** *ACTUAL-BOOK*:  **if not** x *date-due* **null**   **then** x.*is-loaned-book*) **and** (**for every** x **in** *PERSON*:

    **for every** y **in** *ACTUAL-BOOK*:

        **if** x *the-holder-of* y

        **then** x.*is-customer* **and** y.*is-loaned-book*)

### Solution for Problem 5-14 on page 232

**get** student.*LAST-NAME*

    **where** student.*BIRTH-YEAR* = 1967

### Solution for Problem 5-15 on page 232

**get** student.*FIRST-NAME*, student.*LAST-NAME*,
instructor.*FIRST-NAME*, instructor.*LAST-NAME*

    **where**

        **exists** work **in** *WORK*:

        **exists** dept **in** *DEPARTMENT*:

            instructor *INSTRUCTOR-WORK* work **and**

            dept *DEPARTMENT-WORK* work **and**

            dept *MAJOR-ST* student

### Solution for Problem 5-16 on page 232

**get** instructor.*LAST-NAME* **where**

    (**for every** dept **in** *DEPARTMENT*:

        **exists** work **in** *WORK*:

            instructor *INSTRUCTOR-WORK* work **and**

            dept *DEPARTMENT-WORK* work)

### Solution for Problem 5-17 on page 232

**get** instructor.*LAST-NAME* **where**

    (**for every** student **in** *STUDENT*:

     **exists** enrl **in** *ENROLLMENT*:

     **exists** offer **in** *OFFERING*:

        student *STUDENT-ENROLLMENT* enrl **and**

        instructor *INSTRUCTOR-OFFERING* offer **and**

        offer *OFFERING-ENROLLMENT* enrl)

### Solution for Problem 5-18 on page 232

**get**

    **for every** student **in** *STUDENT*:

      **exists** enrl **in** *ENROLLMENT*:

        **exists** quarter **in** *QUARTER*:

        **exists** offer **in** *OFFERING*:

           student *STUDENT-ENROLLMENT* enrl **and**

           quarter.*YEAR* = 1995 **and**

           quarter *QUARTER-OFFERING* offer **and**

           offer *OFFERING-ENROLLMENT* enrl

### Solution for Problem 5-19 on page 232

**get** Teacher: instructor.*LAST-NAME*, Student-taught: student.*LAST-NAME*
**where**

   **exists** enrl **in** *ENROLLMENT*:

   **exists** offer **in** *OFFERING*:

      instructor *INSTRUCTOR-OFFERING* offer **and**

      offer *OFFERING-ENROLLMENT* enrl **and**

      student *STUDENT-ENROLLMENT* enrl

### Solution for Problem 5-20 on page 233

**get** student.*LAST-NAME*,

    (**average** enrl.*FINAL-GRADE* **where**

student *STUDENT-ENROLLMENT* enrl)

**where** student **is a** *STUDENT* **and**

**exists** dept **in** *DEPARTMENT*:

**exists** dept-name **in** *DEPARTMENT-NAMING*:

dept-name.*THE-NAME* = 'Computer Science' **and**

dept *DEPARTMENT—DEPARTMENT-NAMING* dept-name **and**

dept *MAJOR-ST* student

### Solution for Problem 5-21 on page 233

**get** (**average** enrl.*FINAL-GRADE*

**where** enrl **is an** *ENROLLMENT* **and**

**exists** prof **in** *INSTRUCTOR*:

**exists** offer **in** *OFFERING*:

prof.*LAST-NAME* = 'Smith' **and**

prof *INSTRUCTOR-OFFERING* offer **and**

offer *OFFFERING-ENROLLMENT* enrl)

### Solution for Problem 5-22 on page 233

**get** (**count** student **where** student **is a** *STUDENT*)

### Solution for Problem 5-23 on page 233

**get** student.*LAST-NAME*

**where** student **is a** *STUDENT* **and**

60 >

(**average** enrl.*FINAL-GRADE* **where**

enrl **is an** *ENROLLMENT* **and**

enrl *THE-STUDENT* student)

### Solution for Problem 5-24 on page 233

**for every** enrl **in** *ENROLLMENT*:
**for every** enrl2 **in** *ENROLLMENT*:
**if**

     student *STUDENT-ENROLLMENT* enrl **and**

     student *STUDENT-ENROLLMENT* enrl2 **and**

     offer *OFFERING-ENROLLMENT* enrl **and**

     offer *OFFERING-ENROLLMENT* enrl2 **then** enrl=enrl2

### Solution for Problem 5-25 on page 233

**userview subcategory**: student *COMPUTER-SCIENCE-MAJOR*
**where**

     student **is a** *STUDENT* **and**

     **exists** dept **in** *DEPARTMENT*:

     **exists** dept-name **in** *DEPARTMENT-NAMING*:

          dept-name.*THE-NAME* = 'Management' **and**

          dept *DEPARTMENT-DEPARTMENT-NAMING* dept-name **and**

          dept *MINOR-ST* student

### Solution for Problem 5-26 on page 233

**connect** enrl *FINAL-GRADE* 100

     **where**

          enrl **is an** *ENROLLMENT* **and**

          **exists** dept-name **in** *DEPARTMENT-NAMING*:

          **exists** dept **in** *DEPARTMENT*:

          **exists** student **in** *STUDENT*:

          **exists** prof **in** *INSTRUCTOR*:

          **exists** offer **in** *OFFERING*:

**exists** quarter **in** *QUARTER*:
**exists** course **in** *COURSE*:
    dept-name.*THE-NAME* = 'Computer Science' **and**
    dept *DEPARTMENT—DEPARTMENT-NAMING* dept-name **and**
    dept *MAJOR-ST* student **and**
    student *STUDENT-ENROLLMENT* enrl **and**
    prof.*LAST-NAME* = 'Smith' **and**
    prof *INSTRUCTOR-OFFERING* offer **and**
    quarter.*YEAR* = 1995 **and**
    quarter.*SEASON* = 'Fall' **and**
    quarter *QUARTER-OFFERING* offer **and**
    course.*NAME* = 'Databases' **and**
    course *COURSE-OFFERING* offer **and**
    offer *OFFERING-ENROLLMENT* enrl

### Solution for Problem 5-27 on page 233

**disconnect** dn   *DEPARTMENT-NAMING*
  **where** dn.*NAME*='CS' **and**
  dn **is a** *DEPARTMENT-NAMING*

### Solution for Problem 5-28 on page 233

**update** enrl *FINAL-GRADE* 100
  **where**
    enrl **is an** *ENROLLMENT* **and**
      **exists** dept-name **in** *DEPARTMENT-NAMING*:
      **exists** dept **in** *DEPARTMENT*:
      **exists** student **in** *STUDENT*:
      **exists** prof **in** *INSTRUCTOR*:
      **exists** offer **in** *OFFERING*:

    **exists** course **in** *COURSE*:

        dept-name.*THE-NAME* = 'Computer Science' **and**

        dept *DEPARTMENT—DEPARTMENT-NAMING* dept-name **and**

        dept *MAJOR-ST* student **and**

        student.*LAST-NAME* = 'Johnson' **and**

        student.*FIRST-NAME* = 'Jack' **and**

        student *STUDENT-ENROLLMENT* enrl **and**

        prof.*LAST-NAME* = 'Smith' **and**

        prof *INSTRUCTOR-OFFERING* offer **and**

        course.*NAME* = 'Databases' **and**

        course *COURSE-OFFERING* offer **and**

        offer *OFFERING-ENROLLMENT* enrl

### Solution for Problem 5-29 on page 234

**update** enrl    *FINAL-GRADE*    1.1*enrl.*FINAL-GRADE*

    **where**

        enrl **is an** *ENROLLMENT* **and**

        **exists** prof **in** *INSTRUCTOR*:

        **exists** offer **in** *OFFERING*:

        **exists** course **in** *COURSE*:

            prof.*LAST-NAME* = 'Smith' **and**

            prof *INSTRUCTOR-OFFERING* offer **and**

            course.*NAME* = 'Databases' **and**

            course *COURSE-OFFERING* offer **and**

            offer *OFFERING-ENROLLMENT* enrl

**Solution for Problem 6-1 on page 267**

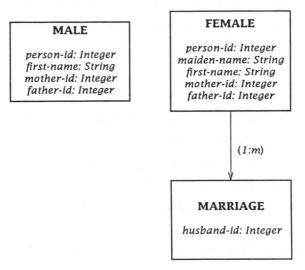

**Figure 8-40.** A hierarchical schema for a clan.

*Some of the Integrity Constraints Generated During Schema Conversion*

(**for every** x **in** *FEMALE*:

   x *mother-id* **null or**

   **exists** y **in** *FEMALE*:  x.mother-id = y.person-id) **and**

(**for every** x **in** *MARRIAGE*:

   **exists** y **in** *MALE*:  y.person-id = x.husband-id) **and**

(**for every** x **in** *FEMALE*:

   **for every** y1 **in** *MARRIAGE*:

     **for every** y2 **in** *MARRIAGE*:

       **if** x *female—marriage* y1 **and** x *female—marriage* y2 **and**
        y1.husband-id = y2.husband-id **then** y1=y2)

**Solution for Problem 6-2 on page 267**

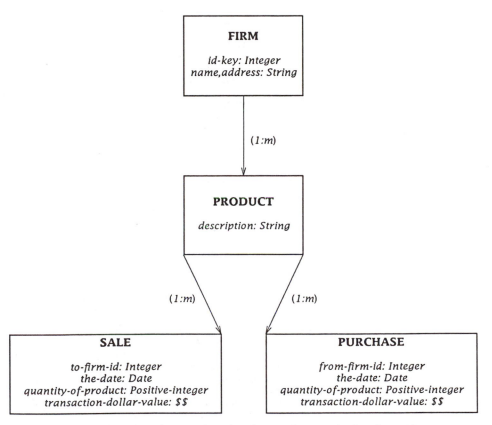

**Figure 8-41.** A hierarchical schema for a wholesaler. Alternative I.

The relation from the root segment *FIRM* means:

- Relation **manufactures** from *FIRM* to *PRODUCT* (*1:m,onto*)

*Some of the Integrity Constraints Generated During Schema Conversion*

(**for every** x **in** *SALE*:

    **exists** y **in** *FIRM*:  x.*to-firm-id* = y.*id-key*) **and**

**(for every** x **in** *PURCHASE*:

   **exists** y **in** *FIRM*:

      x.*from-firm-id* = y.*id-key*)

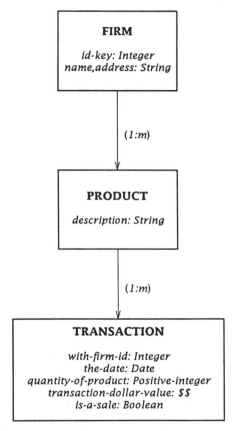

**Figure 8-42.** A hierarchical schema for a wholesaler. Alternative II.

*Some of the Integrity Constraints Generated During Schema Conversion*

**(for every** x **in** *TRANSACTION*:

   **exists** y **in** *FIRM*:

      x.*with-firm-id* = y.*id-key*)

## Solution for Problem 6-3 on page 267

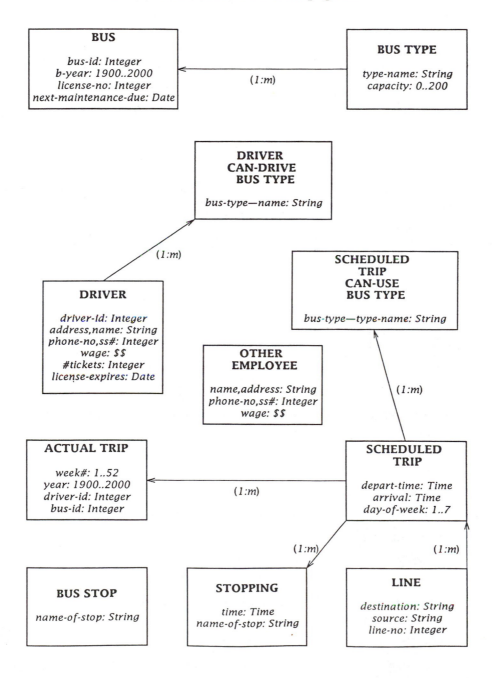

**BUS**

bus-id: Integer
b-year: 1900..2000
license-no: Integer
next-maintenance-due: Date

(1:m)

**BUS TYPE**

type-name: String
capacity: 0..200

**DRIVER
CAN-DRIVE
BUS TYPE**

bus-type—name: String

(1:m)

**DRIVER**

driver-id: Integer
address,name: String
phone-no,ss#: Integer
wage: $$
#tickets: Integer
license-expires: Date

**SCHEDULED
TRIP
CAN-USE
BUS TYPE**

bus-type—type-name: String

**OTHER
EMPLOYEE**

name,address: String
phone-no,ss#: Integer
wage: $$

(1:m)

**ACTUAL TRIP**

week#: 1..52
year: 1900..2000
driver-id: Integer
bus-id: Integer

(1:m)

**SCHEDULED
TRIP**

depart-time: Time
arrival: Time
day-of-week: 1..7

(1:m)    (1:m)

**BUS STOP**

name-of-stop: String

**STOPPING**

time: Time
name-of-stop: String

**LINE**

destination: String
source: String
line-no: Integer

**Solution for Problem 6-4 on page 267**

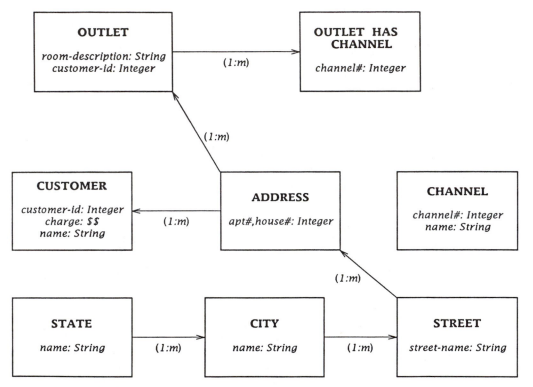

**Figure 8-43.** A hierarchical schema for a cable distribution network.

*Some of the Integrity Constraints Generated During Schema Conversion*

**(for every** x **in** *OUTLET--HAS--CHANNEL*:

    **exists** y **in** *CHANNEL*:    y.channel# = x.channel#) **and**

**(for every** x **in** *OUTLET*:

    **for every** y1 **in** *OUTLET--HAS--CHANNEL*:

        **for every** y2 **in** *OUTLET--HAS--CHANNEL*:

            **if** x --- y1 **and** x --- y2 **and** y1.channel# = y2.channel# **then**
            y1=y2)

**Solution for Problem 6-5 on page 267**

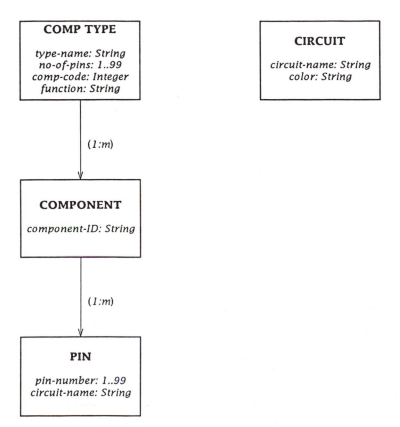

**Figure 8-44.** A hierarchical schema for a circuit board.

*Some of the Integrity Constraints Generated During Schema Conversion*

(**for every** x **in** *PIN*:

    x *circuit-name* **null or**

    **exists** y **in** *CIRCUIT*:     x.*circuit-name* = y.*circuit-name*)

**Solution for Problem 6-6 on page 267**

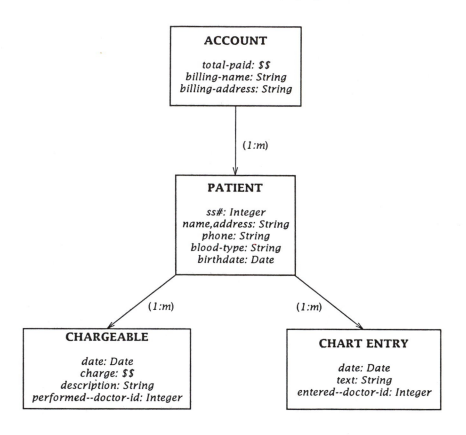

**Figure 8-45.** A hierarchical schema for a medical clinic. Alternative I.

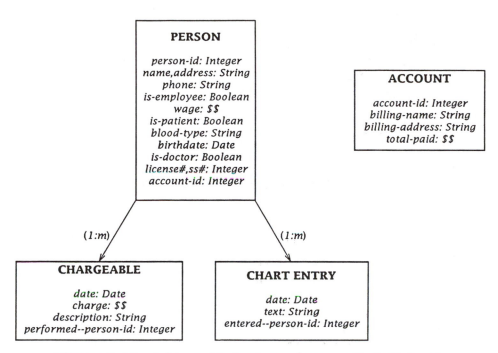

**Figure 8-46.** A hierarchical schema for a medical clinic. Alternative II.

*Some of the Integrity Constraints Generated During Schema Conversion*

**(for every** x **in** *PERSON*:   **if not** x *wage* **null   then** x.*is-employee*) **and**

**(for every** x **in** *PERSON*:   **if not** x *license#* **null   then** x.*is-doctor*) **and**

**(for every** x **in** *PERSON*:   **if not** x *blood-type* **null   then** x.*is-patient*) **and**

**(for every** x **in** *PERSON*:   **if not** x *birthdate* **null   then** x.*is-patient*) **and**

**(for every** x **in** *PERSON*:   **if not** x *account-id* **null   then** x.*is-patient*) **and**

**(for every** x **in** *PERSON*:   **for every** y **in** *CHART-ENTRY*:
    **if** x *the-patient-of* y **then** x.*is-patient*) **and**

**(for every** x **in** *PERSON*:   **for every** y **in** *CHARGEABLE*:
    **if** x *for-of* y **then** x.*is-patient*) **and and**

**(for every** x **in** *CHART-ENTRY*:

    **exists** y **in** *PERSON*:

y.is-doctor **and**

y.person-id = x.entered--person-id)

**and**

(**for every** x **in** *CHARGEABLE*:

    **exists** y **in** *PERSON*:

        y.is-doctor **and**

        y.person-id = x.performed--person-id)

**Solution for Problem 6-7 on page 267**

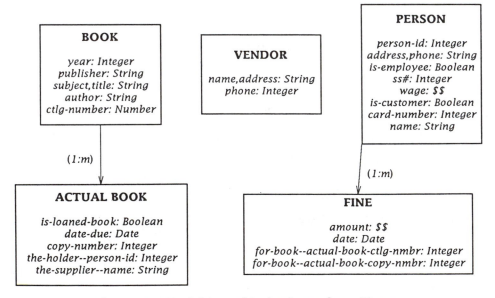

**Figure 8-47.** A hierarchical schema for a library.

*Some of the Integrity Constraints Generated During Schema Conversion*

(**for every** x **in** *PERSON*:  **if not** x *ss#* **null**  **then** x.*is-employee*) **and**

(**for every** x **in** *PERSON*:  **if not** x *wage* **null**  **then** x.*is-employee*) **and**

(**for every** x **in** *PERSON*:  **if not** x *card-number* **null**  **then** x.*is-customer*) **and**

(**for every** x **in** *PERSON*:  **for every** y **in** *FINE*:

    **if** x *must-pay* y **then** x.*is-customer*) **and**

(**for every** x **in** *ACTUAL-BOOK*:   **if not** x *date-due* **null**   **then** x.*is-loaned-book*)

(**for every** x **in** *PERSON*:

> **for every** y **in** *ACTUAL-BOOK*:
>
> > **if** x.person-id = y.the-holder--person-id
> >
> > **then** x.is-customer **and** y.is-loaned-book)

### Solution for Problem 6-8 on page 267

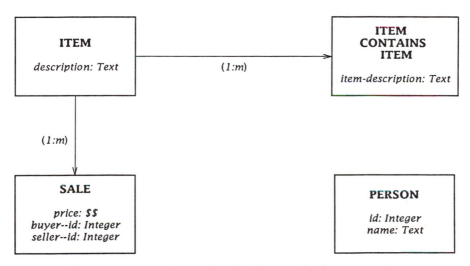

**Figure 8-48.**  A hierarchical schema of sale transaction.

*Some of the Integrity Constraints Generated During Schema Conversion*

(**for every** x **in** *ITEM--CONTAINS--ITEM*:

> **exists** y **in** *ITEM*:   y.description = x.item-description) **and**

(**for every** x **in** *ITEM*:

> **for every** y1 **in** *ITEM--CONTAINS--ITEM*:
>
> > **for every** y2 **in** *ITEM--CONTAINS--ITEM*:
> >
> > > **if** x *contained-item* y1 **and** x *contained-item* y2 **and** y1.item-description = y2.item-description   **then** y1=y2)

### Solution for Problem 6-9 on page 267

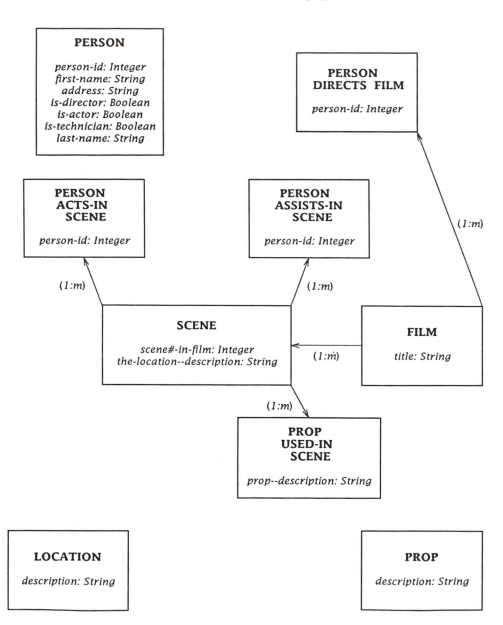

# 9 APPENDIX

# FIFTH-GENERATION LANGUAGES

The optional sections of Chapter 3 are prerequisite to reading this Appendix.

## 9.1. Limitations of Non-procedural Database Languages

Not every query can be specified in the languages based on Predicate Calculus.

---

*Example 9-1.*

A person $x$ *can improve grades of* a person $y$ if $x$ teaches $y$ or $x$ teaches a person who *can improve grades of $y$.* A query to find whether $x$ can improve grades of $y$ cannot be specified in the calculus.

---

*Example 9-2.*

Consider the following relational subschema of the bill of material of items. Each row in the table contains the names of two items where one item has the other as its immediate component.

---

```
┌─────────────────────────────┐
│      COMPONENT              │
│                             │
│  contained-item: String     │
│  containing-item: String    │
└─────────────────────────────┘
```

We cannot specify in Predicate Calculus, or in SQL, or in Relational Algebra the following query:

'Print a list of all the pairs of items which directly or indirectly contain one another.'

The queries of the above examples are *recursive* queries. Some unexpressible recursive queries would become expressible if we extend the calculus with additional constructs, such as the so-called *transitive closure* operator or a more powerful *fixed-point* operator. But whatever additional constructs we add to the Predicate Calculus, it would still be possible to encounter a query which cannot be specified in the extended language. A solution to this problem will be suggested in a later section.

## 9.2. Prolog-like languages

In the section on the calculus for transactions we have used an *insert* operation with the following syntax:

**insert into** *category* (*relation*$_1$: *expression*$_1$ , . . . , *relation*$_k$: *expression*$_k$)
**where** *condition*

Let us consider now a program which iteratively performs a set of **insert** statements and terminates when there is nothing more to insert.

*Example 9-3.*

Let *ITEM-NAME* be a concrete category of strings.

The following program augments the table *COMPONENT* by all the pairs of items which directly or indirectly contain one another.

   **repeat**

      **insert into** *COMPONENT*

         (*CONTAINING-ITEM*: containing,

         *CONTAINED-ITEM*: contained)

      **where**

> **exists** intermediate **in** *ITEM-NAME*:
>
> > *COMPONENT* (*CONTAINING-ITEM*: containing, *CONTAINED-ITEM*: intermediate) **and**
> >
> > *COMPONENT* (*CONTAINING-ITEM*: intermediate, *CONTAINED-ITEM*: contained)
>
> **until** nothing new has been inserted in the last iteration

A **Prolog-like database program** is an equivalent of a program with one *repeat* loop enclosing several *insert* statements:

**repeat**

   *insert-statements*

**until** nothing new has been inserted in the last iteration

(We interpret the *insert* operation as adding only information which is not already there.)

Normally, Prolog-like languages allow only very primitive conditions within the *insert* statements: they do not allow the quantifier **"for every"** or complex expressions within those conditions. In exchange for this limitation, the Prolog-like languages can perform the program by a much faster algorithm than the obvious straight-forward implementation of the loop.

A Prolog-like program can be used for retrieval of information from the database if instead of inserting new objects into the existing categories in the database we perform insertion into output tables.

---

*Example 9-4.*

The following program will produce a table *OUTPUT-COMPONENT* which will be composed of all the pairs of items which directly or indirectly contain one another. The input is the original table COMPONENT which is composed of the pairs of items directly containing one another.

   **repeat**

   > **insert into** *OUTPUT-COMPONENT*
   >
   > > (*CONTAINING-ITEM*: containing,
   > >
   > > *CONTAINED-ITEM*: contained)
   >
   > **where**
   >
   > > *COMPONENT* (*CONTAINING-ITEM*: containing,

*CONTAINED-ITEM*: contained);

**insert into** *OUTPUT-COMPONENT*

(*CONTAINING-ITEM*: containing,

*CONTAINED-ITEM*: contained)

**where**

**exists** intermediate **in** *ITEM-NAME*:

*COMPONENT* (*CONTAINING-ITEM*: containing,
*CONTAINED-ITEM*: intermediate) **and**

*OUTPUT-COMPONENT* (*CONTAINING-ITEM*:
intermediate, *CONTAINED-ITEM*:
contained)

**until** nothing new has been inserted in the last iteration

(\* The first insert statement will be performed only
once. \*)

The above description of Prolog-like languages has a strong procedural flavor
because of the 'repeat...until' loop. We can describe a Prolog-like program
non-procedurally — as an assertion which links the relations of the input
database and the relations to be produced as the output of the query.

*Example 9-5.*

The above query can be non-procedurally regarded as the following
assertion:

**for every** containing **in** *ITEM-NAME*:

**for every** contained **in** *ITEM-NAME*:

**if** *COMPONENT*

(*CONTAINING-ITEM*: containing,

*CONTAINED-ITEM*: contained)

**then** *OUTPUT-COMPONENT*

(*CONTAINING-ITEM*: containing,

*CONTAINED-ITEM*: contained)

**and**

> **for every** containing **in** *ITEM-NAME*:
>> **for every** contained **in** *ITEM-NAME*:
>>> **for every** intermediate **in** *ITEM-NAME*:
>>> **if**
>>>> *COMPONENT* (*CONTAINING-ITEM*: containing, *CONTAINED-ITEM*: intermediate) **and**
>>>>
>>>> *OUTPUT-COMPONENT* (*CONTAINING-ITEM*: intermediate, *CONTAINED-ITEM*: contained)
>>> **then** *OUTPUT-COMPONENT*
>>>> (*CONTAINING-ITEM*: containing,
>>>>
>>>> *CONTAINED-ITEM*: contained)
>
> The pragmatic meaning of such an assertion is:
>> Output a set of tuples which, when regarded as a table *OUTPUT-COMPONENT*, would make the above assertion come true. Do not output any extra tuples which are not needed to make the assertion *true*.

The Prolog-like languages described above are sometimes referred to as **fifth-generation database languages**, although this term can be broadly applied to all powerful non-procedural database languages, particularly the languages based on Predicate Calculus.

The actual syntax of Prolog-like languages is usually somewhat different from the 'insert' notation shown above, but it is equivalent to that notation. The loop specification is omitted. The quantifiers 'exists' in the conditions are implicit. (No ambiguity arises since the 'for every' quantifier is normally not allowed as a part of the insert conditions in Prolog-like languages.)

> *Example 9-6.*
>
> The above program would be written as follows in some Prolog-like languages:
>> *OUTPUT-COMPONENT*(*CONTAINING-ITEM*: containing, *CONTAINED-ITEM*: contained) ←
>>> *COMPONENT* (*CONTAINING-ITEM*: containing, *CONTAINED-ITEM*: contained);
>>
>> *OUTPUT-COMPONENT* (*CONTAINING-ITEM*: containing, *CONTAINED-ITEM*: contained) ←

> COMPONENT (*CONTAINING-ITEM*: containing,
> *CONTAINED-ITEM*: intermediate),
>
> *OUTPUT-COMPONENT (CONTAINING-ITEM*:
> intermediate, *CONTAINED-ITEM*: contained)

The expressive power of Prolog-like database languages, that is, the ability of these languages to express a wide range of queries, depends, in part, on what is allowed to appear on the right side of the '←' statement. However, even if we allow arbitrary first order predicate calculus assertions on the right side of the statements, there would still be many reasonable queries which cannot be specified in the Prolog-like database languages, without sacrificing the non-procedurality of the language.† The cause of such limitation is the limit to what one can do with the "insert until nothing new comes" construct.

## 9.3.  The Maximal Expressive Power

A non-procedural language more powerful than the Prolog-like database languages has been proposed by N. Rishe.*

In this language, a query is specified simply as an assertion about the relations to appear in the output, linking those relations to the information in the input instantaneous database.

> *Example 9-7.*
>
> The previously considered example 9-5 on page 378, which was an assertion equivalent to a Prolog program producing the table of the pairs of components indirectly containing one another, is also an example of a query specification in the language discussed in this section.

---

† Some Prolog-like languages allow specification of functions, which increases their expressive power. However, the use of those functions, which act like subroutines logically defined by the user, greatly reduces the non-procedurality of the language.

* N. Rishe. "Postconditional Semantics of Data Base Queries." *Mathematical Foundations of Programming Semantics.* A. Melton, ed. Lecture Notes in Computer Science, vol. 239. Springer-Verlag, 1986.
The formal foundations of the language and related developments appear in N. Rishe. *Database Semantics.* Tech. Rep. TRCS87-2, University of California, Santa Barbara, 1987.

*Example 9-8.*

The following is an assertion stating that the output shall display the item which indirectly contains all the items (if such a super-item exists).

We assume that the userview has

- Relation **contains** from *ITEM-NAME* to *ITEM-NAME* (*m:m*)

The output is the category *SUPERITEM-OUTPUT*. This category will have at most one object — the superitem. In the formulation of the query we define a temporary relation *INDIRECTLY-CONTAINS*. The assertion states that this temporary relation relates all the pairs of items indirectly containing one another. (This includes an item containing itself.)   This temporary relation will not become a part of the output.

**for every** item **in** *ITEM-NAME*:

    item *INDIRECTLY-CONTAINS* item

**and**

**for every** containing **in** *ITEM-NAME*:

    **for every** contained **in** *ITEM-NAME*:

        **for every** intermediate **in** *ITEM-NAME*:

            **if**    containing *CONTAINS* intermediate **and**
                    intermediate *INDIRECTLY-CONTAINS* contained

            **then** containing *INDIRECTLY-CONTAINS* contained

**and**

**for every** si **in** *ITEM-NAME*:

    **if**

        (**for every** item **in** *ITEM-NAME*:

            si *INDIRECTLY-CONTAINS* item)

    **then** si **is a** *SUPERITEM-OUTPUT*

The pragmatic meaning of such an assertion is:

    Create an instantaneous relation *INDIRECTLY-CONTAINS* and an instantaneous category *SUPERITEM-OUTPUT*, which would make the above assertion come true. Output the

> *SUPERITEM-OUTPUT* category and discard the temporary relation *INDIRECTLY-CONTAINS.* Do not output any extra objects or relationships which are not needed to make the assertion *true.*

---

*Example 9-9.*

The following is an assertion specifying the relation *CAN-IMPROVE-THE-GRADES-OF.*

**for every** s **in** *STUDENT:*

    **for every** i **in** *INSTRUCTOR:*

        (**if** i *TAUGHT* s

           **then** i *CAN-IMPROVE-THE-GRADES-OF* s) **and**

      **for every** middleman **in** *STUDENT:*

        **if**   i *TAUGHT* middleman **and**
           middleman *CAN-IMPROVE-THE-GRADES-OF* s

        **then** i *CAN-IMPROVE-THE-GRADES-OF* s

---

In a sense, this language is a superset of the Prolog-like database languages. A Prolog-like database program can also be regarded as an assertion about the output relations. However, the Prolog-like languages allow only *some* assertions: those assertions which are equivalent to the "insert until nothing new comes" interpretation.

---

*Example 9-10.*

It is known that several items have more components than the item CAR. Display one of those items.

    **exists** output-item **in** *OUTPUT-ITEM:*

        (**count** car-component **where** 'Car' *CONTAINS:* car-component) <

        (**count** item-component **where** output-item *CONTAINS* item-component)

---

The aggregate functions, like the function **count** in the above example, are not strictly necessary in the language. Every query can be expressed without aggregate functions*. The aggregate function can be regarded as convenient abbreviations for non-aggregate constructs.

The following is an informal description of the semantics of a query in this language. This is also a description of the semantics of the Prolog-like languages (since every Prolog-like program can be regarded as an assertion, the Prolog-like programs are a subset of all queries expressed by assertions).

- A query is an assertion about a virtual instantaneous database. This virtual database exists only in the programmer's mind. The virtual database contains all the information of the input instantaneous database and, in addition, the output which the query should produce. Thus, the schema of the virtual database consists of all the relations (including the categories) of the input database and all the relations of the output. The output relations may form the headings of columns and tables in the output. One query can produce several tables in its output, or, in general, any interrelated information, like a whole instantaneous database.

  In addition to the input and output relations, the virtual database may contain intermediate relations which are not in the input, nor are they

---

* The following is a specification of the query of the previous example without the aggregate function count.

**exists** output-item **in** *OUTPUT-ITEM*:

(* There is a relation *MATCHES* between the components of CAR and the components of the output-item. It is m:1 and "total", but not "onto" the components of the output-item: there exists at least one extra component of the output-item not matched by a component of CAR. *)

  (**for every** cc **in** *ITEM-NAME*:    **if** 'CAR' *CONTAINS* cc **then**

    **exists** oc **in** *ITEM-NAME*:

      output-item *CONTAINS* oc **and** cc *MATCHES* oc **and**

      (* The car-component cc matches with nothing else but oc *)

        **for every** z **in** *ITEM-NAME*:    **if** cc *MATCHES* z **then** z=oc)

  **and**

  (* There is at least one *extra* component of the output item *)

    **exists** oc **in** *ITEM-NAME*:    output-item *CONTAINS* oc **and**

      **not exists** cc **in** *ITEM-NAME*:    cc MATCHES oc

The pragmatic meaning of such an assertion is:

Create an instantaneous relation *MATCHES* and an instantaneous category *OUTPUT-ITEM* which would make the above assertion come true. Output the *OUTPUT-ITEM* category and discard the temporary relation *MATCHES*. Do not output any extra objects or relationships which are not needed to make the assertion *true*.

needed in the output, but they are needed to establish connection between the input and the output.

- Now, consider all the potential virtual databases which satisfy the assertion. It is possible that there is no such database at all. Then there is no output. Pragmatically, this means that the program goes into an infinite loop.

- It is possible that there is exactly one such virtual database. The output relations are then extracted from the virtual database and delivered to the user.

- It is possible that there several such virtual databases satisfying the assertion, $vdb_1, vdb_2, \cdots$, but all the information contained in $vdb_1$ is also contained in the rest of them. That means, that in addition to the minimally required output, the other virtual databases contain some extra, possibly irrelevant, information. The database $vdb_1$ is minimal in the sense of information content. Only the minimal possible virtual database will be taken into account by the language interpreter.

- It is possible that there are several possible virtual databases satisfying the assertion where none of the virtual databases contains all the information of any other. This means that there is no single minimal database. In this case, all of those databases are regarded as equally suitable to produce the output for the user. The system will select one of them.

The last case appears in **non-deterministic** queries — the queries in which the user does not wish to bother to specify what exact output he should receive, but only specifies some requirement to be satisfied by the output.

---

*Example 9-11.*

Display the last name of *one* student.

  **exists** s **in** *STUDENT*:

    s.*LAST-NAME* **is an** *OUTPUT-STUDENT-NAME*

---

The capability of non-deterministic specification saves the user's effort and also allows for a greater optimization potential.

---

*Example 9-12.*

In the above example, the system will fetch one student which happens to the first in the physical access path to the database.

> Had the user specified precisely a specific student, it would take longer to deliver that from the database.

This language has no limitation of the expressive power — every query that can be programmed in any procedural data manipulation language also can be specified non-procedurally in Rishe's language.*

While the language can express any query, this generality might also allow for unreasonable queries, that is, queries which would not make any sense.

> *Example 9-13.*
>
> A query to find the average social security number of two persons makes no sense.
>
> A query to find the average between two persons, as if they were integers, makes even less sense.

It may be desirable to prevent the user from asking such queries. Such a constraint would both eliminate some user errors and improve the efficiency of the system. An interesting feature of the language is the capability to restrict itself to the reasonable queries, by accepting criteria of reasonability as a parameter. When such criteria are given as a parameter, those queries which are unreasonable according to the criteria are syntactically screened out. The criteria are defined in terms of the scalar operators which make sense in different concrete categories.

> *Example 9-14.*
>
> The operators meaningful on the final grades are +, −, >, <, and so on. There are no operators except the equality verification (=, ≠) on the id's of the students. Constants of the type *STUDENT-ID* are allowed. (Unlike that, there are no constants in the abstract categories.)

The sublanguage restricted according to the reasonability criteria can express *every* reasonable query that can programmed in any procedural language.†

---

* Formally, this means that if we encode the databases by integers, then every partial recursive function would be expressible. The encoding, though, is not trivial, since the databases are unordered sets of information, and, moreover, contain abstract objects which can be distinguished from each other only by relations in which the objects participate.

† Formally, the set of *reasonable* queries is defined in terms of isomorphisms of databases. Two instantaneous databases are isomorphic if they

The language can also be used to specify integrity constraints, inference rules, userviews, and update transactions. An update transaction can be specified as two sets of facts: a set of old facts to remove from the database and a set of new facts to insert into the database. Those two sets of facts are extracted from an output of a query. The output of a query (specified as an assertion) may contain relations marked with a suffix '-insert'. The facts of those relations are to be inserted. The facts of the relations marked with the suffix '-delete' are to be deleted.

---

*Example 9-15.*

Remove all the grades.

> **for every** e **in** *ENROLLMENT*:
>
> > e     *FINAL-GRADE-delete*     s.*FINAL-GRADE*

---

*Example 9-16.*

Create a new student Veronica. Assume that the category *EXISTING-OBJECT* is the supercategory of all the categories.

> **exists** s **in** *STUDENT-insert*:
>
> > **not** (s **is an** *EXISTING-OBJECT*) **and**
> >
> > s     *FIRST-NAME-insert*     'Veronica'

(The condition '**not** (s **is an** *EXISTING-OBJECT*)' can be stated implicitly.)

---

*Example 9-17.*

Enroll every student in the *Databases* course. It is assumed that at least one offering of the course exists.

> **for every** s **in** *STUDENT*:
>
> > **exists** e **in** *ENROLLMENT-insert*:
> >
> > > **not** (e **is an** *EXISTING-OBJECT*) **and**

---

cannot be distinguished by means of the available operators. A query is reasonable if for isomorphic inputs it produces isomorphic outputs.

> e.*THE-STUDENT-insert*=s **and**
>
> e.*THE-OFFERING-insert.THE-COURSE.NAME =*
>   'Databases'

A problem with this language is that there is no practical efficient implementation for the language. Nevertheless, the language is useful for the following purposes:

- as a high-level language in which to write the specification of a problem, before that specification is translated into a lower-level program in the language supported by the actual DBMS

- as a language model from which sublanguages can be derived and efficiently implemented

- as a tool to compare and evaluate the power of practical database languages

- as a tool to reason about databases.

## 9.4.  User-friendly Interfaces

The predicate languages may be unfriendly to the unsophisticated user. However, user-friendly **"syntactic sugar"** can, and has been, added to some predicate calculus languages to enhance their usability. This "sugar" can range from simple syntactic abbreviations to menu-driven languages and to natural language interfaces in which the user can enter a query in what might look like plain English or Swahili.

An interesting user interface to a relational calculus-based language is the **Query-By-Example** language developed by M. Zloof and now used commercially. In this language, the user specifies his query by drawing, with the system's assistance, tables on a two-dimensional screen.

> *Example 9-18.*
>
> The following table will be an on-the-screen specification of the query
>
>> 'Print the names and the seasons of the course offerings prior to 1900.'

**COURSE OFFERING**

| INSTRUCTOR-ID | COURSE-NAME | YEAR | SEASON |
|---|---|---|---|
| | **print** | <1990 | **print** |

---

*Example 9-19.*

The following table will be an on-the-screen specification of the query

> 'Print the names and the seasons of the course offerings by
> the instructors who also taught *Databases*.'

This query uses a variable _dbinstructor in order to specify a relationship (join) between different rows of the table, so that the related rows have the same value in the column *INSTRUCTOR-ID*. The variables in this language are preceded by an underscore ('_').

---

**COURSE OFFERING**

| INSTRUCTOR-ID | COURSE-NAME | YEAR | SEASON |
|---|---|---|---|
| _dbinstructor | **print** | <1990 | **print** |
| _dbinstructor | Databases | | |

Some Prolog-based languages have user-friendly interfaces to subsets of the languages. The Rishe language described in the previous section also has a user-friendly interface which can be used only for intermediate specifications of data manipulation tasks — it is not used to write the actual programs since there is no efficient implementation.

# BIBLIOGRAPHY

ACM. *Proceedings of the fifth ACM SIGACT-SIGMOD symposium on principles of database systems: March 24-26, 1986, Cambridge, Massachusetts.* New York, N.Y.; Association for Computing Machinery, 1985.

ACM. *Proceedings of the fourth ACM SIGACT-SIGMOD symposium on principles of database systems, March 25-27, 1985, Portland, Oregon.* New York, N.Y.; Association for Computer Machinery, 1985.

ACM. *Proceedings of the third ACM SIGACT-SIGMOD symposium on principles of database systems, April 2-4, 1984, Waterloo, Ontario, Canada.* New York, N.Y.; Association for Computing Machinery; 1984.

Agosti, Maristella. *Database design: a classified and annotated bibliography.* Cambridge [Cambridgeshire]; New York; Cambridge University Press, 1986.

Alagic, Suad. *Relational database technology.* New York; Springer-Verlag, 1986.

Albano, A., De Antonellis, V., and Di Leva, A., eds. *Computer-aided database design: the DATAID project.* Amsterdam; North-Holland, 1985.

Andersen, D., Cooper, C., and Dempsey, B. *dBase III: tips & traps.* Berkeley, Calif.; Osborne/McGraw-Hill, 1986.

Appelrath, Hans-Jurgen. *Von Datenbanken zu Expertensystemen.* Berlin; Springer-Verlag, 1985.

Ariav, Gadi, and Clifford, James. *NYU symposium on new directions for database systems.* Norwood, N.J.; Ablex Pub. Corp., 1986.

Ausiello, G. , and Atzeni, P., eds. *ICDT '86: International conference on database theory, Rome, Italy, September 8-10, 1986: proceedings.* Berlin; Springer-Verlag, 1986.

Banet, Bernard A., Davis, Judith R., and Marshak, R. T. *Data base management systems: the desk-top generation.* New York; McGraw-Hill, 1985.

Barnes, Lan. *Introducing dBase III.* New York; McGraw-Hill, 1985.

Bell, D. A. *Database performance.* Maidenhead, Berkshire, England; Pergamon Infotech, 1984.

Benton, Charles J. *The data base guide: how to select, organize, and implement data base systems for microcomputers.* Bowie, Md.; R.J. Brady, 1984.

Berg, J.L., ed. *Data base directions II: the conversion problem.* U.S. Department of Commerce, Washington, D.C.; ACM-SIGDB Data Base and ACM-SIGMOD Record, vol. 12, no. 2, Jan. 1982.

Berg, J.L., ed. *Data base directions — the conversion problem.* U.S. Department of Commerce, Washington, D.C.; NBS Special Publication 500—64, 1980.

Bernstein, Philip A., Hadzilacos, V., and Goodman, N. *Concurrency control and recovery in database systems.* Reading, Mass.; Addison-Wesley, 1987.

Bonczek, Robert H., Holsapple, C.W., and Whinston, A. B. *Micro database management: practical techniques for application development.* New York; Academic Press, 1984.

Booth, G.M. *The design of complex information systems: common sense methods for success.* New York; McGraw-Hill, 1983.

Brackett, Michael H. *Developing data structured databases.* Englewood Cliffs, N.J.; Prentice-Hall, 1987.

Bramer, M.A., and Bramer, D. *The fifth generation: an annotated bibliography.* Reading, Mass.; Addison-Wesley, 1984.

Brathwaite, Ken S. *Data administration: selected topics of data control.* New York; Wiley, 1985.

Brodie, M. L., and Mylopoulos, J., eds. *On knowledge base management systems: integrating artificial intelligence and database technologies.* New York; Springer-Verlag, 1986.

Brodie, M.L. *Data abstraction, databases, and conceptual modelling: an annotated bibliography.* U.S. Department of Commerce, Washington, D.C.; NBS Special Publication 500-59, 1980.

Brodie, M.L., Mylopoulos, J., and Schmidt, J. *On conceptual modelling.* New York; Springer Verlag, 1984.

Brodie, M.L., Mylopoulos, J., and Schmidt, J. W., eds. *On conceptual modelling: perspectives from artificial intelligence, databases, and programming languages.* New York; Springer-Verlag, 1984.

Byers, Robert A. *Everyman's database primer: featuring dBASE III.* Culver City, Calif.; Ashton-Tate, 1984.

Cardenas, Alfonso F. *Data base management systems.* Boston, Mass.; Allyn and Bacon, 1985.

Carrabis, Joseph-David. *dBase III advanced programming.* Indianapolis, Ind., Que Corporation, 1985.

Carrabis, Joseph-David. *dBase III plus: the complete reference.* Berkeley, Calif.; Osborne/McGraw-Hill, 1987.

Castro, L., Hanson, J., and Rettig, T. *Advanced programmer's guide: featuring dBase III and dBase II.* Culver City, Calif.; Ashton-Tate, 1985.

Ceri, S., and Pelagatti, G. *Distributed databases: principles and systems.* New York; McGraw-Hill, 1984.

Chen, P.P., ed. *Entity-relationship approach to system analysis and design.* New York; North-Holland, 1980.

Chorafas, Dimitris N. *Databases for networks and minicomputers.* Princeton, N.J.; Petrocelli Books, Inc., 1982.

Chou, George Tsu-der. *Using Paradox.* Indianapolis, Ind.; Que Corp., 1986.

Chou, George Tsu-der. *dBase III handbook.* Indianapolis, Ind.; Que Corporation, 1985.

Chu, Wesley W., Gardarin, G., and Ohsuga, S., eds. *Very large data bases: proceedings.* Los Altos, CA, USA; Distributed by Morgan Kaufmann Publishers, 1986.

Chu, Wesley W., ed. *Distributed systems.* Dedham, Mass.; Artech House, 1986.

Cobb, D.F., Cobb, S. S., Richardson, K.E., Cobb Group. *The Paradox companion.* Toronto; Bantam Books, 1986.

Cohen, Leo. *Creating and planning the corporate database system project.* Englewood Cliffs, N.J.; Prentice-Hall, 1982.

Date, C. J. *A guide to DB2: a user's guide to the IBM product IBM Database 2 (a relational database management system for the MVS environment) and its companion products QMF and DXT.* Reading, Mass.; Addison-Wesley, 1984.

Date, C. J. *An introduction to database systems.* Reading, Mass.; Addison-Wesley, 1986.

Date, C. J. *Relational database: selected writings.* Reading, Mass.; Addison-Wesley, 1986.

Date, C.J. *A guide to DB2.* Reading, Mass.; Addison-Wesley, 1984.

Date, C.J. *An introduction to database systems, Vol. I..* Reading, Mass.; Addison-Wesley, 4th ed. 1986.

Date, C.J. *An introduction to database systems, Vol. II.* Reading, Mass.; Addison-Wesley, 1982.

Date, C.J. *Database: a primer.* Reading, Mass.; Addison-Wesley, 1983.

Dayal, Umeshwar, ed. *Proceedings, tenth international conference on very large data bases, Singapore, August 27-31, 1984.* Saratoga, Calif.; VLDB Endowment, 1984.

DeWitt, D. J., and Boral, H., eds. *Database machines: fourth international workshop, Grand Bahama Island, March 1985.* New York; Springer-Verlag, 1985.

Deen, S. M. *Principles and practice of database systems.* Basingstoke; Macmillan Education, 1985.

Delobel, C., and Adiba, M. *Relational database systems.* Amsterdam; North-Holland, 1985.

Dinerstein, Nelson T. *Database and file management systems for the microcomputer.* Glenview, Ill.; Scott, Foresman, 1985.

Dinerstein, Nelson T. *Paradox for the programmer.* Glenview, Ill.; Scott, Foresman, 1986.

Dinerstein, Nelson T. *Rbase 5000 for the programmer.* Glenview, Ill.; Scott, Foresman, 1986.

Dinerstein, Nelson T. *dBASE II for the programmer: a how-to-do-it book.* Glenview, Ill.; Scott, Foresman, 1984.

Dinerstein, Nelson T. *dBASE III for the programmer: a how-to-do-it-book.* Glenview, Ill.; Scott, Foresman, 1985.

Durell, William. *Data administration: a practical guide to successful data management.* New York; McGraw-Hill, 1985.

Emerson, S., and Darnovsky, M. *Database for the IBM PC.* Reading, Mass.; Addison-Wesley, 1984.

Erickson, J., and Baran, N. *Using RBase 4000.* Berkeley, Calif.; Osborne/McGraw-Hill, 1985.

Erickson, J., and Baran, N. *Using Rbase 5000.* Berkeley, Calif.; Osborne/McGraw-Hill, 1986.

Everest, Gordon C. *Database management: objectives, system functions, and administration.* New York; McGraw-Hill, 1986.

Fadok, G.T. *Effective design of CODASYL data base.* London; Macmillan, 1985.

Fadok, George T. *Effective design of CODASYL data base.* London; Macmillan, Collier Macmillan, 1985.

Fernandez, E.B., Summers, R., and Wood, C. *Data base security and integrity.* Reading, Mass.; Addison-Wesley, 1981.

Fife, D.W., Hardgrave, W. T., and Deutsch, D.R. *Database concepts.* Cincinnati; South-Western, 1986.

Flavin, M. *Fundamental concepts of information modeling.* New York; Yourdon Press, 1981.

Flores, I. *Data base architecture.* New York, N.Y.; Van Nostrand Reinhold, 1981.

Fong, Elizabeth. *Guide on logical database design.* Washington, D.C.; U.S. Department of Commerce, National Bureau of Standards, 1985.

Freedman, Alan. *dBase II for the first-time user.* Culver City, Calif.; Ashton-Tate Pub. Group, 1984.

Freshman, Ron. *System design guide featuring dBASE II.* Culver City, Calif.; Ashton-Tate, 1984.

Frost, R. A. *Introduction to knowledge base systems.* London; Collins Professional and Technical, 1986.

Frost, R. A., ed. *Database management systems: practical aspects of their use.* London; New York; Granada, 1984.

Gallagher, L.J., and Draper, J.M. *Guide on data models in the selection and use of database management systems.* Washington, D.C.; U.S. Dept. of Commerce, National Bureau of Standards, 1984.

Gallagher, L.J., and Salazar, S. *Report on approaches to database translation.* Washington, D.C.; U.S. Dept. of Commerce, National Bureau of Standards, 1984.

Gallaire, H., Minker, J., and Nicolas, J.M., eds. *Advances in database theory.* New York; Plenum Press, vol. 1, 1981, vol. 2, 1984.

Gardarin, G. and Gelenbe, E., eds. *New applications of databases.* Orlando, Fla.; Academic Press, 1984.

Gardarin, G., and Gelenbe, E., eds. *New applications of data bases.* Orlando, Fla.; Academic Press, 1984.

Ghosh, S.P. *Data base organization for data management.* Orlando, Fla.; Academic Press, 1986.

Gillenson, Mark L. *Database: step-by-step.* New York; Wiley, 1985.

Goldstein, Robert C. *Database: technology and management.* New York; Wiley, 1985.

Gorman, Michael M. *Managing database: four critical factors.* Wellesley, Mass.; QED Information Sciences, Inc., 1984.

Gorney, Leonard. *Invitation to database processing.* Princeton, N.J.; Petrocelli Books, 1985.

Gray, Peter M. D. *Logic, algebra, and databases.* New York; Halsted Press; Chichester, West Sussex, England; Ellis Horwood, 1984.

Grundy, A.F., ed. *Proceedings of the fourth British national conference on databases, University of Keele, 10-12 July 1985.* Cambridge [Cambridgeshire], New York; Published by Cambridge University Press on behalf of the British Computer Society, 1985.

Hawryszkiewycz, I. T. *Database analysis and design.* Chicago; Science Research Associates, 1984.

Hawryszkiewycz, Igor T. *Database analysis and design.* Chicago, Ill.; SRA, 1983.

Hecht, Myron. *File and database management programs for the IBM PC.* New York; Wiley, 1985.

Hogan, Rex. *Diagnostic techniques for IMS data bases.* Wellesley, Mass.; QED Information Sciences, 1986.

Hubbard, G.U. *Computer assisted data base design.* New York; Van Nostrand Reinhold DP series, 1981.

Hubbard, George U. *IMS data-base organization and performance.* New York; Van Nostrand Reinhold Co., 1986.

Humphrey, S.M., and Melloni, B.J. *Databases: a primer for retrieving information by computer.* Englewood Cliffs, N.J.; Prentice-Hall, 1986.

IBM Corp. *IMS II, System and application design guide.* IBM DPD, SH20-0910.

IBM Corp. *Introduction to data management.* IBM SC20-8096.

IBM DPD. *SQL/Data system concepts and facilities.* IBM, 1981, GH24-5013-0, File No. S370-50.

IBM DPD. *SQL/Data system general information.* IBM, GH24-5012-0, 1981.

IEEE. *International conference on data engineering, February 5-7, 1986, Los Angeles, California, USA.* Washington, D.C.; IEEE Computer Society Press; 1986.

IEEE. *International conference on data engineering: April 24-27, 1984, Los Angeles, California, USA.* Silver Spring, Md.; IEEE Computer Society Press; 1984.

IEEE. *The 4th International conference on entity-relationship approach: October 28-30, 1985, Chicago, Ill.;* Silver Spring, Md.; IEEE Computer Society Press; 1985.

IEEE. *Trends and applications, 1984: making database work. Proceedings, May 23-24, 1984, National Bureau of Standards, Gaithersburg, Maryland.* Silver Spring, Md.; IEEE Computer Society Press, 1984.

Information Builders. *FOCUS users manual: release 5.0.* New York; Information Builders, 1985.

Inmon, W.H. *Effective data base design.* Englewood Cliffs, N.J.; Prentce-Hall, 1980.

Inmon, W.H., and Bird, T.J. *The dynamics of data base.* Englewood Cliffs, N.J.; Prentice-Hall, 1986.

Inmon, W.H., and Friedman, L.J. *Design review methodology for a data base environment.* Englewood Cliffs, N.J.; Prentice-Hall, 1982.

Jacobs, Barry. *Applied database logic, vol. 1: fundamental database issues.* Englewood Cliffs, N.J.; Prentice-Hall, 1985.

Johnson, L.F., and Cooper, R.H. *File techniques for data base organization in COBOL.* Englewood Cliffs, N.J.; Prentice-Hall, 1986.

Jones, Edward. *Using dBASE IIIR plus.* Berkeley, Calif.; Osborne/McGraw-Hill, 1987.

Jones, Edward. *Using dBASE III.* Berkeley, Calif.; Osborne/McGraw-Hill, 1985.

Jones, J. A. *Databases in theory and practice.* London; Kogan Page, 1986.

Kapp, D., and Leben, J. *IMS programming techniques: a guide to using DL/I.* New York; Van Nostrand Reinhold, 1986.

Kerschberg, L., ed. *Expert database systems: proceedings from the first international workshop.* Menlo Park, Calif.; Benjamin/Cummings, 1986.

Kim, W., Reiner, D.S., and Batory, D.S., eds. *Query processing in database systems.* New York; Springer Verlag, 1984.

Kim, W., Reiner, D.S., and Batory, D.S., eds. *Query processing in database systems.* Berlin; Springer-Verlag, 1985.

King, J.M. *Evaluating data base management systems.* New York, N.Y.; Van Nostrand Reinhold, 1981.

King, Jonathan J. *Query optimization by semantic reasoning.* Ann Arbor, Mich.; UMI Research Press, 1984.

Knecht, Ken. *Practical Paradox: applications and programming techniques.* Blue Ridge Summit, Penn.; Tab Books, 1986.

Kokoreva, L. V., and Malashinin, I. I. *Proektirovanie bankov dannykh.* Moskva; Nauka, Glav. red. fiziko-maticheskoi lit-ry,

Korth, H.F., and Silberschatz, Abraham. *Database system concepts.* New York; McGraw-Hill, 1986.

Kroenke, D. and Nilson, D.E. *Database processing for microcomputers.* Chicago, Ill.; Science Research Associates, 1986.

Kruglinski, David. *Data base management systems for MS-DOS: evaluating MS-DOS data base software.* Berkeley, Calif.; Osborne/McGraw-Hill, 1986.

Kruglinski, David. *Data base management systems: a guide to microcomputer software.* New York; Osborne/McGraw-Hill, 1983.

Krumm, Rob. *Understanding and using dBase II and III.* Bowie, Md.; Brady Communications Co., 1985.

Larson, J.A., and Rahimi, S. *Tutorial: distributed database management.* Silver Spring, Md.; IEEE CS, 1985.

Larson, J.A., and Rahimi, S., eds. *Tutorial, distributed database management.* Silver Spring, Md.; IEEE Computer Society Press, 1985.

Laurie, Peter. *Databases: how to manage information on your micro.* London; Chapman and Hall/Methuen, 1985.

Li, Deyi. *A PROLOG database system.* Letchworth, Hertfordshire, England; Research Studies Press Wiley, 1984.

Lima, Tony. *dBASE II for beginners.* Englewood Cliffs, N.J.; Prentice-Hall, 1985.

Longstaff, J., ed. *Proceedings of the third British national conference on databases, Leeds 11-13, July 1984.* Cambridge [Cambridgeshire]; New York; Published by Cambridge University Press on behalf of the British Computer Society, 1984.

Maier, D. *The theory of relational databases.* Rockville, Md.; CS Press, 1983.

Marcus, Claudia. *Prolog programming: applications for database systems, expert systems, and natural language systems.* Reading, Mass.; Addison-Wesley, 1986.

Martin, Daniel. *Advanced database techniques.* Cambridge, Mass.; MIT Press, 1986.

Martin, J. *An end user's guide to data base.* Englewood Cliffs, N.J.; Prentice-Hall, 1981.

Martin, J. *Fourth generation languages.* Englewood Cliffs, N.J.; Prentice-Hall, 1985.

Martin, J. *Managing the database environment.* Englewood Cliffs, N.J.; Prentice-Hall, 1983.

Mayne, Alan. *Data dictionary systems: a technical review.* Manchester, Eng.; NCC Publications, 1984.

McClelland, Trish. *Creating the perfect database using DB MASTER.* Glenview, Ill.; Scott, Foresman, 1985.

McFadden, F.R., and Hoffer, J.A. *Data base management.* Menlo Park, Calif.; Benjamin/Cummings, 1985.

McFadden, Fred R. and Hoffer, Jeffrey A. *Data Base Management.* Menlo Park, Calif.; Benj. Cummings, 1985.

McHugh, K., and Corchado, V. *Selecting the right data base software for the IBM PC.* Berkeley, Calif.; SYBEX, 1984.

Melton, A., ed. *Mathematical foundations of programming semantics.* Lecture notes in Computer Science, vol. 239. Berlin, Heidelberg; Springer-Verlag, 1986.

Merrett, T. H. *Relational information systems.* New York, N.Y.; Reston, 1984.

Merrett, T.H. *Relational information systems.* New York; Reston, 1983.

Mohan, C. *Tutorial, recent advances in distributed data base management .* Silver Spring, Md.; IEEE Computer Society Press, 1984.

Neal, S., and LeTraunik, K. *Data base management systems in business.* Englewood Cliffs, N.J.; Prentice-Hall, 1986.

Neuhold, E.J., and Furtado, A.L. *Formal techniques for data base design.* Berlin; Springer-Verlag, 1986.

Nilson, D.E., and Kroenke, D.M. *Managing information with microcomputers: featuring RBase series database management systems.* Bellevue, Wash.; Microrim, 1984.

Oxborrow, E. A. *Databases and database systems: concepts and issues.* Bromley, Kent; Chartwell-Bratt; Lund, Sweden; Studentlitteratur, 1986.

Oxborrow, E.A., ed. *Proceedings of the fifth British national conference on databases, University of Kent at Canterbury, 14-16 July 1986.* Cambridge [Cambridgeshire]; New York; Cambridge University Press on behalf of the British Computer Society, 1986.

Ozkarahan, Esen. *Database machines and database management.* Englewood Cliffs, N.J.; Prentice-Hall, 1986.

Papadimitriou, C.H. *The theory of database concurrency control.* Rockville, Md.; Computer Science Press, 1986.

Pergamon Infotech. *The corporate database.* Maidenhead, Berkshire, England; Pergamon Infotech, 1985.

Perkinson, R.C. *Data analysis: the key to data base design.* Wellesley, Mass.; QED Information Sciences, 1984.

Pirotte, A., and Vassiliou, Y., eds. *11th International conference on very large data bases, Stockholm, August 21-23, 1985.* Brussels; Presses universitaires de Bruxelles, 1985.

Prague, C.N., and Hammitt, J.E. *Programming with Rbase 5000.* Blue Ridge Summit, Penn.; Tab Books, 1986.

Rishe, N. *Database semantics.* Tech. rep. TRCS87-2, University of California, Santa Barbara, 1987.

Rosenfeld, Pilar N. *Investigation of DBMS for use in a research environment.* Santa Monica, Calif.; Rand Corp., 1985.

Ross, S.C. *Understanding and using dBaseR III: including dBase IIR.* St. Paul; West, 1986.

Rumble, J.R., and Hampel, V.E., eds. *Database management in science and technology: a CODATA sourcebook on the use of computers in data activities.* Amsterdam; North-Holland; 1984.

Salzberg, Betty Joan. *An introduction to data base design.* Orlando, Fla.; Academic Press, 1986

Schmidt, J.W. and Brodie, M.L., eds. *Relational database systems.* New York; Springer-Verlag, 1983.

Schwartz, Andrew N. *Using Smart.* Indianapolis, Ind.; Que, 1986.

Sheppard, Charles L. *Guide for selecting microcomputer data management software Charles L. Sheppard.* Gaithersburg, Md.; U.S. Dept. of Commerce, National Bureau of Standards; Washington, D.C.; 1985.

Simpson, Alan. *Advanced techniques in dBASE III PLUS.* Berkeley; SYBEX, 1986.

Simpson, Alan. *Mastering Paradox.* Berkeley, Calif.; SYBEX, 1986.

Simpson, Alan. *Understanding Rbase 5000.* Berkeley, Calif.; SYBEX Inc., 1985.

Smith, Peter D., and Barnes, G.M. *Files and databases: an introduction.* Reading, Mass.; Addison-Wesley, 1987.

Sood, A. K., and Qureshi, A. H., eds. *Database machines: applications and modern trends.* Berlin; Springer-Verlag, 1986.

Stanford University. Information Technology Services. Data Resources Group. *Microcomputer data base management systems: their selection and evaluation.* Stanford, Ca.; Information Technology Services, 1984.

Stocker, P. M., Gray, P., and Atkinson, M. P., eds. *Databases, role and structure: an advanced course.* Cambridge [Cambridgeshire]; New York; Cambridge University Press, 1984.

Stonebraker, M., ed. *The INGRES papers: anatomy of a relational database system.* Reading, Mass.; Addison-Wesley, 1985.

Stonebraker, Michael. *The INGRES papers: anatomy of a relational database system.* Reading, Mass.; Addison-Wesley, 1986.

Sundgren, Bo. *Data bases and data models.* Lund, Sweden; Studentlitteratur; Bromley, Kent; Chartwell-Bratt, 1985.

Swan, Tom. *Pascal programs for data base management.* Hasbrouck Heights, N.J.; Hayden Book Co., 1984.

Tay, Y. C. *Locking performance in centralized databases.* Boston, Mass.; Academic Press, 1987.

Taylor, Allen G. *Rbase 5000 user's guide.* Indianapolis, Ind.; Que Corp., 1986.

Townsend, Carl. *Mastering dBase III: a structured approach.* Berkeley, Calif.; SYBEX Inc., 1985.

Tsichritzis, D., and Lochovsky, F. *Data models.* Englewood Cliffs, N.J.; Prentice-Hall, 1981.

Turk, Thomas A. *Planning and designing the data base environment.* New York; Van Nostrand Reinhold, 1985.

Ullman, J.D. *Principles of database systems, 2nd ed.* Potomac, Md.; Computer Science Press, 1982.

Ullmann, Julian R. *A Pascal database book.* Oxford [Oxfordshire]; Clarendon Press; New York; Oxford University Press, 1985.

Vasta, Joseph A. *Understanding data base management systems.* Belmont, Calif.; Wadsworth, 1985.

Vesely, E.G. *The practioner's guide for logical and physical database design.* Englewood Cliffs, N.J.; Prentice-Hall, 1986.

Vesely, Eric Garrigue. *The practitioner's blueprint for logical and physical database design.* Englewood Cliffs, N.J.; Prentice-Hall, 1986.

Vetter, M. and Maddison, R.N. *Data base design methodology.* New Jersey; Prentice-Hall, 1981.

Walter, R. Kenneth. *Introduction to data management and file design.* Englewood Cliffs, N.J.; Prentice-Hall, 1986.

Weber Systems Inc. *dBase III user's handbook.* New York; Ballantine Books, 1985.

Wertz, Charles J. *The data dictionary: concepts and uses.* Wellesley, Mass.; QED Information Sciences, 1986.

Wiederhold, G. *Database design*. New York; McGraw-Hill, Computer Science Series, 2nd ed., 1983.

Yang, Chao-Chih. *Relational databases*. Englewood Cliffs, N.J.; Prentice-Hall, 1986.

Yao, S. Bing., ed. *Principles of database design*. Englewood Cliffs, N.J.; Prentice-Hall, 1985.

Yao, S.B., Benigni, D.R., and Hevner, A.R. *Benchmark analysis of database architectures: a case study*. Gaithersburg, Md.; U.S. Dept. of Commerce, National Bureau of Standards; Washington, D.C., 1985.

Yao, S.B., Hevner, A.R., and Benigni, D.R. *A guide to performance evaluation of database systems*. Gaithersburg, Md.; U.S. Dept. of Commerce, National Bureau of Standards; Washington, D.C., 1984.

Yormark, B., ed. *SIGMOD '84: proceedings of annual meeting, Boston, MA, June 18-21, 1984*. New York, N.Y.; Association for Computing Machinery; 1984.

Zemankova-Leech, M., and Kandel, A. *Fuzzy relational data bases: a key to expert systems*. Koln; Verl. TUV Rheinland, 1984.

# INDEX

The following is a comprehensive index to the database concepts covered in this text. The labels in brackets indicate the topic or field in which the term is used. Thus, the entry 'Application [databases], 2' means: the term *application* in the general field of *databases* is explained on page 2, where it appears in bold face.

# QUICK REFERENCE SCHEMAS FOR THE UNIVERSITY CASE STUDY

The following are the binary, relational, network, and hierarchical schemas for the university case-study application. These schemas are referred to in most of the examples in this text.

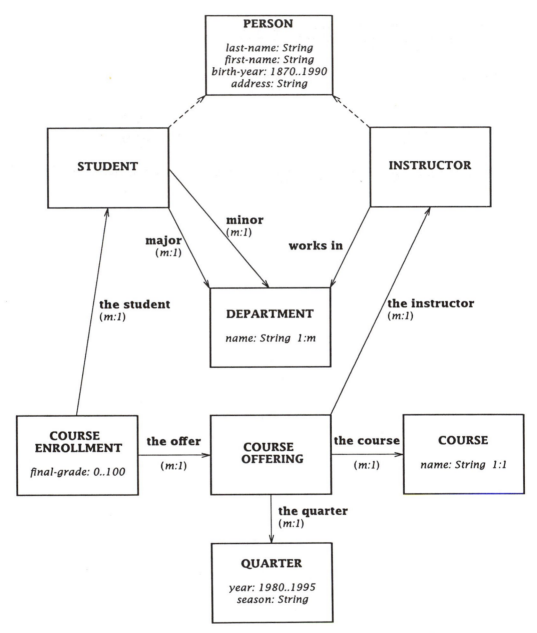

**Figure Ref-1.** A binary schema for a university application.

**DEPARTMENT NAMING**

*name-key: String*
*main-name: String*

**WORK**

*instructor-id-in-key: Integer*
*department-main-name-in-key: String*

**STUDENT**

*id-key: Integer*
*last-name: String*
*first-name: String*
*birth-year: 1870..1990*
*address: String*
*major-department-main-name: String*
*minor-department-main-name: String*

**INSTRUCTOR**

*id-key: Integer*
*last-name: String*
*first-name: String*
*birth-year: 1870..1990*
*address: String*

**DEPARTMENT**

*main-name-key: String*

**COURSE ENROLLMENT**

*instructor-id-in-key: Integer*
*course-name-in-key: String*
*year-in-key: 1980..1995*
*season-in-key: String*
*student-id-in-key: Integer*
*final-grade: 0..100*

**COURSE OFFERING**

*instructor-id-in-key: Integer*
*course-name-in-key: String*
*year-in-key: 1980..1995*
*season-in-key: String*

**COURSE**

*name-key: String*

**QUARTER**

*year-in-key: 1980..1995*
*season-in-key: String*

**Figure Ref-2.** A relational schema for the university application.

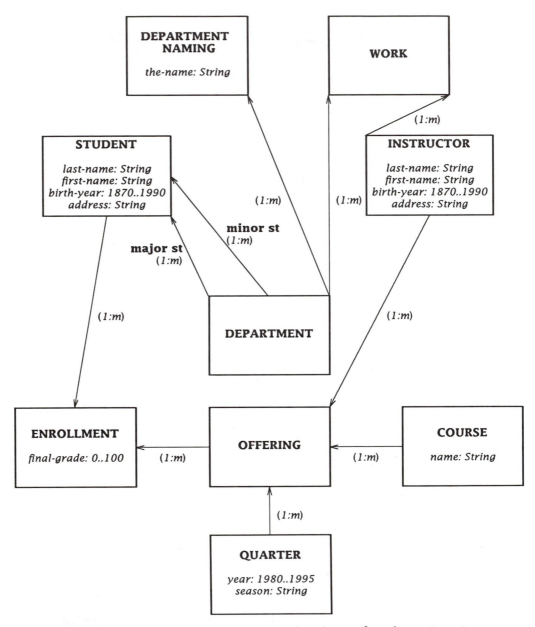

**Figure Ref-3.** An order-less network schema for the university application.

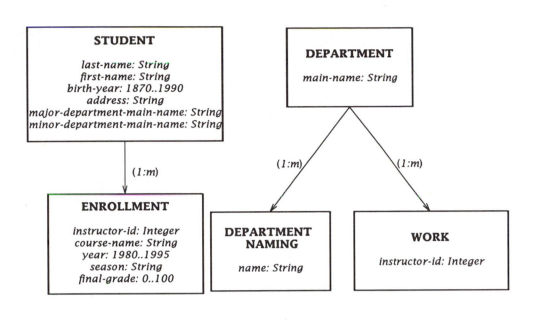

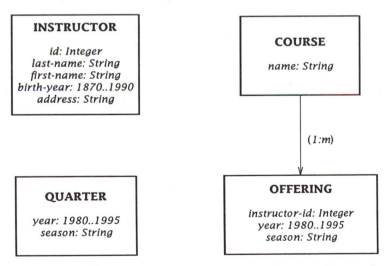

**Figure Ref-4.** An order-less hierarchical schema for the university application.